The Agape Road

Journey to Intimacy with the Father

Other Titles by Bob Mumford

Books
Fifteen Steps Out
Take Another Look at Guidance
The King & You
The Purpose of Temptation
Dr. Frankenstein & World Systems

Bible Studies
The Agape Road
Breaking Out (also in Spanish)
Knowing, Loving, & Following Jesus
Leading Leaders in Agape
Unshared Love

Booklets
Below the Bottom Line
Church of My Dreams
Correction Not Rejection
The Difference Between the Church and the Kingdom
Forever Change
Grace: God's Rubber Room
The Implications of Following Jesus
On Being Scandalized
Prison of Resentment
Psalm for Living
Renegade Male
Riddle of the Painful Earth
Standing in the Whirlwind
Three Dimensional Reality
Water Baptism
Why God?
(and many others)

Bob Mumford

The Agape Road

Journey to Intimacy with the Father

LIFECHANGERS®
LIBRARY SERIES
COOKEVILLE, TENNESSEE

Bob Mumford

The Agape Road: Journey to Intimacy with the Father
by Bob Mumford
2004 © Lifechangers®
P. O. Box 3709, Cookeville, TN 38502
www.lifechangers.org
ISBN 1-884004-50-4

Editor and cover design: Keren Kilgore

Table of Contents

Preface

This book was not just written, it was a birthing process. It has been difficult in that I am more of a teacher than a writer and a very ordinary person through whom God has chosen to pour Himself. My one foundational concern has been that the theme of this book be given suitable opportunity to be read, understood, and hopefully, assimilated.

I dedicate this work to our friends who we identify as Underwriters. Without these co-workers, I could not have continued. I personally thank each one for their incalculable sacrifices, unwavering confidence, innumerable acts of lovingkindness, and immeasurable patience.

My personal and virtually inexpressible debt of gratitude goes to my daughter, Keren Alene Kilgore, who gave herself untiringly in carrying this manuscript with her editing and technical skills in such a way as to bring this book to birth. She participated like a midwife, apart from whose help and assistance the child being born would have been in much danger. As the author, I need to say that without Keren I am not sure this book could have known a healthy and useful existence.

Caution is advised to those who may simply have picked this book up or innocently had someone give you this copy. We have made an effort to take you on a journey called the *Agape* Road. You will soon realize that, like blind Bartimaeus, Jesus is calling you, wanting to heal your spiritual blindness so that you can walk in intimacy with Him. This *Agape* Road journey does get difficult in places encouraging us to run, hide, or shift blame. But, it is a journey that we truly believe the Lord Jesus Christ has called us to walk, and hopefully, help others to discover. I have discovered that it is literally impossible to know God as He really is and not love Him. This is my own testimony; hopefully it will be yours as well.

May Father's glory be revealed in the earth,

Bob Mumford

Bob Mumford

Love has a hem to her garment
that trails in the very dust;
It can reach the very stains
of the streets and lanes,
and because it can, it must.
Unknown

Chapter 1
Journey to the Father

Along the journey we commonly forget its goal.
Nietzsche

 When I was 13 years old, my father abandoned me. My parents were in the middle of an ugly divorce. I had been visiting my father in Tampa, Florida, and he was driving me home to Atlantic City, New Jersey, where I lived with my mother and five sisters. Like a typical know-it-all teenager, I was arguing with my Dad and heatedly defending my mother. We were nearing Baltimore, Maryland, when the argument became overly intense. Suddenly, he stopped the car and said, "Get out." I thought he wanted me to see if we had a flat tire, so I walked around the car to check out the problem. When I got to his window, he rolled it down and I leaned toward him so he could tell me what he thought was wrong with the car. With rage on his face he looked at me and said, "*You* are no good. You never *have been* any good. You never *will be* any good." He rolled up the window and drove away, leaving me standing by the side of the road more than 100 miles from home with less than a dollar in my pocket.

Stunned by what had just happened, I stood in the street for the longest time feeling absolutely abandoned, trying to figure out what I was going to do. My sense of what it meant to be a Mumford was severely shaken. My street-kid survival skills kicked in, and I hitchhiked home, subtly trying to let the different drivers know I had not eaten. I made it to Atlantic City about 15 hours later very hungry. This experience left deep impressions in my person.

Serious Consequences

When I arrived home, something deep and unexplainable had changed in me; I felt like an entirely different person. In order to deal with my rejection, shame, and sense of failure and loss, I chose anger and superiority as a cover up. Like many young people, I remember making a childhood vow to "never, ever trust another person as long as I lived." The following year, I dropped out of school, taking menial employment in order to support my Mom and five sisters in my father's absence.

I finished my GED in the Navy, graduated from college, and earned my Masters of Divinity Degree, but even after several decades of successful ministry, the consequences of my father's rejection were very much alive. Eventually, I was forced to recognize that I had deep, internal *anger* directed at no one in particular, accompanied by fear, more accurately *free-floating anxiety*—both without any obvious source or cause. The fear and anger revealed themselves in a *critical mouth* and false superiority. These problems were very real, and I knew they were displeasing to God, but I was unable to get free from them. Reading more Bible verses or ministering to more people certainly did not deal with the issues. I knew that *anger, fear,* and a *critical mouth* were not normal and that these problems would always present a barrier to the intimacy with God for which my heart longed. Like many who have preceded me in this search, I felt bound in heart and conscience to find answers to these problems both for me personally and for others.

Because we must live in a less than perfect world, human failure, mistakes, and injuries, like my Dad's rejection of me, take their toll on us, often appearing and reappearing many years later. Failure, disappointment, or betrayal from any loved one is always difficult to manage. However, if God can restore me, He can restore you. It is not magic. What I have to say is not *experience* oriented; it is a journey. These lessons have come at great personal expense, so have one on me! Allow me, by means of the illustrations and diagrams in this book, to take you toward God's Land of Promises.

Barriers to Intimacy

In order to deal with barriers to intimacy, we must put the things that hinder us from having an intimate relationship with God and with others into a personal context. First are the *satanic and demonic* hindrances. Satan is very real regardless of what our culture, modern philosophy, or liberal Christianity thinks. Satan's goal—whether he uses us against ourselves or attempts to push us into thoughts or behaviors that are cruel or unusual—is to keep us from the Father.

The second hindrance is the *original fall,* the effect of which has caused us to turn in upon ourselves. This is depicted by the death line which is explained in the next section. We live in a fallen world. The result is unpredictable people and unfulfilled expectations. God often gets blamed for life not working out as we might expect. Most Bible-centered people have a fairly good grasp on these first two hindrances. This book addresses the third category.

The third hindrance to intimacy with the Father is *human failure.* This predicament is the result of the first two. Human failures are mistakes and injuries whose origin and source, for the most part, come from us. They take their toll on us. My dad's injury toward me as a young teenager falls in this category, revealing itself so many years later. Failure, disappointment, or injury from any loved one is very difficult to embrace. When I became the father of four children, I understood human failure. I saw how inadequate and unprepared I was to be a parent. The fact that my four children (and all their children) are serving God is a miracle! It certainly was not because of my parenting skills, but simply a result of the grace of God on us as a family.

Being Welcomed Home

When God created man in His image, His desire and intent was to have a relationship of unbroken intimacy with us. Originally, nothing was hidden between God and Adam and Eve. They felt at home resting and abiding with God and they felt no shame. Then God said, "But from the tree of the knowledge of good and evil you shall not eat, for in the day that you eat from it you shall surely die" (Genesis 2:17). When Adam and Eve transgressed, it caused a separation between God and His creation and *death* came upon all men (Romans 5:12). The death line represents this broken relationship between God and His creation and as a result, sin, shame, and guilt came upon all humanity. The death line is the entrance of sin into the world that alienated us from God, from ourselves, and from each other. Our human

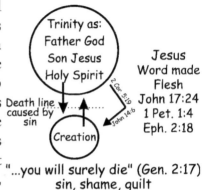

response, like Adam and Eve's, was to run, hide, and shift blame. Paul, many years later, said, "you were dead in your trespasses and sins" (Ephesians 2:1).

God, however, transcended the death line by sending us Jesus who came to take us back home to the Father. Our path to God is Jesus, the Word of God made flesh, the Scriptures, and the Holy Spirit. We cross the death line by way of the New Birth or being born again. Because Jesus and the Father are One (John 10:30), and because we are one with Jesus (1 Corinthians 6:17), intimacy is possible. He made a way for us to be included in fellowship within the relational structure of the Trinity (Matthew 28:19; John 16:27; 17:22-26). It is impossible for rivalry to exist within the Trinity; God, as a Father, designed a route to Himself so that we could enjoy the same intimacy with Him, as does His Son. Ephesians 2:18 says, "for through Him we both have our access in one Spirit to the Father." Christ came as God Incarnate in order to show us the way home and give us the opportunity to be restored to intimacy with God our Father (2 Corinthians 5:19). The journey home to intimacy with the Father is more than salvation; it is His promise (John 14:21-23).

While ministering in Peru some years ago, a 90-year-old Quechua tribal Indian elder came up to the platform and began talking to me in his dialect, which was then translated into Spanish and then into English for me. He said, "I want to know the God you are talking about. Why didn't somebody tell me and my tribe about this sooner?" So, back and forth through the interpreters we introduced him to Jesus. I felt such compassion for him; even at his age, there had awakened within him a real hunger for God. I prayed that God would baptize him in the Holy Spirit and receive him into His intimate fellowship. Suddenly, the Indian started talking rapidly, and, by the joy on his face, it was obvious that he was enjoying something. I asked what he was saying and the interpreter, puzzled, said he did not know. Gradually we discovered that he was enjoying a new-found relationship with God the Father. He had been welcomed back home. We were humbled by the realization that the Father had suddenly and powerfully set His love on a man who had never heard the Gospel before. Like Cornelius in Acts 10, he had been invited into *immediate* fellowship and intimacy with the Trinity.

We all remember the weeks after our new birth when we were so full of His love that we could hug a tree! The love of God that broke loose in my own spirit in 1954 has been reapprehended as a result of understanding this *Agape* Road journey. Now, after many years, not only are my lights on, but somebody is home! A whole new sense of wanting to share the life and love of the Lord to a hurting generation has been rekindled.

The *Agape* Road

Jesus said, "I am the way, and the truth, and the life; no one comes to the Father but through Me" (John 14:6). Jesus' job description was to bring us to the Father, restoring our relationship of love and intimacy that went astray because of the fall. God, the Father, was seeking us through the Person of His Son. Christ intends to bring us to intimacy by way of the *Agape* (ä-gä′pä) Road. The route, as well as the goal, is "not of our ourselves, it is the gift of God" (Ephesians 2:8). The fact that He had to come to us is proof that we could not come to Him.

The moment we are born again, we *do* have intimacy with God, but it is sporadic, and often interrupted. This intimacy is new and immature (1 Peter 2:2), needing to be cultivated into an abiding relationship. *Agape* is the Greek word for love and the *Agape* Road is just that—a road of love that He created to bring us to Himself.

It is important to understand that heaven is not the goal. If you are a Christian and you die, you have to go to heaven, there is no place else to go! I believe in heaven—

I AM the Way to the Father
I AM the Truth about the Father
I AM the Life of the Father

it is real and beautiful. It is everything and more than we could imagine. But, many people have mistakenly made heaven to be the goal or the object of their life. There is life after being born again. God, as a Father, wants to know us (1 Corinthians 8:3) and longs for us to know Him in this present life on earth. John 17:3 says, "This is eternal life that they might know Thee and Jesus Christ whom Thou hast sent." It is such an important theme in the New Testament that Jesus uses the term "sent Me" 40 times. He wants us to be comfortable in God's Presence. As a Father, God wants to be known and experienced (2 Corinthians 6:18). Jesus was sent to reintroduce us to our loving heavenly Father.

Intimacy

Another way of understanding the word "intimacy" is into-me-He-sees. God's heart cry is that we know Him and open ourselves so that He can know us. *Agape* is a way of knowing. Learning the principles of the *Agape* Road facilitates our finding each other. He is the One who planted in us the Eternal Seed. The Eternal Seed is the ultimate source of intimacy by reason of the New Birth (1 Peter 1:23). When Christ is formed in us (Galatians 4:19), intimacy between God and us becomes possible. We now seek to nourish, cultivate, and protect it until it comes to maturity and fruitfulness.

Intimacy is so important to God that He made a promise which reveals His Father's heart: "For all will know Me, from the least to the greatest of them..." (Hebrews 8:11). We can see His basic intent in the Scripture "And I will be a Father to you, and you shall be sons and daughters to Me" (2 Corinthians 6:18). We do not have to wait for this intimate relationship with our Father to happen until we are in heaven. The abiding relationship gained on the *Agape* Road allows God to see into us and for us to see into Him. Out of this comes a joining or a heart relationship. This intimate relationship with God is a mystery that is difficult to define, but very much the normal Christian life which belongs to every one of us as believers.

When my awareness of Who the Father is and what He is really like began to increase, the fear and anger within my person began to subside. I began to experientially understand that Jesus was eager for me to walk this *Agape* Road to come to a relationship with His Father. When we begin to know what the Father is really like, we start to love Him. As one of the early Church fathers said, "It is impossible to know God as He really is, and not love Him."

God Desires Three Things From Us

God, as a Father, seeks something specific from a relationship with us. The question we need to ask is: are we willing to give Him what He is seeking?

First, *He wants to see our face.* Most people are only aware of seeking God's face–it never dawns on them that He might want to see their face. It still amazes me that God Almighty even *wants* to see our face (1 Corinthians 8:3). "O my dove, in the seclusion of the clefts in the solid rock, in the sheltered and secret place of the cliff, let me see your face, let me hear your voice; for your voice is sweet, and your face is lovely" (Song of Solomon 2:14 AMP). Most of us feel intimidated to show our real face or personality to anyone, let alone to God. Guilt, shame, and self-condemnation cause us to run, hide, and shift blame (Genesis 3:10-13).

We all wear masks and create impressions to prevent others from knowing who we really are. Scripture tells us that God is no respecter of persons (Deuteronomy 10:17) meaning He does not show partiality. The Greek word for *persons* means *masks*–God is no respecter of masks. God wants to go past the mask and get to know the real person even when we are running, hiding, or shifting blame.

When Jacob wrestled with God he said, "I have seen God face to face, yet my life has been preserved" (Genesis 32:30). I am sure he was remembering Cain saying, "Behold, You have driven me this day from the face of the ground; and from Your face I will be hidden" (Genesis 4:14). Only by grace are we allowed to see the face of God and have Him see our faces. When God sent His Son to break the death line, He made this kind of intimacy available to us. Intimacy is a *process*, not just a onetime experience. This process will come clear as our understanding of the *Agape* Road unfolds. 1 Corinthians 8:3 tells us that God has given us the privilege of knowing Him and seeks the privilege of being known by Him.

Intimacy with God must start with our new birth because before that we are spiritually dead. Once we have acknowledged Jesus as Lord and Savior and embrace water baptism, we are given the privilege to penetrate the veil where we see the face of God in the person of Jesus Christ (John 14:9; 2 Corinthians 4:6). We can see God and live for the simple reason that we have been buried with Christ in water baptism.

Second, *He desires to spend time with us communing together.* Many of us love God but do not want to be with Him because we are not comfortable in His presence. God did not create us like this; it is a direct result of the death line. Adam and Eve had fellowship or closeness with God–He walked in the Garden in the cool of the day *looking for them* (Genesis 3:8-9), but that closeness or intimacy was broken when Adam and Eve refused His limits. Since then, all of mankind has had to deal with that inner desire to return to a place of intimacy with his or her Creator (2 Corinthians 6:18).

Third, *God desires our unshared love.* He guards this love *jealously.* He does not want us to share our love for Him with anything that is illegal. It may seem strange to apply that word to God, but the Scripture does. Exodus 34:14 says, "the Lord, whose name is Jealous, is a jealous (impassioned) God." In its pure form, 'jealous' means vigilant in guarding something or loving protection. This describes the way God cares for each of His children. God is jealous *for* us, He is not jealous *of* us. Another translation of James 4:6 says, "the Spirit which He made to dwell in us, jealously yearns for the *entire devotion* of the heart.[1]" In other words, God, by the person of the Holy Spirit is always seeking to cultivate a love relationship with those of us who will respond. It is our love for Him and His love for us that protects and guards us from that which is injurious.

When I joined the Navy, all my needs were met including clothes, food, haircuts, travel, medicine, etc. Of course, the Navy does not take care of everyone in this way, just those who have enlisted in the Navy. This is the essence of God causing all things to work together for good to those who love Him (Romans 8:28-30). God as a Father does not function by determinism or fatalism. The only people this scriptural prescription works for are those who *seek* a relationship with Him as Father. God acts on behalf of those who *love* Him (Isaiah 64:4). It is stated in the Old Testament like this, "You shall love the Lord your God with all your heart and with all your soul and with all your might" (Deuteronomy 6:5). Father God wants us to set our *love* upon Him in such a way that we will not share it illegally with anyone or anything. God, as a Father, asks that we gather up all we are, all we have, and all we hope to be and place our affection on Him as evidence of our love. This we do without reservation or compromise. This is the meaning of "seek first the kingdom of God" (Matthew 6:33)

God has the ability to *govern* all things in our journey toward His purposes. Romans 8:28-30 requires us to acknowledge that God knows us, that the circumstance we are in will do something in our character, and that it is God Who is at work, not luck, or cosmic powers. God has a purpose in every event–to conform us to His likeness. Thus, He is increasing our *capacity* to know Him and for Him to know us (John 17:3). The intended result is intimacy with Father God (2 Corinthians 6:16-18).

---

[1]Joseph Mayor, *The Epistle of St. James* (London: MacMillan and Co., Limited, 1807), 137.

How God Wants to be Known

For years, my concept of God's glory was splendor like an extraterrestrial glow or the power of God coming in some supernatural way. I never thought it had anything to do with His character or nature. When Moses asked God to *show him His glory*, God said He would proclaim the *name* of the Lord before him (Exodus 33:18-19). God then, in self-revelation, explains to Moses the content of His glory which is His seven hidden attributes:

> [5]And the Lord descended in the cloud and stood there with him as he called upon the name of the Lord. [6]Then the Lord passed by in front of him and proclaimed, "The Lord, the Lord God, *compassionate* and *gracious, slow to anger* and *abounding in lovingkindness* [mercy] and *truth*; [7]who keeps *lovingkindness* [faithful] for thousands, who *forgives* iniquity, transgression and sin...."
>
> Exodus 34:5-7

God's DNA

Compassion
Grace
Slow to Anger
Mercy
Truth
Faithful
Forgives:
    Iniquity
    Transgression
    Sin

God's *character* or DNA is the content of His glory and the significance of His Name. The breadth of meaning in these seven words that God uses to reveal Himself is spectacular. "For since the creation of the world God's invisible qualities—his eternal power and divine nature—have been clearly seen, being understood from what has been made, so that men are without excuse" (Romans 1:20 NIV). This is not Bob Mumford's idea of what God is like; it is God's personal revelation of Himself. If God had not revealed Himself, we could not know Him (2 Corinthians 2:8-16). God's *glory* is the manifestation of His communicable *attributes* that are *hidden* from the world (John 17:25). God is a Spirit; He cannot be known unless He chooses to reveal Himself.

Of course, the depths and complexities of God are ineffable or impossible to clearly explain. God also has incommunicable attributes: He is eternal, omnipresent, omniscient, immutable, and self-revealed (we cannot know Him unless He reveals Himself). When Jesus was on earth, He laid aside the incommunicable attributes–picking them up again after His death and resurrection (John 17:5). When sin entered the world, it released the twisted desire for us to be like God, grasping for the incommunicable attributes and essentially rejecting the *communicable*. For example, stubbornness is actually immutability perverted. The communicable attributes consist of the image of God that is restored to us in Christ. These are the aspects of His Person that Father God wants the world to know about. The only way the world can see God's hidden nature or what He is actually like is by means of the Person of Christ revealing Himself through the body of Christ–you and me (Hebrews 1:3; John 14:9). As Christ is "formed in us" (Galatians 4:19), God's personality becomes evident in us. Matthew 5:43-48 teaches us to love our enemies that we may be the sons and daughters of our Father. This shows us the necessity of God's love being replicated. Without the effective and active presence of His attributes, we are not allowing His glory to come through our own person. Jesus, in teaching us the implications of this, states it clearly, "Let your light shine before men in such a way that they may see your good works, and glorify your Father who is in heaven" (Matthew 5:16). The objective evidence that God is our Father is that His DNA is revealed in us as His very own family. We will look at each of God's seven communicable attributes.

Compassion (Strong's #7349 / #3628). It is pity or empathy, inward affection, and tender mercy. The Greek word *splagchnon*—splangkh'-non is used 111 times in Scripture and means bowels of compassion or mercy (see Philippians 2:1). Webster's 1828 Dictionary gives us the best explanation of compassion without attempting a full word study.

> Suffering with another; painful sympathy; a sensation of sorrow excited by the distress or misfortunes of another; pity; commiseration. Compassion is a mixed passion, compounded of love and sorrow; at least some portion of love generally attends the pain or regret, or is excited by it. Extreme distress of an enemy even changes enmity into at least temporary affection.

Compassion means my insides are moved for you in a supernatural way. It is different than sympathy, which is easier to experience. Scripture says that Jesus "being full of *compassion*, forgave their iniquity" (Psalm 78:38). The father of the prodigal son "had *compassion*, and ran and fell upon his neck and kissed him" (Luke 15:20). Paul asked for *compassion* to be present in the Philippian church (2:1) wondering at its lack or absence. Compassion was missing in the Levite but not in the Samaritan. The New Testament states clearly that compassion is something we should be exerting (Colossians 3:12).

Grace (Strong's #2587 / #5485). This is one of the most beautiful words in Hebrew, but it is not easily translated into English. This word is the very source of understanding God's Person. It means to find favor, kindly, friendly, benevolent, courteous, disposed to show or dispense grace and forgive offenses, and to impart unmerited blessings. "But You are a God of forgiveness, *gracious* and merciful (compassionate), slow to become angry, and full of unfailing love and mercy" (Nehemiah 9:17 NLT). "And all were speaking well of Him, and wondering at the *gracious* words which were falling from His lips" (Luke 4:22). *Graciousness* is the mark of the Lord Jesus who is the exact representation of God's character (Hebrews 1:3). Christ was gracious because God is gracious.

Slow to anger (Strong's #639/ #750 / #3115). Longsuffering is fortitude, forbearance, or patience. It means not being easily provoked and able to patiently bear injuries. "The Lord is *slow to anger* and abundant in lovingkindness (mercy), forgiving iniquity and transgression..." (Numbers 14:18). "Do you think lightly of the riches of His kindness and *tolerance* [forbearance] and *patience*..." (Romans 2:4)? "But everyone must be quick to hear, slow to speak and *slow to anger*" (James 1:19).

Personally, nothing causes me to press into Jesus more than my own weakness of anger. When we understand how slow to anger God really is and then see ourselves, we can be overwhelmed by the chasm. When we think that we are a representation of Father God to our children and others close to us, it is no wonder they often struggle to find Him. As living epistles, we fail to reveal God's glory to the very ones He loves so deeply.

The Agape Road

It was anger that caused Moses, the meekest man on earth, to miss God's highest for his own life. When Moses struck the rock in anger (Numbers 20), it was a distortion of the glory of God. Moses misrepresented God as One who was easily angered. Amazingly, the water flowed irrespective of Moses' anger; however, he was refused the privilege of entering the Promised Land with the people whom he had led. It is important to note that Moses did not lose his salvation–he appears later on the Mount of Transfiguration with Jesus (Matthew 17:3), but he lost the opportunities and privileges which were part of his earthly inheritance.

Mercy (Strong's #2617 / #1656). Mercy is mildness and tenderness of heart which disposes a person to overlook injuries or to treat an offender better than he deserves. There is no word in English precisely synonymous with mercy in its original language. "The Lord is slow to anger and abundant in *mercy*, forgiving iniquity and transgression..." (Numbers 14:18 NKJV). "I desire *mercy* and not sacrifice" (Matthew 9:13 NKJV). "Be *merciful*, just as your Father is merciful" (Luke 6:36). Again, the appeal is for us to reveal mercy *because* God is merciful. This is the essence of the Christian life, leading us on the journey to the freedom that He promised. The injury of the Church toward a hurting world has been failing to give mercy after receiving His mercy in such abundance. Behaving like this is a fast way to get into trouble with the Father.

Truth (Strong's #571 / #225). Truth is conformity with fact or reality; exact accordance with that which is, has been, or shall be. Jesus said "I am the way, and the truth, and the life; no one comes to the Father but through Me" (John 14:6). Truth is a Person, the Lord Jesus Christ, Who is the Word of God. "My mouth will utter *truth*" (Proverbs 8:7). "Sanctify them in the *truth*; Your word is truth" (John 17:17). Truth is the nature of God because God is reality. The closer we get to reality, the closer we are to God. It was truth, Jesus said, which would make us free (John 8:32).

Faithfulness (Strong's #2617 / #4103). The Greek word is *hesed* meaning fixed, determined love, to be kept, guarded, watched over, and preserved. This is covenantal faithfulness. Once God gives Himself covenantally, it is impossible for Him to desert or abandon the person or the covenant (Hebrews 13:8). It is firm adherence to truth and duty, true to allegiance, careful to observe all compacts, treaties, contracts, or vows. In other words, true to one's word. God's *affection* is what makes the covenant. "Know therefore that the Lord your God, He is God, the faithful God, who keeps His covenant and His lovingkindness to a thousandth generation with those who love Him and keep His commandments" (Deuteronomy 7:9). No one reading the Old Testament could ever doubt the covenantal faithfulness of God. We need only read Nehemiah 9 or Psalm 78 to be overwhelmed at the manner in which God is seen faithfully cultivating the relationship with Israel who does nothing but violate the relationship and rebel against Him.

Christ is the covenant maker–the agreement is between Him and His Father, not between God and us. Hebrews 7:20-22 explains that the covenant between the Father and the Son is forever. This arrangement cannot and will not change. Jesus explains that "no one comes to the Father but through Me (John 14:6). This exclusive place of coming to God by means of Christ the Son is seen in Paul's writing when he uses the phrase "in Christ" 88 times. Christ keeps the covenant on our behalf; we enter as participants of His grace and recipients of His covenant faithfulness. No matter where we go or what we do, God will remain faithful to love, cultivate us out of our sin, and, if necessary, discipline us into the freedom of His Kingdom. In light of this, the Scripture, "I will never leave you nor forsake you" (Hebrews 13:5 NKJV) can be seen as more of a threat than a promise. If we think we are going to escape God, we are mistaken. When He sets His covenant faithfulness on us, we only have two ways to go: the easy way or the hard way. As a backslider for 12 years, I can testify to the covenant faithfulness of God; He was faithful when I was not.

Forgive (Strong's #5375 / #5746). This word means pardoning, remitting, disposed to forgive, inclined to overlook offense, mild, merciful, and compassionate as a forgiving temperament. "And *forgive* us our debts, as we *forgive* our debtors" (Matthew 6:12). Someone said to me, "God doesn't forgive intentional sin." Well, I don't know any other kind! We wanted to do it, so we did. How thankful I am that God, as a Father, made provision for all our failures in the Person of His Son. God forgives because it is His nature; it is why the redemptive plan was executed in the Person of Christ. "God was in Christ reconciling the world to Himself" (2 Corinthians 5:19). Psalm 51 allows us to see three distinctions of failure.

> [1]Be gracious to me, O God, according to Your lovingkindness; according to the greatness of Your compassion blot out my *transgressions*. [2]Wash me thoroughly from my *iniquity* and cleanse me from my *sin*. [3]For I know my *transgressions*, and my *sin* is ever before me.
>
> Psalm 51:1-3

Sin has degrees of intensity and varying amounts of accountability which elicit different responses from Father God. Note the words: *iniquity, transgression,* and *sin*[2] and how David deals with each separately in Psalm 51. His iniquity is washed, his transgression is blotted out, and his sin is cleansed.

The first level is *iniquity* (Strong's #5771 / #458). There are 11 different words translated as 'iniquity' in the Old Testament. The New Testament uses 'lawless.' The most prominent in the Old Testament is *awon* used some 215 times meaning crooked, that which is not straight, to bend, go astray, or deviation from the right path.

The second level is *transgression*. The word 'transgression' occurs 80 times and it's meaning is essentially a rebellious *attitude*. This is intentionally going beyond known limits, breaking or violating a law, principle, or relationship. It is deciding that the "No Parking" sign is for other people, not for us, so we intentionally go beyond the known limit and park there anyway.

The third level is *sin*. The Hebrew root of this word means 'to miss the mark' or what is more commonly understood as failing, omitting, or refusing to do what we ought to do. All of these result in our inability

---

[2]*International Standard Bible Encyclopedia*, Electronic Database 1996 Biblesoft.

to reveal God's glory or as Paul stated, "all have sinned and come short of the glory of God" (Romans 3:23). Sin is used 430 times in both the Old and New Testaments and includes both Jews and Gentiles. To use the word *sin* is important because, unlike ignorance or chance, it involves some degree of choice, intention, and culpability. Answers for sin and evil lie outside the sphere of education; we are talking moral responsibility which does not resolve itself by more learning. How thankful I am that Father God has made provision for all of these in the Person of His Son. God forgives because it is His nature. This is why the redemptive plan was executed in the Person of Christ (2 Corinthians 5:19).

The only part of the Lord's Prayer that Jesus took time and effort to more thoroughly explain was the urgent need for us to understand the necessity of forgiveness. "For if you forgive others for their transgressions, your heavenly Father will also forgive you. But if you do not forgive others, then your Father will not forgive your transgressions" (Matthew 6:14-15). When we receive forgiveness from the Father but refuse, withhold, or fail to give it to others, we may find ourselves in trouble with the Father. Many of us have serious difficulty forgiving. People do us wrong and we simply do not *want* to forgive them, yet we wrong others and then expect them to forgive us. We seriously jeopardize our journey toward intimacy when we refuse to forgive. Our stubbornness causes us to fail to reveal Father's hidden attributes to others and to misrepresent Him to those who are seeking to know Him. This we do much in the same way as Moses striking the rock in anger, misrepresenting the Father Whom we serve.

When Israel failed God miserably (Numbers 14), God comes on the scene, and though He was *slow to anger*, He was quite displeased because the Israelites disfigured His glory and contaminated everything He intended the nations to see. Then God swore an oath, "But indeed, as I live, all the earth will be filled with the glory of the Lord" (Numbers 14:21). It is *inevitable* that the hidden attributes of His glory are going to be revealed in the earth. This declaration describes and defines God's inexorable purpose in the earth.

When people are able to see through us a Father who is compassionate, gracious, slow to anger, merciful, truthful, faithful, and forgiving, their lives will change. This is and will be the source of society's renewal. These things are not what Father God *does* but *who He is*. When I rediscovered God as a Father, I stopped measuring all fatherhood by an earthly standard. After experiencing such rejection from my earthly father, I found myself wanting to know how to love and enjoy unlimited access to my heavenly Father.

Having an intimate relationship with Father God is what the *Agape* Road is all about. He made this clear when He instructs us to love Him with all our heart, soul, mind, and strength" (Deuteronomy 6:5; Mark 12:30). God wants our affection. In the following chapters we will discover the reasons for His request.

Jesus, Revealer of God's Glory

One of the most beautiful, unfolding insights into Christology is Jesus coming as *Agape* Incarnate for the express purpose of introducing us to the Father (see Appendix for the explanation of the Greek word *Agape*). "And the Word became flesh, and dwelt among us, and we beheld His glory, glory as of the only begotten from the Father, full of grace and truth" (John 1:14). Because the incarnation was for the sole purpose of allowing us to see what God was like, when Jesus said, "If you have seen Me, you have seen the Father" (John 14:9), we know that what Jesus really came to do was reveal His Father to a hurting world. He was "the radiance of His glory, the exact representation of His character" (Hebrews 1:3).

Compassion
Gracious
Slow to Anger
Mercy
Truth
Faithful
Forgiving

Understanding the glory leads us to knowing the Father. Paul said in 1 Corinthians 2:8, "...none of the rulers of this age has understood; for if they had understood it they would not have crucified *the Lord of glory.*" Jesus really is the Lord of the glory (literal Greek translation) and it is His responsibility, along with the Holy Spirit, to teach us. We are learning how to bring honor to God, our Father. The glory consists of the hidden attributes of God being revealed or replicated within His

Own people. This is the essence of Jesus saying that if we follow Him, He will take us to the Father (John 14:6). Every hidden attribute of God is revealed in the Person and activities of Christ. When we see Jesus, we see God's compassion, grace, mercy, truth, faithfulness, and forgiveness revealed in the earth.

God as a Father is an important concept in Scripture. He was a *Father* before He was a *Creator* or a *Redeemer*. He was the Father of the Lord Jesus Christ in eternity before the world began, so that through Fatherhood we can come to know Him (John 17:3). Nothing in American society has been more twisted and damaged than the concept of Father. No one in the history of the world has been more misrepresented than God the Father. He is easy to malign, condemn, and speak against because He does not defend Himself. However, in the damaging of the concept of Father, our whole society is bereft of *security, identity,* and *belonging*. It is urgent that we see the Fatherhood of God restored. This is what Jesus came to do (John 14:6).

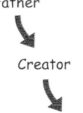

Father

Creator

Redeemer

Throughout Scripture, God's unrelenting goal seems to be to give His glory away. Yet, in the Old Testament He said, "I am the Lord, that is My name; I will not give My glory to another..." (Isaiah 42:8). I always thought that meant God's glory was unattainable, until one day, in a flash of illumination, the Lord said to me, "You're not another, you are My body." In John 17:22 Jesus says, "The glory which You have given Me *I have given to them*, that they may be one, just as We are one." We are bone of His bone and flesh of His flesh. He gives us His glory for the purpose of His character being formed in us as His people so that a hurting world can see through us to the Father.

As we come to know this God, the One who revealed Himself, we start feeling comfortable in His presence. We have a wonderful Father! How I wish that when I was young in the faith someone had helped me to more clearly understand that Christ came to take me to His Father. My idea of a father was displays of male testosterone in the futile attempt to acquire, possess, and control. I knew little to none of His character or the hidden attributes of God's nature.

The Name

A child represents his father's name. If my child is causing trouble or doing something good and someone says, "Oh, that's Mumford's son," he is representing my name.

When Moses wanted to see God's glory, God's response was that He would "proclaim the name of the Lord before you" (Exodus 33:18-19). Then the Lord gave Moses a clear self-revelation of His seven DNA attributes. This biblical writer connects God's glory and God's Name. The content of His Name is God's glory; His Name reveals His character. When we pray in God's Name, we are using His authority which He gave His body to use (John 1:12; 17:22). God's glory is seen when His hidden attributes are revealed through us. His Name is His revealed character, all that He wants us to know of Him. To call upon His Name is to worship Him. We need a deep, gut-wrenching reformation that can help us respond to our call to reveal His glory. Remember that God vowed that all the earth would be filled with His glory (Numbers 14:2).

Every time we pray for someone in Jesus' Name, we are revealing at least one of His seven character traits. Apart from these seven aspects of God's own character, there is no ministry because *Agape* must find a way to reach hurting people. God is *Agape* (1 John 4:16) and He

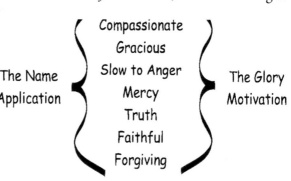

is so eager to reach them that He even uses you and me! He gave us His Name (His reputation) and His Glory in order for us to accomplish this. When we use the authority of His name to pray for people, we are making application of His DNA. This must be done with proper motivation as Paul states in 1 Corinthians 10:31, "Whether, then, you eat or drink or whatever you do, do all to the glory of God."

When the Lord emphasizes physical healing and deliverance, we can sense love, mercy, and compassion flowing through us to those who are captive, sick, hurt, and injured. We can actually perceive something of the glory, the nature of the Father, reaching out from within us. God's love refuses to remain inactive in the presence of human need. I remember ministering with an evangelist who had been in a car accident and crushed his shoulder. He was wearing an "airplane cast" with a stabilizing bar to keep his arm and shoulder from moving. As he laid his cast on people, the life of God flowed through him and they were healed. The simple lesson is that our infirmity does not lesson or obstruct the life of God flowing through us. Healing ministries are born when we touch God's compassion and His searching love for a hurting world. He gives us His name so we can do something about it.

God desires that we represent His name and reflect His glory to the world. However, if you finish reading this with a task list of new things to do in order to reveal God's glory, you will have missed the point. We need simply to *learn to love God.* Scripture says that "to everyone who has, more shall be given, and he will have an abundance" (Matthew 25:29), so it is *God's initiative.* Jesus is both the originator and the finisher of our faith (Hebrews 12:2). Eternal life is when we know what the Father is really like, come to trust Him, and begin to respond to His love.

Coming Short of the Glory

God's goal is that we be formed into the likeness of His Son, reflecting His glory. However, "all have sinned and fall short of the glory of God" (Romans 3:23). Because the image of God in man has been distorted, people, for the most part, do not look to the Church for answers (Ephesians 3:21). As a result, many are left in confusion and darkness.

"Coming short of the glory" is failing, neglecting, refusing, or perhaps being totally ignorant of the necessity of our seeking to accomplish that for which we were created—to show forth God's glory.

Two dramatic illustrations of coming short of God's glory are Moses and David. Moses who received the revelation of God's character first hand, struggled with anger. He was told to speak to the rock (which was a type of Christ) and God would provide water for the Israelites. In anger, Moses struck the rock rather than speaking to it. Because his action distorted the representation of God's glory, he was banned from the Promised Land. King David was also a human representative of God's government. Scripture says that David had a heart after God, yet the ungoverned desires he expressed toward Bathsheba facilitated a series of events, including adultery and murder, which totally distorted the image of God's Nature. This cost him his son and a broken relationship of intimacy with God (Psalms 51:11). Like Moses and David, we, too, have fallen woefully short of God's glory. When people look at us as living epistles, they hope to see God through our life, but often, it is obscured or misrepresented.

Summary

We began by understanding the barriers to intimacy and what it means to be welcomed home. God, in a self-sacrificing act of love, sent Jesus to transcend the death line for one purpose—so that we could love God and others as He originally created us to do. God's self-revelation came to us in the Person of His Son, Jesus Christ: *compassion, grace, slow to anger, mercy, truth, faithful* and *forgiving*. Father God made full compensation for the fact that we have, indeed, "come short of the glory." That is, we have failed to reveal God as He wants and intends to be known. In the next chapter, we'll see how deep this problem really goes and how we have been given the preferential choice between two kinds of love.

Chapter 1 Glossary

Agape Road: (ä-gä′pä) *Agape* is the Greek word for love. The *Agape* Road is a road of love that God created to bring us to intimacy Himself. Jesus is the road–the Way, the Truth, and the Life–to the Father (John 14:6).

Barriers to Intimacy: Three main categories hinder us from having an intimate relationship with the Lord: the satanic or demonic, the original fall, and as a result of the first two, human failure—the mistakes and injuries whose origin and source, for the most part, come from us.

Compassion: (Strong's #7349 / #3628) Greek word *splagchnon*—splangkh'-non; meaning bowels of compassion or mercy (Phil. 2:1). The word means suffering with another; painful empathy; a sensation of sorrow excited by the distress or misfortunes of another; pity; commiseration. Compassion is a mixed passion, compounded of love and sorrow; at least some portion of love generally attends the pain or regret, or is excited by it. Extreme distress of an enemy even changes enmity into at least temporary affection. Compassion means my very insides are moved in concern and care toward you in a supernatural way.

Death Line: When Adam and Eve transgressed, it created a separation between God and His creation causing *death* to come upon all men (Romans 5:12). The death line represents the broken relationship between God and His creation and as a result, sin, shame, and guilt came upon all humanity. God, however, transcended the death line by sending us Jesus. Our path to God is the Holy Spirit, the Scriptures, and Jesus as the Word of God made flesh. These three things are the source of life for those who have been brought over the death line.

Faithfulness: (Strong's #5375 / #5746). The Greek word is *hesed* meaning fixed, determined love. God, Himself, causes His love to be kept, guarded, watched over, and preserved. Once God gives Himself covenantally, it is impossible for Him to desert or abandon the person or the covenant (Heb. 13:8). It is firm adherence to truth and duty, true to allegiance, careful to observe all compacts, treaties, contracts, or vows. In other words, true to one's word. (Deut. 7:9; Heb. 13:5).

Forgiving: (Strong's #5375 / #5746). Forgive means pardoning, remitting, inclined to overlook offense, mild, merciful, and compassionate as a forgiving temper (Matt. 6:12). It is one of God's hidden attributes. Forgiveness is part of His Nature.

The Agape Road

God's DNA/Nature: God's DNA is His communicable attributes, His nature which are able to be imparted to humans (Gal. 5:23). He is compassionate, gracious, slow to anger, merciful, truthful, faithful, and forgiving (Ex. 34:6-7). God also has incommunicable attributes: He is eternal, omnipresent, omniscient, immutable, and self-revealed. When Jesus was on earth, He laid aside the incommunicable attributes, picking them up again after His death and resurrection (John 17:5).

God's Name: God's reputation (Ex. 33:18-19). His Name is His identity, authority, and revealed character; it is all that He wants us to know about Him. To call upon His Name is to worship Him. When we pray for someone in God's Name, we are revealing at least one of His seven character traits.

Gracious: (Strong's #2587 / #5485). It means to find favor, be kind, friendly, benevolent, courteous, disposed to show or dispense grace and forgive offenses, and to impart unmerited blessings. Gracious is a substitute for the name of God.

Iniquity: (Strong's #5771 / #458). A biblical term meaning lawlessness, crooked, that which is not straight, to bend, go astray, deviation from the right path. It is the result of the fall of man when ungoverned desire caused Adam and Eve to go their own way (Gen. 3:6). Iniquity defines the innate and ubiquitous desire that has broken loose from God's restraint, motivating us to go our own way and do our own thing (Is. 53:6). (See Transgression, Sin).

Intimacy: Into-me-He-sees. God wants us to know Him (Heb. 8:11) and He wants to know us (1 Cor. 8:3). This is the normal Christian life made possible through Jesus.

Land of Promises: The New Testament fulfillment of the Promised Land. In the Old Testament, all that was type and shadow (Col. 2:17) is brought to spiritual reality in the Person of Christ. Rom. 8:1-39 is the most succinct description of the Land of Promises.

Mercy: (Strong's #2617 / #1656). Mercy is mildness, tenderness of heart, which disposes a person to overlook injuries or to treat an offender better than he deserves. There is no word in the English language precisely synonymous with mercy.

Sin: The Hebrew root of sin means 'to miss the mark' or failing, omitting, or refusing to do what we ought to do. All of these result in our inability to reveal God's glory. Sin involves some degree of choice, intentions, and culpability. (Rom. 3:23). (See Iniquity, Transgression).

Slow to Anger: (Strong's #639/ #750 / #3115). Longsuffering is God's forbearance or patience and involves not being easily provoked but able to patiently bear injuries or provocation for a long time. (Num. 14:18; Rom. 2:4; Jam. 1:19).

Transgression: Intentionally going beyond known limits, breaking or violating a law, principle, or relationship. The word 'transgression' occurs 80 times and it's meaning is essentially a rebellious *attitude*. (See Iniquity, Sin).

Truth: (Strong's #571 / #225). Truth is conformity with fact or reality; exact accordance with that which is, has been, or shall be. Truth is a Person, the Lord Jesus Christ, who is the Word of God. (Prov. 8:7; John 17:17).

Chapter 2
The Human Dilemma

Sin is the radical twist with a supernatural originator, and salvation is a radical readjustment with a supernatural Originator.[1]

Oswald Chambers

 A paradigm shift is a complete change or reversal in the way something is perceived. This drawing[2] of two ladies is a classic example of a paradigm shift. One is a beautiful young lady, the other an old lady who is not so beautiful. The young lady is wearing a choker and a scarf on the back of her head. She is looking off to her right so that we see only her left profile. The old lady is looking down. The young lady's jaw has become the old lady's rather large nose. The left ear of the young lady is now the left eye of the old lady, the choker is her mouth, and a scarf covers the old lady's head from side to side. Can you see each of them now? If not, take time to do so; they illustrate what I mean by a paradigm shift–a complete change in the way something is perceived. In this instance, we see a shift of many years as we move from the young lady to the old one in the same illustration.

---

[1]Oswald Chambers, *The Philosophy of Sin: And Other Studies on the Problem of Man's Moral Life* (Hants UK: Marshall, Morgan & Scott, 1996, 1960).

[2]Paradigm shift–Stephen Covey materials.

A paradigm shift is needed in the definition of the word *love*. In order to understand the full meaning of the word, we need to understand that love has several "faces." Determining exactly which type or definition of love we are dealing with is important.

Four Faces of Love

The Greek language, from which our English New Testament was translated, has several words for "love" while the English language has only one. We use the same word when we say "I love God" and "I love my dog," but they certainly do not have the same depth of meaning. While we will be focusing on *Eros* and *Agape* in this book, it is important that we have a basic understanding of each of the Greek words for love –*Storgos, Phileo, Agape,* and *Eros.*[3]

Storgos

The essential meaning of *Storgos* or *Astorgos* (Strong's #724 / #845) is without love, heartless, or without family or natural affection. It speaks of the hardening and loss of affection toward our kin or relations. It is used twice in the New Testament, both in negative connotations. In Romans 1:31, the word "unloving" is used, implying that the natural bond a mother has for her children has been lost or destroyed. This can be seen in our day in the increase of abortion to avoid personal inconvenience. In 2 Timothy 3:3 it is used to describe a degenerating society.

Phileo

The essential meaning of *Phileo* (Strong's #5387 / #5384) is "tender affection." It is a love that is reciprocal, expressing friendship, trust, and openness. *Phileo* is friendship moved by qualities inherent in the one loved. The word is used most remarkably of Father and Son in John 3:35 and 5:20. *Phileo* is essentially reciprocal–I love you because you love me. John 12:25 states that "he who loves (*Phileo*) his life loses it." To love (*Phileo*) life from an undue desire to preserve it, forgetful of the real object of living, causes us to lose our life. To love (*Agapao*) life as

---

[3] *Vine's Expository Dictionary of Biblical Words* (Nashville: Thomas Nelson Publishers, 1985).

used in 1 Peter 3:10, is to explore with confidence and risk the true interests of living. Here the word *Phileo* would be quite inappropriate.

Agape

God is *Agape* (1 John 4:16). The essential meaning of *Agape* (Strong's #25) is an exercise of the divine will in deliberate choice, made without assignable cause save that which lies in the nature of God Himself (Deuteronomy 7:7-8). It is God's absolute by which He measures all things (Acts 17:31). It is ultimate reality. It is used both as a noun and a verb. Agape does *not* love because of beauty or value discovered; it is a love that comes out of His own nature. While *Phileo* is reciprocal, *Agape* always reveals God's own character. *Agape*, when understood, quickly reveals our need for Christ, who is *Agape* Incarnate.

Agape unfolds in three progressive steps:

1. Love God with all of my heart, soul, mind, and strength (Mark 12:30).

2. Love myself because God loves me (Matthew 22:39; Romans 5:8). He has given me value and worth by pouring His Own love into me while I was yet a sinner.

3. Love others, even our enemies, in the same manner and degree that He loved us and gave Himself for us (Matthew 5:43-48). This is God's love replicated in His own.

In this chapter we will look at what happens when we fail to understand in our mind and grow in our capacity to love in all three of these ways.

Eros

Eros is a Greek word, but it is not used in the New Testament because of its sexual corruption. (See *Necessity for Creating the New Word Agape* in the Appendix.) The essential meaning of *Eros* is the desire or intention to possess, acquire, or control. *Eros* does not seek to be accepted by its object, but to gain possession of it.[4] *Eros* has an appetite or yearning desire that is aroused by the attractive qualities of its object. *Eros,* in

---

[4]Anders Nygren, *Agape and Eros* (Philadelphia: Westminster Press), viii-xvi.

Greek philosophy, came to mean that which is loved for the purpose of personal satisfaction. It is from this posture that the word *Eros* took on its sexual and ultimately pornographic connotation. The word is not primarily sexual, but has more to do with living for my own personal advantage. The Greek word "evil" in many places in the New Testament is *"porneia"* (Strong's #4190) where we get the word pornography. William Barclay in his book *Flesh and Spirit*[5] says that essentially *porneia* is a love which is bought and sold. This, he adds, is no love at all.

Porne is the link that joins *Eros* and original sin. Moffatt translates *porne*, the King James word for 'evil', as 'selfishness'. "If your eye is selfish, your whole body will be filled with darkness" (Matthew 6:23). Because the New Testament uses *porne* for its description of evil, it is saying something like, "all evil is love for God that has been twisted and sold for something else." Paul explained evil as fallen man "exchanging God's glory" for his or her own desires (Romans 1:23).

Love that has personal reward and self-satisfaction as its motive (Philippians 2:21) has the tendency and capacity to annul the *Agape* of God. "Self-will, that which is self-pleasing, is the negation of love to God."[6] If my love is twisted, everything is twisted. This takes us to the center of all Christian truth, namely that our love for God *must* be accompanied by renunciation of our old self. *Eros* is self-referential, causing us to lose the central appeal of Jesus Christ to "take up your cross and follow Me" (Matthew 16:24). The loss of *Agape* and its demand for self-renunciation leads us to "Cross-less Christianity" (Philippians 3:18). Christianity, apart from the Cross of Christ, has reappeared frequently in Church history.

Eros is the mother of all sins. It can be recognized because it is *always* self-referential. It is not only self-centered, but it becomes self-consuming, turning increasingly inward upon itself in a tighter and tighter spiral. There is a story of a crow that wanted to know where the center of the universe was. He landed on the highest tree he could find and looked to the horizon on his left and on his right; each was the

---

[5]William Barclay, *Flesh and Spirit: An Examination of Galatians 5:9-23* (Nashville: Abingdon Press / SCM Press LTD, 1962), 23.

[6]*Vine's Expository Dictionary of Biblical Words* (Thomas Nelson Publishers, 1985).

same distance apart. Just to be sure, he flew further and landed on another tall tree and again looked at the distant horizons on his left and right. Again, they were equidistant. On the third tree, he looked around then said to himself, "Oh, I see, *I* am the center of the universe!"

The Greek symbol for *Eros* is actually a serpent consuming its own tail. It is a highly refined form of self-interest and self-seeking. It is a love that has become so distorted that its only purpose is to meet its own needs. When Jesus referred to religion that turned us in upon ourselves, He said, "how great is that darkness" (Matthew 6:22-23). He was talking about selfishness which leads to a form of darkness

Greek Symbol
for Eros

that has deadening results. Jesus challenged the deadening effect of *Eros*-motivated religion with these words, "But blessed are your eyes, because they see; and your ears, because they hear" (Matthew 13:16). If that light reverts to darkness, we are then like the serpent who is eating his own tail.

The nature of evil is selling or sharing our love that belongs to God in an illegal manner. God jealously asks for all our love—heart, soul, mind, and strength—to the limit of our capacity because He knows it is the *one force* that releases us from ourselves and exerts the capacity to keep us from evil. We do, indeed, become what we love. We are faced with the inexorable truth that no one can set us free from that which we still love–especially an illegal love for ourselves!

Norman Snaith[7], a conservative scholar, says:

> Dr. A. Nygren has dealt with the matter in connection with what his earlier translator, Father A. G. Hebert, has called '*the fatal confusion between Agape and Eros which now obscures the meaning of Christianity*' [italics mine].... What is Christianity? There can be no answer to the question, except by a clear view of the real meaning of the *Agape* of the New Testament, and its difference from the pagan *Eros*."

---

[7]Norman H. Snaith, *The Distinctive Ideas of the Old Testament* (London: Epworth Press, 1944, 1962), 187-88.

Three Arrows

A philosopher/theologian named Cornelius VanTil lectured in the Episcopal Seminary that I attended in Philadelphia and taught the following principle: If you want to know whether the theory with which you are working is accurate, press it out to its fullest extreme. If you follow *Agape* to its fullest extreme, you find God. God is not faith or hope; God *is* love (*Agape*). If you take *Eros* out to its full end, you come to Satan who wants to possess, acquire, and control. The father of lies passed the whole package of evil desires on to us when Adam and Eve sinned against God. C.S. Lewis explained it most clearly, "When sin entered, all the world was bent."[8] Redemption has to do with God straightening what was bent.

Understanding this has helped me to interpret both the Old and New Testaments and has led me to three very interesting truths:

1) *There is no evil in the world other than Eros manifested as selfishness.*

2) *There is no good in the world other than Agape as God's Own Person revealed.*

3) *All of life can be reduced to three arrows: straight, crooked, or a mixture of the hook and arrow.*

Eros is illustrated by a bent arrow or hook because it is always self-referential, turning back upon itself. *Eros* is the cause and the result of the original fall, causing us to run, hide, and shift blame. When sin entered the world, the effect was that the very nature and center of our **Eros Hook** being became self-serving and was changed from God to ourselves. *Eros* can be overtly worldly or very religious. This hook can be blatant or very subtle. There is a story of two long-time friends who happened to meet again. One of them talked about how he was doing for quite a while, then turned to his friend and said, "We've been talking about me, now let's talk about you. How did you like my new book?" Can you see the hook in that conversation?

---

[8]Charles Huttar, *Imagination and the Spirit*, quoting C.S. Lewis (Grand Rapids: Eerdmans Publishing Company, n.d.).

Agape is illustrated by a straight arrow. If you take *Agape* out to its full end, you arrive at the seven **Agape Arrow** hidden attributes of God's own nature —His DNA.

Again, God is not faith or hope; He *is* love. Unfortunately the word *love* has semantically lost its meaning. With four different Greek words, meaning 'love', we have to decide what we mean when we say, "I love you."

Most of us are a mixture of the hook and the arrow, rather than a full-blown representation of one or the other. As I would read various stories in my Bible, I would draw either an arrow or a hook in the margin, depending on whether the story described *Agape* or *Eros*. For **Mixture** example, as I read the story of Ananias and Sapphira (Acts 5:1-11), I drew a little hook beside it. There are hooks and arrows all over my Bible; it has been fascinating to study the Word in this way.

Jeremiah 15:19 talks about extracting the precious from the worthless. The dividing of soul and spirit is a biblical description of straightening the hook (Hebrews 4:12). This is not easy. The separation is delicate and can be very painful. We cannot and must not attempt this separation in ourselves or for someone else. The Father has reserved the separation and pruning process for Himself. All we have to do is be willing to be brought to maturity in *Agape*.

As we look around, we become increasingly aware of the hooks existing in all sorts of relationships—friendships, marriage, business arrangements, social life, and Christian fellowship. If we are not careful, we can become so cynical that we think everyone who approaches us has a hook. We become suspicious thinking, "What are they after? Why are they saying that?"

Nature of Original Sin

The following pre-suppositional statements[9] may help us better understand the nature of original sin:

---

[9]With due acknowledgement to H.C.G. Moule, M.A., *Outlines of Christian Doctrine* (London: Hodder and Stoughton, 1890), 174-175.

1. *An evil ground of being exists in my nature* as seen in Romans 7:20, "But if I am doing the very thing I do not want, I am no longer the one doing it, but sin which dwells in me."

2. *Eros exists in my will, mind, and emotions* affecting my consciousness, thinking, decisions, feelings, and plans. Everything I think and do is self-referential.

3. *Eros is antecedent to any choice or act.* It is a source or motivation of the act or choice itself.

4. *Eros permeates my person* and was there before any assignable moment in time.

5. *Eros is a mystery* difficult to understand, but alive and active nonetheless. It is implicit rebellion which produces real guilt.

6. *Eros is an aspect of my true personality* even though I may try to hide my humanly-created personality with a mask.

7. *Eros is encompassing*; it affects every aspect of my being. It is at the center of my person, so that there is nothing deeper within me that will enable me to conquer or change it.

8. *I am Eros;* I do not merely "do" *Eros.*

We have all created a personality or a mask for others to see while the real person is permeated with the self-referential hook. On one occasion, I had preached a powerful message and God had done many wonderful things in the meeting, and I said something like this to Him, "Now, Lord, that is my real self." Strangely, there was no response. About two weeks later I was in another meeting that seemed to be an absolute catastrophe and it was entirely my fault. Then the Lord said very quietly, "That's your real self." The person I thought was the real me was actually an image I had created to impress others. The real me was in great need of God's grace.

Lack of Capacity

When we experience the lack of capacity to love God, others, and ourselves, we are presented with two choices:

1. *Fake it.* This is stated in Romans 12:9, "let *Agape* be without hypocrisy." Hypocritical, religious love has destroyed many in the body of Christ, embarrassing God and effectively injuring His reputation.

2. *Face it.* Take an honest look at our lack of ability to love God, ourselves, and others on command as God instructs us. This reveals our need for Christ, Who alone can increase our capacity. Honestly admitting this lack, without condemnation or guilt (John 13:34-35), puts us on the *Agape* Road, so that our capacity to love as God loves can be increased, allowing *Agape* to be perfected in us.

Eros Toxicity

When I was in Japan in 1955 as a Navy medic, I participated in a discussion with the hospital staff about the health issues of Japanese women working in factories. These women would dip their brushes first in water, then in radium, and with their mouth would make a fine point on the brush in order to paint the illuminated dials on watches. Within a short time, they developed cancer of the mouth, digestive, and urinary tract. Because radium does not have a taste or smell, they were completely unaware of the dangers involved. Nursing mothers would then pass the radiated poison on to their babies who suffered and died as well.

Eros, like radium, is odorless, tasteless, and is not easily detected, but it is lethal. *Eros* is so prevalent in our society that even "mother's milk" of the Church (1 Peter 2:2) has become seriously infected with *Eros.* That which should heal and deliver us from our selfishness has the capacity to inadvertently injure us by reinforcing all that is self-referential, i.e., learning how to get things from God. Ordinarily, we would go to church for the purpose of allowing Christ to rule our desires, learn to deny ourselves, embrace the Cross, love God, and seek first the Kingdom. As we feed from an *Eros*-centered Church, we will likely get a double dose of the *Eros*-infection which was our problem before we came to Christ. We have often been taught statements like, "Get your inheritance, get all you can from God, He only wants to bless you." "Pay your tithe in order to gain God's blessings." "We are children of the King, and God intends that all His children live like King's kids." "You should have been at the service last night, you would have received a blessing."

It is not wrong to make Christians aware of their inheritance (along with the conditions necessary to receiving it), to teach that God blesses us, or to encourage church attendance. What is terribly wrong is to be motivated not by our love for God, but rather by what we can get out of Him. We attend church expecting to be taught *Agape,* but we are taught *Eros* both by concept and example.

Eros Capacity to Mutate

Eros is the presence of an element within our heart and will which is alien to our original creation. It is universal in its presence. Every nationality from Aborigines in the outback of Australia to a proper English gentleman has one thing in common—*Eros.* It ever seeks to possess, acquire, and control us in such a manner as to disturb internal and external harmony in every sphere of life and at every level of human existence. It lays dormant when undisturbed, but rages uncontrollably when exposed or challenged. *Eros* causes us to betray each other for personal advantage and is identifiable as the source or cause of that betrayal, even from one we could not imagine possible (Luke 22:48). That which is earthly, sensual, and demonic energizes it. *Eros* is capable of horrendous evil and unimaginable manipulation. It is recognizable by its incredible resiliency and ability to metamorphose for the purpose of survival. Each strain of *Eros,* like a virus that has emerged from attempts to eradicate it, becomes increasingly more lethal and resistant to countermeasures. Except for the viral metamorphosis of the *Eros* strain, one effective repentance or spiritual breaking should be sufficient, but it seldom is. Like any deadly virus, if we do not recognize and seek to slay the *Eros* virus, it quickly goes through the metamorphosis process, continues to develop immunity in a different form, and rapidly re-emerges in religious clothes quoting Bible verses. This is the manner in which Cross-less Christianity is explained in Philippians 3:18. Thus, we can see the necessity of the Cross because nothing in heaven or earth can meet and defeat *Eros* other than embracing the Cross of Jesus Christ.

Suppose a successful, powerful man who is full of *Eros* and has the need to be in control gets saved. *Eros* goes into the death and resurrection of the new birth with him, but it is not exterminated. This is what happened to Diotrophes, a first century church leader, who loved to be first (3 John 9). He used control to exert himself and maintain that position. *Eros* goes through a metamorphosis and reappears in the Christian life with the same need to be in control, only now it is in the church and uses Bible verses to promote itself. This is explained clearly in James 3:14. We rejoice with Diotrophes in his salvation, but the same *Eros* strain has now reappeared in a different form in his life. *Eros*, like a deadly strain of viral infection, can only be matched by the totality of the Cross (Galatians 2:20). We will examine this problem and the solution in greater detail later.

Eros as Lawlessness

Lawlessness is the failure or refusal to bring my entire personality, including my love and affection, into conformity with the likeness of Jesus Christ. *Eros*, undiscovered and untreated, is the hidden source of atheism. *Eros* seeks exceptions and is determined to exploit every personal advantage. It can create plausible demands and is increasingly clever in use of Bible verses to make excuses for itself. *Eros* has the acquired ability to be noticed and observed. Its characteristic is to scheme unrelentingly and without relief, depending upon its ability to outtalk and outsmart others. *Eros* is competitive and self-promoting in that it takes the credit for ideas, opportunities, and suggestions of other people. *Eros* or lawlessness is egocentric or centered in itself, even using God's Name and reputation as a means to its own end. God, the Father, is sought not for Himself, but simply to satisfy our own desires. This is the nature of "original sin" as described in Romans 5.

Lawlessness in the Old and New Testament is often translated iniquity. Iniquity is a power, force, or spirit that must be purged, not forgiven. Matthew 7:21-23 is the pivotal text for understanding the concept of iniquity/lawlessness in the New Testament:

> [21]Not everyone who says to Me, "Lord, Lord," will enter the kingdom of heaven, but he who does the will of My Father who is in heaven will enter. [22]Many will say to Me on that day, "Lord, Lord, did we not prophesy in Your name, and in Your name cast out demons, and in Your name perform many miracles?" [23]And then I will

declare to them, "I never knew you; depart from Me, you who practice lawlessness."

Explaining how successful ministry can arise out of an essentially lawless motivation is difficult. Paul explains this in 2 Timothy 3:5. Arthur Way translates it most accurately, "They will wear the mask of religion, while they have denied all its influence on their character."

Many of us will remember when a prominent evangelist went repeatedly to a hotel room with a prostitute. The woman undressed on the bed, assumed lewd and suggestive poses, but because he never physically touched her, he reasoned that he was not sinning. This is lawlessness. *Eros* was driving him. The presence of *Eros* in the Church is not new. Paul even identified it at work among the apostolic team. He had to send Timothy to see about the conditions of the church because he had no one else to send "for they all *seek after their own interests*, not those of Christ Jesus" (Philippians 2:21).

Lawlessness includes giving other people truthful advice, but not applying it to our own life. *Eros* refuses to give itself to the process of allowing *Agape* to change the manner in which we live and love. The outward form has never satisfied God. He will never rest until we have understood His intent for us to think and act in accordance with His Son. From the original Greek language, lawlessness is translated something like: I do not *want* to do the things that religion presents as necessary. The idea of *lawlessness* is quiet rebellion, a sweet refusal to do the will of God. It is desire and intent which are determined to go their own way. We were not designed nor are we free to please ourselves (Romans 15:1; Galatians 5:17). 1 John 3:4 says, "Everyone who practices sin also practices lawlessness; and sin is lawlessness." Lawlessness reveals the inner motivations of the heart. Unless the heart and the intent are accompanying the outward obedience, it is the same as resisting being conformed to the image of God. It is the cosmic conflict of two wills–God's and mine!

We are capable of being *Eros* driven in our heart, even if we are not in outward actions. Years ago I read a phrase that said "I am sitting down in my chair, but I am standing up in my heart." That same day I was trying to get my toddler to sit down in his high chair so we could eat our evening meal. I had to repeatedly ask him to sit. When he finally gave in and sat down, he was gritting his teeth and the look on his face told me that he was still standing up in his heart. Each of us has attempted to fulfill God's law while gritting our teeth. Heart obedience is a realm without rules (Romans 6:17).

Jesus, as *Agape* Incarnate, seeks to straighten our hook, turning our *Eros* into internal holiness. He reaches for the driving and motivating factors that are resident deep within our person. This is what He was conveying in the misunderstood text of Matthew 5:27-30, "everyone who looks at a woman with lust for her has already committed adultery with her in his heart." With this as the standard, much of the Church lives in adultery and does not even realize it. The sensuality and self-referential conduct within the larger body of Christ is a scandal which discredits the Kingdom of God. Nothing can release us from *Eros* and precipitate our willingness to embrace self-denial apart from the Cross. No one can free us from that which we still love.

The Nature of *Agape*

> Love for the neighbor is love for him in all his strange, irritating, distinct createdness.... Love is eternal, leveling righteousness (Kierkegaard), because it justifies no man according to his desire. Love edifies the fellowship because it seeks fellowship only. Love expects nothing, because it has already reached the goal. Love does not intend, because it has already done. Love asks no questions, it already knows. Love does not fight, it is already the victor. Love is not *Eros*, that lusteth ever, it is *Agape* that never faileth.[10]
>
> Karl Barth

---

[10]Karl Barth, quoted by Romano Penna, *Paul the Apostle: Wisdom and Folly of the Cross* (Collegeville, Minnesota: Liturgical Press, 1996), 200.

The word *Agape* has to do with the nature of God. 1 John 4:8 says, "God is *Agape*." God is not only the origin of the command to love; He is also the source to release that love. He does not give love as a gift, He gives Himself because He is the source of *Agape*. The Son is the begotten *Agape* Incarnate. The Holy Spirit is the manifestation of *Agape* proceeding from the Father and the Son. Love, biblically understood, is a longing and intention toward another person, object, or experience. God's *Agape* creates a *longing* and *intention* toward Himself. He is the One who retains the initiative. *Agape* does not need to be discovered or observed. It absorbs our own failure as well as the failure of others; it seeks to be there in someone's need or crisis; it depends upon truth and faithfulness; it functions as a team in mutuality; it seeks to build up, release, and encourage. *Agape* is an inner authority that is not controlling or possessive. One cannot receive God's command to love and remain unchanged.

In 1 Corinthians 13:4-7 (Message) *Agape* is personified. *Agape* is the *character* traits of Jesus (Hebrews 1:3). These are the seven hidden attributes of God's Person, now made Incarnate–the Word made flesh:

> Love never gives up.
> Love cares more for others than for self.
> Love doesn't want what it doesn't have.
> Love doesn't strut,
> Doesn't have a swelled head,
> Doesn't force itself on others,
> Isn't always "me first,"
> Doesn't fly off the handle,
> Doesn't keep score of the sins of others,
> Doesn't revel when others grovel,
> Takes pleasure in the flowering of truth,
> Puts up with anything,
> Trusts God always,
> Always looks for the best,
> Never looks back,
> But keeps going to the end.
> Love never dies.

These attributes can be seen in the following eight aspects of the nature of *Agape*:

1. *Agape loves without a self-referential bent.* God's *Agape* goes out to a hurting world without seeking return and comes to us from God, as a Father, without personal advantage or selfish gain. Which Greek word is used in this Scripture, "For God so *loved* the world..."? It is *Agape*, of course. Even

1 Corinthians 13 Compared to Exodus 34	
Patient	Slow to anger
Kind	Gracious
Not jealous	Merciful
Does not brag	Truth
Is not arrogant	Truth
Does not act unbecomingly	Gracious
Does not seek its own	Compassion
Is not provoked	Slow to anger
No account of wrong suffered	Forgiveness
Not rejoice in unrighteousness	Truth
Bears all things	Faithfulness
Believes all things	Faithfulness
Hopes all things	Faithfulness
Endures all things	Faithfulness
Love never fails	Faithfulness

though the world rejects, spurns, and refuses to acknowledge God, He continues to pour out His gracious love upon us. *Agape* never disappears.

My wife and I were traveling in the car and she was reading to me aloud from T. W. Hunt's description of the crucifixion.[11] I wept until I didn't think I could see the road. He described how Jesus had to push against the nails in His feet and slide His bleeding back up the Cross to get enough breath to say, "Father, forgive them." I suddenly saw the hook and arrow more clearly than I had ever seen them in my life. As Jesus was hanging there, just moments from death, His concern was for others–that the two soldiers who crucified the Son of God would be forgiven before they were required to stand in the presence of God Almighty and that His Mother was cared for. He was concerned for everyone except Himself.

If I had been hanging there, everything would have centered upon me. I would have been saying, "What's the matter with you people? Don't you understand how innocent I am? Can't you see how I'm suffering?" I began to see how bent in upon myself I had become and felt so unworthy and incapable of expressing *Agape*.

---

[11]T. W. Hunt, Claude King, *The Mind of Christ* (Nashville: LifeWay Press, 1994).

2. *Agape requires preferential choice.* Fortunately, *Agape* is not dependent on us. We simply choose to accept God's love or resist it. This preferential choice breaks the darkness. We will discuss preferential choice in more depth in a later chapter. Perhaps God's intention for permitting evil at all was because He wanted to be wanted. Love that is not based on our preferential choice is not love at all—it is bought and sold and God will not be bought. This is why salvation is a free gift; it can never be bought with good works.

3. *Agape responds first.* We love God because He first loved us (1 John 4:19). We respond effectively to God when, like a sponge, we absorb His love and return it to Him in as pure a form as we are capable. He instills in us the desire and then enjoys our response. Is that not what fathers are like? We give our child a bicycle and then enjoy them enjoying it.

4. *Agape controls us* (2 Corinthians 5:14). Paul sees *Agape* as the reins that control our desires. It is like the harness that goes out to the Clydesdale horses pulling the cart or the steering wheel of the Christian life. It is not human will power, but *Agape* that controls and governs us. 1 Corinthians 8:3 says, "but if anyone loves God, he is known by Him." *Agape*, then, becomes the *absolute* by which a Christian is identified, and is *more than a virtue.*

5. *Agape creates community.* It brings us to *being* rather than *doing.* "If I do not *have* love, I am nothing" (1 Corinthians 13:2). The reason we are nothing is because *Agape* is what gives us identity, revealing us to ourselves and to each other. Because *Agape* is relational, we would have to say, "We love, therefore we are" (1 Corinthians 8:3). It is by the instrumental means of *Agape* that the body builds itself up in love (Ephesians 4:16). *Eros* does not build anyone or anything but itself. While *Agape* covers and tells no one but the person involved, *Eros* tells everyone. The relational differences are like night and day. *Eros* says, "Look what they are doing to me!" *Agape* says, "Forgive them, Father, they don't know what they are doing." *Eros* seeks to be like God; *Agape* is God.

6. *Agape will never go away.* Love never fails. If I am manufacturing love, it will fail. If love is the real thing, it will stand. This helps us

understand how the early church could face terrible persecution and death. I remember reading about a man condemned to die for his faith. He was in prison for about three weeks before execution and the presence of the Lord lifted from him during that time. He kept asking the Lord why he was being forsaken, but the Lord never answered. On the final morning the guards came to get him, and as he stepped into the hall, the presence of God came over him. That was all he was waiting for. He walked through martyrdom with the real joy of the Lord.

7. *Agape loves even our enemies.* To be measured as authentic, *Agape* must reach even to our enemies (Matthew 5:44; Romans 12:14). We are not talking about our feelings or emotions for our enemies, but our *intention* to do them good. Matthew 5:48 says, "you must be perfect [mature] as your Father is perfect [mature]." Measuring yourself by this, how far do you have to go? To love our enemies is a totally new and unique concept that Jesus is presenting about Christ's Kingdom. Remember *Phileo* involves liking someone in a friendship capacity, while *Agape* means we unselfishly seek someone's highest interest and intend to do them good no matter what. Our first thought towards an enemy is usually to do him in. Almost every movie involves revenge towards the bad guy. Ask God specifically for a baptism in His love. It is a choice—God set His *Agape* on us and our choice is to replicate His love. Setting our affections on someone is a learned behavior because, in general, people are unlovable.

8. *"Our God is a consuming fire"* (Deuteronomy 4:24; Hebrews 12:29). Fire is an outward manifestation of God's jealousy. It consumes all that is not eternal and uncreated. Thus, we can understand the importance of the fire of Acts 2 at Pentecost. The inward manifestation of *Agape* is what gives us the adjectives and verbs that describe the mystical realm the saints have talked about down through the ages. However ineffable, this inward realm is described as repentance, tears, gratitude, vision, clinging, unsatisfied desire, light, and heat. It is an inner-penetration of His Spirit leaving the one who is seeking with an unshakable confidence and a certain kind of knowing, which can only be attributed to God as a Father. It is *Agape*, and no other, which has come to us. God came Himself in the Person of His Son!

Hooks and Arrows in Daily Life

Just as all of life reduces to three arrows–hooks, arrows, and mixture–there are also three kinds of people–givers, takers, and mixture. If we love God according to the definition of *Eros*, we are going to love others the same way. If people could really see this, it would make a tremendous impact in our society.

When I first saw that my love for God was mixed with all kinds of things causing me to attempt to *use* God for my personal benefit, even in my prayer life, I did not think I could survive. Most of my prayers were a mixture of *Agape* arrows and self-referential hooks. I shared this with a friend one time. When it dawned on him that he was doing the same thing, he said, "You've ruined my prayer life." Most of us do not know any other way to pray.

Hooks and arrows definitely apply to marriages, too. The husband may be going into the relationship with nothing but hidden agendas. His testosterone is at work, and he is only looking for sexual fulfillment, while his wife may approach marriage with the purest of motives. The reverse could be true—he approaches marriage without hooks, but she has her own hidden agenda such as happiness, security, money, etc.

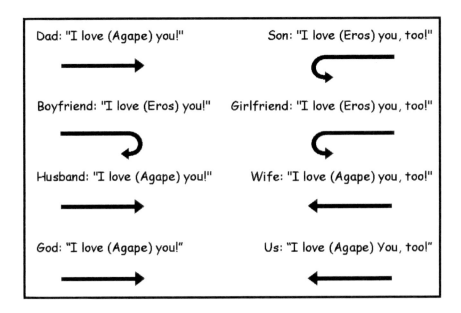

Both may approach the other with *Eros* motives resulting in something psychologists describe as co-dependency, the act of staying together simply because of mutual need. Divorce courts today are full of people saying, "He (or she) did not meet my needs."

Ideally, marriage will be based on an *Agape-Agape* relationship, each partner loving the other unconditionally, each seeking first the other's highest interest. What word for love do you suppose is used in Ephesians 5:33? "...Each individual among you also is to love his own wife even as himself." The word *Agape* is used. It is only when two straight arrows meet each other that God's ideal marriage can occur. "I want to marry you simply because I love you, not because of what you will do for me or what I can get from you."

God intended marriage to reflect the glorious relationship between Jesus Christ and His Bride, the body of Christ, not just to meet the needs of individuals. Satan, the liar and deceiver, has effectively used *Eros* to pervert God's beautiful design of marriage.

Suppose two Christians enter into a business deal together. One has honorable intentions—to build a good business; the other is motivated by *Eros* and only intends to personally profit. Does this ever happen among Christians? You had better believe it! If they were both pursuing a Kingdom standard, they would not only be successful, but God would be glorified.

What about parents and children? The parent says, "I love (*Agape*) you." The child says, "I love (*Eros*) you, too," but leaves unsaid, "for the money I will inherit from you." Or turn it around. The child says, "I love (*Agape*) you." The parent says, "I love (*Eros*) you, too," but leaves unsaid "because I expect you to look after me in my old age."

Consider pastors and congregations. Perhaps the congregation loves the pastor, but the pastor seeks only his self-advancement, using the congregation as a stepping-stone until he can move on to something bigger and better. Or, perhaps the situation is reversed. The pastor is seeking to do God's will, but the congregation is only using him until he can be replaced with someone more to their liking, better educated, or more personable. Believe me, this happens more often than we would like to admit. There is also the possibility that both the pastor *and* the congregation are self-seeking and approaching the relationship in *Eros*. But, sometimes God's will triumphs with the pastor loving his congregation with an *Agape* love and the congregation responding with the same sort of love—no hooks, just straight arrows. The climate in such a congregation is different than in most churches.

Judith and I had been married 30 years when our last child married and left home. One would think that in all those years we would have come to know each other pretty well. We found that the intimacy that should have developed between us over the years was both scarce and very fragile. At that time we were not aware of the *Eros/Agape* principle and its damaging effect upon intimacy. One day Judith said to me, "I think you are one of the most selfish persons I have ever encountered! You outtalk me, bulldoze over me, and intimidate me." I grieved over that particularly because I knew it was true. I was absolutely crushed because the picture I had of myself was heroic, selfless, someone out saving the world, loving everyone, and doing it purely for God. In my male pride, I resented what she had said and I literally did not know how to respond. I thought, "How can this be?" But, over the last several years, I have realized how accurate her appraisal was. Ministry carries its own *Eros* phenomenon, all wrapped in Bible verses and good intentions.

One of the things the Lord used to break this *Eros* self-centeredness was a calcium pill. Every night before bed my wife would get out a calcium pill for each of us. She did this faithfully for many years. One night I was going to bed early, so I got a calcium pill out and took it. She came in the bedroom a little while later and said, "Where's my calcium pill?" I was lying in bed and felt like I had been shot. For so many years she gave me the calcium pill, loved me, served me, and cared for me. When I wanted to go to bed early, who did I think of? Me. She was not even in the periphery of my thinking. I laid there and grieved. Judith said, "I'm sorry you feel so bad about this." I said, "You don't need to take the bullet out, I'm already dead, I just haven't stopped bleeding yet."

The Lord used my wife and that small, painful circumstance to adjust something at the foundation of my soul. My hook was bent into a little straighter arrow. The *Eros/Agape* paradigm has completely changed our marriage! Judith and I are sharing a measure of intimacy we did not know existed. Through these and many other experiences, we began to realize that what was coming out of us (internal) was even more important than what was coming at us (external). What was in us needed to be dealt with first. This is what Jesus meant when He said, "It is not what enters into the mouth that defiles the man, but what proceeds out of the mouth, this defiles the man" (Matthew 15:11).

Loving Others

As previously stated, one of the religious delusions that I carried for many years was the idea that I could be a better Christian if I simply *decided* to be one. If I would just pray, fast, and study the Word more, it would automatically happen. If I just *tried* harder, I could be more spiritual, physically whole, and materially successful. However, after years of trying this, my delusion was broken. Jesus said, "Apart from Me you can do nothing" (John 15:5). I realized that if God in His love did not carry me through, all of my prayer, fasting, study, and works would not only yield nothing, but I would become increasingly frustrated and despondent, which, of course, would lead to anger. What I needed was not just a personal revival, but a reformation based on an undiluted love for God.

After commending the church at Ephesus for its good works, its perseverance, and its ability to endure hardships for His Name, God said, "But I have this against you, that you have left your first love" (Revelation 2:4). I was determined that this would never be said about me, so I read more, fasted more, and "cranked it up" thereby proving to Christ that I would never leave Him–He could depend on me as an overcomer. Then I discovered Moffatt's translation of this verse, "But, I have this against you: you have given up *loving one another* as you did at first." The New Living Testament says it this way, "But I have this complaint against you. You don't love me or each other as you did at first!" This was a pivotal point in breaking my religious delusion.

The shock of this discovery continued for months as I began to understand the meaning of the verse, "If someone says, 'I love God,' and hates his brother, he is a liar; for the one who does not love his brother whom he has seen, cannot love God whom he has not seen" (1 John 4:20). I felt cornered, frustrated, and somewhat paralyzed. According to this Scripture, there was no doubt that I had departed from my first love of the believers God had given me to walk with on my journey. It was not my supposed love for Jesus that was the biblical standard, but my love for Father's other children that gave Him the evidence of my love for Him. I repented deeply and unsparingly.

When we forsake or leave our first love for others, our intimacy with God severely suffers. It is interesting to note, that the verb used is *to send away* or *leave* rather than *lose*. Scripture does not say that Ephesus had lost its first love, they *left* or departed from Christ's command to love others (John 13:34). The distinction is important, for what we have forsaken or misplaced, we can go back and find again.

Hooks and Bible Verses

Consider the *Eros* spin that can be put on the Scripture Jesus gave us that it is "more blessed to give than to receive" (Acts 20:35). The original intent of this Scripture was to provide for our own necessities and labor to support the weak. We put an *Eros* spin on the verse in such a way that it is now used to get money from people for "God's cause." It happens every day. What was originally given in *Agape* has been twisted to our own advantage by *Eros* in order to manipulate and control. This is an infection in the body of Christ. We distort His Word—the very thing God gave us to take the hook out is used as a hook itself. The light is in danger of turning into darkness.

While teaching *Eros* and *Agape* to a small group, I noticed a very masculine man in the front row with tears in his eyes. He said that he and his wife had just recently started attending a new church. One of the church members invited them over for dinner and they were thrilled at the possibility of a new friendship. Halfway through the meal his host tried to get him involved in a multi-level marketing business. The whole reason they had them over was to throw out a hook. It hurt them deeply. The motivation was not *Agape*, but *Eros* in its raw form.

Eros is like a pirate ship flying a flag with the straight arrow on it that says, "*Agape*—I really love you!" As the ship sails into our harbor just past the point where we can defend ourselves, the *Agape* flag is pulled down and an *Eros* flag is hoisted up. It is a form of deception and because of our ignorance of the *Eros/Agape* paradigm, we often fall for it.

Is *Eros* really at work in the lives of Christians despite the redeeming work of Jesus Christ? Absolutely. Just think of some religious television programs. Recently, one of my pastor friends was asked to speak to a church in another city. On his return, he called me and was reacting all over the place. He told me that he was asked how many prayer lines he wanted after the meeting. Not quite sure what the issue was, he replied, "Just one, we will stay with it until everyone has been prayed for." "No," said the leader, "I mean the $1,000 dollar line, the $500 dollar line, and the other line." Suddenly it all came clear to him—indulgences had returned to the Church. As the money increases, so does the *quality* and the *anointing* of the prayer. After 500 years, Tetzel had returned from Luther's day saying, "As the money drops into the box, souls fly out of purgatory." What is most puzzling is that God, in His eagerness to express His *Agape*, will heal and release many of those who are prayed for. The gifts of the Holy Spirit continue to function in the absence of *Agape* (1 Corinthians 13:1-4).

I once met a young man who wanted to be a missionary. We were having a good conversation on the porch when suddenly he said, "Bob, that's my oldsmobile over there." I thought that was strange because it really did not fit in the flow of conversation. Then he said, "The muffler fell off yesterday," and immediately I knew what was coming. For once I saw the hook before it was set. He began a calculated *Eros* symphony as he told me the story about how he and his family were planning to be missionaries and how they needed the car for God's work. He romanced me with all sorts of Bible verses until he finally came to the bottom line: A new muffler would cost him $150. Unfortunately, he had been well taught by some *Eros* professionals on how to sell an effective guilt trip and what needs to be said to manipulate emotions. He even used the Scripture to meet his own needs. If he had just said, in a straight arrow fashion, "Bob, the muffler fell off my car and I don't have the $150 to fix it. Could you help me?" I would have done so in an instant. However, because I understood hooks and arrows, to respond would be to reinforce his error and it was not the time and place to make the whole *Eros/Agape* paradigm clear to him. As there was nothing else I could do, I finally said, "I'm sure the Lord will provide."

Paul identified Timothy as the only man he could send to the Philippian church who did not have a hook (Philippians 2:19-20). Timothy's mother and grandmother, two godly women who loved the Lord had raised him, and he had been discipled by Paul. In effect Paul was saying, "When I send Timothy to you, you can trust him unconditionally, because he will love you as I love you with God's own love."

Selfish and Unselfish

From childhood we are taught about being unselfish. To be selfish is to think, speak, or act in the expectation of reciprocal benefit, even blessing. We give because it is expected. We give to get. We act for a reward. We pray only to ask for "things"—even good ones—instead of understanding prayers as the route to intimate fellowship with God. The arrow we send forth is expected to capture something and return it to us; thus, it becomes a hook. With a hook we can reel our catch back in, and then "testify" to God's provision. As someone once said, "faith without hints is dead!"

To be unselfish is to turn our focus away from ourselves, concentrate on what pleases or benefits someone else and acknowledge that God's will is more important than our own. Unselfishness is like an arrow directed toward someone, with no intention of it retracing its flight path back to its origin. In other words, our love, time, talent, and treasure are directed toward the good of another human being or people group without thought of gaining blessing or benefit. We determine *from the beginning* that the lack of reward or reciprocation will not cause us to cease "spending ourselves" in the other's behalf. We love God because He is God, not because He rewards those who seek Him. We love Jesus because He suffered and died in our place for sins He did not commit, not because He saved us from damnation. We love our spouse because we desire their good, not because he or she gratifies us in some way. If necessary, we "spend" ourselves and get nothing in return, not even a tax deduction for tithing! (I wonder how many American Christians would stop tithing if the tax laws were to change?) To love God because He is God is *Agape*—unselfish. To love God only because He rewards is *Eros*—selfish.

When we follow the implications of *Eros* and *Agape* to their logical conclusions, we find that all of life's thoughts, words, and deeds are rooted in either selfishness or unselfishness. Because of Adam's fall, our sinful nature (*Eros*) tends to dominate us; only in Christ can we be rescued from *Eros*, transformed into God's own *Agape*, and learn to please God rather than ourselves.

Chapter 2 Glossary

Agape: (ä-gä′pä) (Strong's #25) is an exercise of the divine will in deliberate choice, made without assignable cause save that which lies in the nature of God Himself (Deut. 7:7-8). It is a quality of life and is used both as a noun and a verb. *Agape* unfolds in three progressive steps, none of which can be omitted: *1. Love God* with all of our heart, soul, mind, and strength (Mark 12:30); *2. Love myself* because God has given me value and worth by pouring His Own love into me while I was yet a sinner (Rom. 5:8). *3. Love others*, even our enemies, in the same manner and degree that He has loved me and gave Himself for me (Matt. 5:43-48). God Himself is *Agape* (1 John 4:8). His love—covenantally faithful, unconditional, and self-giving—is depicted as a straight arrow. *Agape* is God's absolute by which He judges all things and is His Nature imparted to His own. *Agape* is ultimate reality.

Eros: (er′os′) The original unreality and vanity that entered at the fall of man and it holds all creation in bondage (Rom. 8:19-21). *Eros* is a Greek word, but it is not used in the New Testament because of its sexual corruption. *Eros* does not seek to be accepted by its object, but to gain possession of it. *Eros* has an appetite or yearning desire that is aroused by the attractive qualities of its object. It is man-centered, self-centered love recognized by three manifestations—possess, acquire, and control, and is depicted by the hooked arrow.

Eros Toxicity: Like radium, *Eros* creates spiritual toxicity when we are taught by our culture, including the Church, to be self-referential and how to get things from God. *Eros* toxicity is not easily detected, and it is deadly. The Church, seriously infected with *Eros*, passes on a double-dose of the infection that was our problem before we came to Christ.

Eros Virus: When we are taught by the Church to be self-referential and to get things from God, *Eros*, like a virus, emerges. Attempts to eradicate it make it increasingly lethal and resistant to counter measures, even giving it the ability to mutate. Like a viral strain, one dose of repentance or spiritual breaking is seldom sufficient to kill *Eros*; it goes through a metamorphosis, continues to develop immunity in a different form, and rapidly re-emerges in religious clothes quoting Bible verses.

Lawlessness: Failure or refusal to bring my entire personality, including my love and affection, into conformity to the likeness of Jesus Christ. Lawlessness in the Old and New Testament is often translated 'iniquity'. It includes giving other people truthful advice, but not applying it to our own life. It is desire and intent determined to go its own way; quiet rebellion; and sweet refusal to do the will of God. (1 John 3:4).

Agape Road

Love: Our English word "love" is translated from four very different Greek words: *Storgos, Phileo, Agape,* and *Eros.* "I love God" and "I love my dog" have different meanings. See individual definitions of these words.

Mother's Milk: "Mother's milk" of the Church (1 Pet. 2:2) has become seriously infected with *Eros.* As we feed from an *Eros*-centered church, we will likely get a double dose of the *Eros*-infection that was our problem before we came to Christ. The nourishment which should heal and deliver us from our selfishness has the capacity to inadvertently injure us by reinforcing all that is self-referential.

Paradigm Shift: A complete and expanded change in the model or the pattern of the way something is perceived. The human mind sees different things when looking at the same object, seeing more of what was there all the time, often in a different manner. This is especially true of spiritual concepts. It requires a paradigm shift to accept the New Birth and to see the Kingdom of God.

Phileo: A *reciprocal* friendship; a relationship characterized by affection aroused by certain qualities seen in another.

Preferential Choice: Choosing to accept God's *Agape* rather than resist it. It is a matter of how we set our love. God gave us preferential choice because He wanted to be wanted. Love that is not based on our preferential choice is not love at all—it is bought and sold.

Storgos/Astorgos: Without love, heartless, or without family or natural affection. Used to describe a degenerating society. (Rom. 1:31; 2 Tim. 3:3).

Chapter 3
The Eros Prison

We have grown used to a Godless universe, but we are not yet accustomed to one which is loveless as well, and only when we have so become shall we realize what atheism truly means.

Joseph Wood Krutch[1]

 Freedom involves choices. We have both the capacity and the ability to make choices and to abuse the freedom God has given us, but we are *not* free to choose the consequences of our choices. A person is free to choose alcoholism, but his choice may cost him— DUI arrest, the possibility of killing or injuring someone with the car, financial disaster, etc. People are literally put in prison because of their choices. The consequences of our freedom are facts. Choices have destinations; only truth enables us to make the right choices and preserves our true freedom. We need to be careful that we keep our freedom on the right track (1 Peter 2:16) because certain railroad tracks lead to a place of bondage and suffering.

The concept of choices and *Eros* prisons makes this a difficult chapter. We can always be safe as long as we do not get too specific. Our pain and reactions comes from the scandal of the particular, i.e., I did or did not make the right choice. In this chapter, we will identify some serious and unpleasant issues. Be encouraged that the following chapters do bring hope and answers to these complex problems.

---

[1]Joseph Wood Krutch, *A Lover's Quotation Book, ed.* Helen Handley (New York: Penguin Books, 1986), 26.

Creation is Bent

C. S. Lewis said that original sin caused the entire creation to be bent.[2] We were born with a hook. This bend is the original fall, the sin nature that we inherited from Adam. The *Eros* prison is very real and is the one common denominator of all humanity; it is not limited to believers or unbelievers. *Eros* is the one state of being that binds human beings together all over the globe, in all financial or educational levels, because *"all* have sinned and come short of the glory of God" (Romans 3:23).

How this *Eros* prison works is a very serious issue in the life of every believer. As a brand new Christian, we start our journey on the *Agape* Road, but we can miss the road on either side, religious or worldly. Our objective is to get on the *Agape* Road and stay on it, however unpredictable or uneven our journey might be. Jesus is leading us to the place of intimacy with the Father. When we move off this main road, for whatever reason, we find ourselves heading toward an *Eros* prison. We deviate from the *Agape* Road by pursuing something we love more than God.

All movement off the *Agape* Road starts with a choice made in the

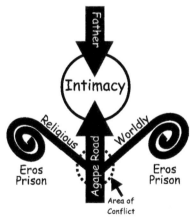

area of conflict. When we go off to the left in religious or legalistic behavior, we are trying to please God with our own human efforts, attempting to improve on all that God has given us. When we go off to the right in worldly behavior, we believe that there is something up there that God has been withholding from us. Very quickly, we discover that neither of these deviations yield what we thought they would. After finding ourselves at a dead end, traveling in ever

---

[2]Charles A. Huttar, *Imagination and the Spirit*, quoting C.S. Lewis (Grand Rapids: William B. Eerdmans Publishing Company, 1971), 200-201.

tightening circles, we recognize that our life is out of whack. Anger, criticism, and anxiety are some of the fruits of this cyclical behavior.

Bars Stronger Than Iron

When God judges something, He sends it in circles. This is what happened to the Israelites when they repeatedly circled the same mountain in the wilderness. While teaching this theme in various prisons and substance abuse programs, I began to see the fruit of this cyclical behavior in the lives of those men and women. It was frightening because I could see more deeply into the spiritual reasons they were there, but their focus was on their struggle with substance abuse or their remaining time in the state penitentiary. Most of them were in an *Eros* prison with bars stronger than iron—built gradually, not overnight.

A lot of attention is put on the prison with concrete walls and steel bars, but that physical prison is nothing compared to the emotional and spiritual one so many of us discover within ourselves. The *Eros* prison is the consummate prison which causes us to think that it may be easier to run, hide, and shift blame than face ourselves and God.

Think of a totally selfish five-year-old who is undisciplined and throws temper tantrums when he or she does not get their way. This behavior only gets worse as the child grows older unless something is done about it. Any human being can find him or herself in an *Eros* prison. The problem is that we do not realize we are in a prison or that the bars are stronger than iron. Each of us is capable of this kind of denial. Jesus establishes this principle when He says, "Everyone who commits sin is the slave of sin" (John 8:34). Once an addict or an alcoholic wanders off the *Agape* Road, he or she becomes a captive and five cycles through a rehab program do not seem to be able to set them free. What is scary is that the *Eros* prison is even more probable when we are given to self-righteousness and

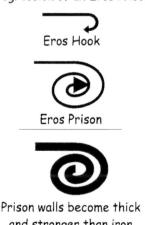

Progression of an Eros Prison

Eros Hook

Eros Prison

Prison walls become thick and stronger than iron

are heading up the religious road. Religion can be an addiction and self-righteousness a real danger for every believer. Once we give ourselves to the *Eros* process, it closes in on us and the walls become thicker and stronger. An *Eros* prison gets us so turned in upon ourselves that we are in an indefensible position. Unless help comes from the outside, we are unable to set ourselves free because we are trapped within the forces that are turning us in upon ourselves.

Ephesians 6:12 says, "For our struggle is not against flesh and blood, but against the rulers, against the powers, against the world forces of this darkness, against the spiritual forces of wickedness in the heavenly places." Notice there are two conflicts, not one—world forces and spiritual forces. Both come against us seeking to provoke us toward departure from the *Agape* Road. Spiritual and worldly forces can be so strong that we feel overwhelmed. If we give into them, we circle in upon ourselves and end up in either a religious or worldly *Eros* prison.

The longer we are in this prison, the thicker the walls become.

Spiral Downward

Once we are trapped in an *Eros* prison, we begin a downward spiral. There are three fairly clear stages in the creation of this *Eros* prison. *First,* as we are spinning down, we are heading to a place where we find ourselves alone. The nature of the Eros prison is to turn us in upon ourselves, creating an increased sense of loneliness. We all know that being in the presence of other people does not mean we are not alone. Each of us have experienced the feeling of being lonely in a crowd. When we discover ourselves alone, we begin to experience fear. No matter how big and bad we think we are, the sensation of loneliness soon introduces us to fear and anxiety.

Alone
Mean
Rage

Second, we become meaner than a junk yard dog. I call it "Christian demeanor." The further we move toward being alone, "da meaner" we become. We will hurt and injure people. We will do anything to have our own way. Paul states this very clearly when he says, "we bite and devour one another" (Galatians 5:15). The worst place in the world to be is at the bottom of this *Eros* prison. When we miss the purpose of God for our life by reaching for something that was forbidden, we experience a form of a free-floating anxiety—the kind of fear that moves toward frustration and anger because we cannot focus on the real issue.

Third, comes the rage itself. As we continue the downward spiral feeling the increasing sense of being alone, anxiety and rage result. This can be a frightening experience, but God, in His mercy, provides a way out of this involutional spiral.

Prison is Not Limited to Unbelievers

Remember the *Eros* symbol of the snake eating his tail? I have known hundreds of Christians who have been this convoluted. They have turned in on themselves to such a degree that they end up examining their own belly button. They cannot function in freedom because they are trapped in an *Eros* prison. If God, as a Father, does not reveal the spiritual issues, we will never know the freedom Jesus promised.

Greek Symbol for *Eros*

In my very first pastorate I inherited an organist who tried to control everything and everyone in the church, including me. One Sunday, I carefully and lovingly told her that it was her last service on the organ. The next Sunday she arrived early and was waiting for me at the church. In anger, she said, "Nobody takes me off the organ!" I had not been out of the Navy all that long and my own self-referential nature was alive and well, so my response to her was less than godly. I said, "Well, you just saw it happen." She was so livid that she literally spit in my face. I could feel my arm drop back and saw my balled fist just coming up past my eye, when I realized that I was about to punch my own church member right in the mouth! By some unknown miracle, something stopped my autonomic reaction in midair. In my mind I could see the headlines in the paper: "Local Pastor Decks His Organist." It was awfully close. The Lord used that experience to begin setting me free from my *Eros* prison. I began to understand that Christ intended for me to be like Him—someone who was slappable and spitable.

What the Bible describes as "the fear of man" (Proverbs 29:25) is an *Eros* prison. Suppose the Holy Spirit urges us to witness to the person seated next to us. We think, "Oh, I can't do that! What will they think?" Our heart palpitates, and we feel sick just thinking about it. The Lord wants us to witness for two reasons—for that person to hear the gospel *and* for our own release from the *Eros* prison. God could certainly use someone else to do the job, and whether or not the man responds is up to the Lord, not us. What God is looking for is our response to His request, so that He can deliver us from our own internal prison.

A person in an *Eros* prison says, "Bless me, help me, visit me, show me, pray for me, teach me, work with me,"—it is truly a spiritual black hole. While we are in our prison, we cannot understand why God would possibly resist us because we see ourselves as eager to do His will. However, when the walls thicken, our light has the frightening capacity to turn to darkness. There is no one in the world harder to reach than someone in an *Eros* prison, especially a religious one (Proverbs 18:19). We can manipulate people and worship to our own advantage and even use God and Scripture in an *Eros* manner. To continue to do so sustains us in the prison rather than helping us get out.

Essentially, if we love darkness (John 3:19), we may not fully recognize nor desire God's freedom. We may want our way no matter what it costs. Certainly we mix in just enough of God to sustain us, but not enough to interfere with our own personally planned future. We may not actually want out of the self-referential prison because He is liable to send us somewhere we do not care to go. Jesus does not want to just sustain us, He may be coming to make war with us (Revelation 2:16), insisting, by the release of His truth in circumstantial events, that, one way or another, we find our way out of our *Eros* prison. God wants us to choose what He wants—the Lordship of Christ.

The *Eros* Shift

In order to understand how *Eros* affects us personally, we need to look at the *Eros* shift from a global and Christian culture perspective and see our place within the large scheme. The *Eros* shift carries with it the idea of breaking loose as seen in Exodus 32:25: "Now when Moses saw that the people were out of control — for Aaron had let them get out of control to be a derision among their enemies." The marginal reading in most Bibles translate it "let loose/go loose." Aaron, in the role of priestly leader, was held responsible for the actual breaking loose. Exodus 32:27-35 describes the inevitable and unavoidable consequences of any society that breaks loose. Once society is living without effective restraint, it is difficult to get it back under control apart from serious or cataclysmic events.

The prophet Isaiah also warned the Israelites about the possibility, even the probability, of their light being turned into darkness. "Woe to those who call evil good, and good evil; who substitute darkness for light and light for darkness; who substitute bitter for sweet, and sweet for bitter!" (Isaiah 5:20). This *Eros* shift accurately describes both western society and the western Church. Like Israel who had a covenant with God, we acknowledge Him in the founding of our country, in the Declaration of Independence, the Constitution, the Pledge of Allegiance, and even on our money; we call ourselves a Christian nation. Under different kings, Israel had powerful revivals; over the years America also has also had powerful revivals. In the meantime, though, because of an *Eros* shift, Israel was sliding down to a judgment that brought about her loss of the Kingdom as inheritance (Matthew 21:43). Despite many revivals in the western Church, as a nation, we too, are moving in an *Eros* shift just as Israel did. Unless God responds with a gut-wrenching reformation which begins in the basement of our souls and which rests upon a Kingdom understanding of *Agape*, America will also experience chaos and upheaval. It is not judgment, but the law of sowing and reaping.

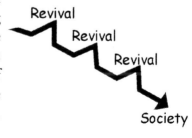

Unfortunately, the *Eros* shift is not unique to America; it is happening all over the planet. Europe, the seat of Luther's reformation, has radically departed from its biblical roots. In Great Britain the people spit on the Prime Minister and watch the Royal family injure themselves with adultery and divorce. Many other nations' capitals are full of *Eros* and are set for social and spiritual upheaval if they fail to understand the issues. However, we have biblical precedent that a city or a nation can reverse the *Eros* shift in a manner similar to Nineveh's leaders who responded to God's appeal (Jonah 3:5-10).

Revivals occur with greater frequency than reformations. They are the product of the Christian Church's attempt to be obedient to the Scriptures. But, they cannot prevent or reverse a paradigm shift until they assume the proportions of a reformation; even then it requires an extended amount of time, even a lifetime or more, to bring society back on course. Despite our revivals, we are still on a downward course, for nothing resembling a *personal reformation* has yet occurred in the twentieth century. What has happened is that a reformation in reverse has taken place in the Church. It is almost complete (see *Eros* Shift Chart). Thus far, Christians have been unable to diagnose it, let alone attempt to reverse it.

This diagram only depicts the *Eros* shift in our society during the past 100 years from a state of controlled or governed desires to a state of uncontrolled or ungoverned desires. The chart also gives us some insight into the idea of momentum and velocity; we find that it is almost complete. The pendulum is swinging from light into darkness both socially and religiously. Robert Bork, whom I have the privilege to know personally, was nominated for judge in the Supreme Court. In his book, *Slouching Toward Gomorrah*[3], he says that the *Eros* shift began 250 years ago, but by the 1900s it finally broke loose because liberalism began to exert more influence.

I was born in 1930 when the influence of the *Agape* culture could still be felt. When a man or woman gave you their word on something,

---

[3]Robert H. Bork, *Slouching Toward Gomorrah* (New York: ReganBooks, HarperCollins Publishers, 1996).

Eros Shift Chart
Galatians 1:4

An *agape*-motivated culture

An *eros*-motivated culture

Reformation in Reverse--Once society is out of control, broken loose, unstrained or unbridled, consequences are inevitable.

Governed Desires
Human desires under the influence of Judeo-Christian tradition or Christian culture rooted in *agape*.

Ungoverned Desires
Human desires under the influence of a culture driven by *eros*

1880-1900s
Strong influences of the ideas of Rousseau (1712-1778)
His basic premise: "Man is born free but is everywhere in chains."
1. Modern idea of education: State owns the children
2. Subjectivism: feelings, careless attire, "Bohemian" lifestyle
3. Man's corruption as excuse
4. Individualism: leads to anarchy
5. Social contract: State as god and father

1910s
First World War. The demise of the European Empires and hierarchical society, the Communist revolution. Broad disillusionment with the traditional society and the Church that led to such destruction.

1920s
Roaring 20s with hedonism, prohibition, and the strong influence of Freud--soul without God. Marx--economy without God, and Darwin--universe without God. By now, the traditional "bottom" does not hold for many.

1930s
Great Depression and widespread disillusion with western capitalism; the New Deal by Franklin D. Roosevelt--the American Social Revolution.

1940s
The Second World War with the destruction of the remaining European states and Japan; the advent of nuclear warfare: severe angst in the human community; the establishment of the United Nations, i.e., Global community.

1950s
Post-war license, abundance, and careless ease (Ezk. 16:49); social and cultural upheaval: return of GIs, women in factories; Cold War and the threat of nuclear annihilation.

1960s
Beatles and Elvis, free love. Hippies "broken loose"; increased substance abuse. Entitlement: do your own thing. Church: happy, free, fulfilled. Divorce, sexual freedom in church and society: tolerance to an exalted position; political correctness (new "Molech").

1970s
Vietnam's division and effect: national corporate identity destroyed; sexual revolution, abortion on demand; TV in every home--camera taking us where we have no right to be. Woodstock: religious/political

1980s
War on poverty ($128 billion); homosexuals "out of the closet"; mega-church and marketing of religious social conditioning.

1990s
Addictive society, absence of restraint in:
1. Media: TV/Radio
2. Computer: internet, virtual reality
3. Music: Gangsta-Rap

2000s+
Consummate eros with consequences that are inevitable; an alternate society mocking Kingdom values.

it was like a signed contract. Some years ago a friend of mine shook hands with a buyer in an agreement to sell a piece of property for $50,000. Forty-five minutes later another man came along and offered $65,000 for the same piece of property. Nothing was signed and no money had been exchanged, but his reply to the offer was "I am sorry, but the land is sold." He never thought twice about it, because he walked according to the *Agape* culture. That kind of integrity in our culture has essentially disappeared. The fact that we are willing to break our word rather than take personal loss is the *essence* of the *Eros* shift. We will do whatever we need to do to preserve our self-interest. We can observe this in everything from marriages and finances to business dealings on Wall Street resulting in the exposure of corporate *Eros*. Christians and non-Christians alike buy into individualism and entitlement living without restraint regardless of how it affects anyone else. "If it feels good, do it" becomes the motto. Restraints or guidelines are not politically correct, and political correctness is a god that must be worshiped. Sadly, the Church has fallen in with this as well and has decided that its mission should be helping people to feel happy, free, and fulfilled. Cross-less Christianity, whether it is religious or worldly, leads inexorably to an *Eros* prison.

Five Steps of an *Eros* Shift in the Church

For most of my 50 years walking with the Lord, I was unable to see that the religious road was equally if not more dangerous to my following Jesus than the worldly one. As a young Christian I always assumed that the Church would become more and more spiritual. To my surprise, the organized Church is becoming more outwardly secular, employing worldly methods and models, while the secular world is becoming increasingly enchanted with the supernatural in the form of the satanic and the cultic. Understanding the dangers of aberrant religious behavior is pivotal. By religion, I mean conscious attempts to possess, acquire, and control. In this definition, religion is used in the broadest sense and with negative connotation. When religion itself deviates from the *Agape* Road, it takes God's people with it as Isaiah states in 9:16, "For the leaders of this people cause them to err...." Few things seek to control and possess as do the leaders of institutional religious entities. Consider the following steps as the process of an *Eros* shift:

1. *Religious Passion.* The most frightening aspect of religious activity is the *passion* that it carries. Greek philosophers interpreted this passion as demonic using the word *entheos*: *en* is Greek meaning 'dwelling within' and *theos* meaning 'indwelt by a god or a demonic force'. Our word enthusiasm came from this root. Of course, this indwelling has a positive application: God (*Agape*) dwells in our hearts through faith (Ephesians 3:17). Religious enthusiasm can never be a substitute for that quiet confidence of the Kingdom of God in our lives. The strange thing about religion that I am seeking to identify can best be seen in India or the Middle East where religion is motivated and driven by consummate control.

2. *Religion is nourished in self-righteousness.* Because *Eros* has not been discovered, acknowledged, or exposed, the religious process increasingly moves toward a human encroachment upon God's prerogatives. Man attempts to move toward the noncommunicable attributes of God, seeking to be all-knowing and all-powerful, and ascends into God's own sphere. The lust for power, as seen in Adolph Hitler, Josef Stalin, or Saddam Hussein, illustrates the strength and ferocity that comes as a result.

3. *Religious violence.* As we have discovered, when *Eros* is denied or resisted, it moves toward violence and murder (James 4:2). Dostoyevsky, in his treatise *The Grand Inquisitor*, identifies this as the "second order of evil." Simply explained, religion is capable of severe persecution and punishment when we fail or refuse to do what is expected or demanded from us. When I discovered that Calvin, one of my heroes, had his religious enemy, Servetus, burned alive, I was chagrined and disillusioned. The violence attached to religion can be seen in Russia, the radical Muslim world, and the religions of Japan and the Far East, all of which readily qualify as candidates for the violence we may call "the second order of evil." Church history is full of violence and murder. The inquisition conducted its "witch hunts" for years with the second order of evil as its intentional agenda. Catholics tortured Protestants, and Protestants responded in like manner. Then, both Protestants and Catholics employed violence toward those who would dare oppose them.

4. *Training by concept and example in the skills of intrigue and suspicion.* Nothing is more sophisticated and dangerous than religious politics. An *Eros*-driven elders' meeting is a prime example. The damage wrought by strife or selfish ambition (James 3:14) is immeasurable. Once intrigue and suspicion enters, the *Eros* shift is nearly complete. This helps us understand how our light can turn to darkness. Thus, the principles of *The Prince and the Discourses* by Niccolo Machiavelli appear and reappear demonstrating the persistence and reality of corrupt and totalitarian forms of government both in the Church and in politics.

5. *Buried in disgrace.* Selfish ambition enters through wisdom that does *not* come from above (James 3:15). In the drive and passion of the project or vision, we are fully prepared to run over someone "for Jesus." Because we are both self-referential and self-righteous, we can and will crush others for their failure. In the momentum of the second order of evil, we are capable of violence toward others, and do it for Jesus' sake. When intrigue and suspicion displaces *Agape,* even the gifts and ministries of the Holy Spirit are reduced to *Ichabod* meaning the glory has departed (1 Samuel 4:21).

In my 50 years, I have observed and participated in five different visitations of the Holy Spirit, each of which quickly became infected with selfish ambition and religious politics followed by intrigue and suspicion. This is the consistent testimony of almost every movement, denomination, and restoration emphasis. Once the *Eros* shift has taken place, the consequences of that shift become inevitable and consequential. It is not necessarily God's judgment, but the inexorable principle that what we sow, we will eventually reap. Departure from our position of keeping ourselves in the *Agape* of God (Jude 21) will eventually lead to failure and disgrace. This is Cross-less Christianity.

Biblical Examples of an *Eros* Shift

Once an individual or a corporate people break loose, two things happen which result in an inexorable third event. When a person rejects moral restraints, it results in a personal *Eros* prison. These individual prisons contribute to the formation of an *Eros* shift. An *Eros* shift and

Agape Road

an *Eros* prison can also be reciprocal, feeding and building one upon the other. The end result is the demise of the entity, including entire civilizations. These principles are clearly demonstrated in the progressive fall of the Roman Empire.

Looking at some biblical examples–both personal and corporate–of the *Eros* prison that lead to an *Eros* shift is important so that we can better understand how our entire Christian culture has become so separated from its foundations. Sufficient numbers of personal *Eros* prisons create a movement, understood as the *Eros* shift–an entire culture doing its own thing. As David asked, "If the foundations are destroyed, what can the righteous do?" (Psalm 11:3).

❖ *Sodom and Gomorrah.* When God was about to bring judgment upon Sodom and Gomorrah, Abraham asked Him to withhold His judgment if ten righteous people could be found living in the city (Genesis 18). Both Sodom and Gomorrah had made a full-blown *Eros* shift, making it impossible to identify even a few who had not been carried away with the *Eros* culture.

❖ *Jerusalem.* Jerusalem as the city of God was supposed to represent God and His glory. However, both in the Old and New Testaments, the majority of those living in Jerusalem were swept up in an *Eros* shift; only a remnant were faithful to the God of the covenant. Once this shift was complete within the residents of the city, judgment came. Isaiah 1:21 says, "How the faithful city has become a harlot, she who was full of justice! Righteousness once lodged in her, but now murderers." Jerusalem who was called to be light had now become darkness (Matthew 4:16). After Isaiah prophesied, the city was judged and the Babylonian captivity, a type of an *Eros* prison, followed. The remnant left in Jerusalem was persecuted; those who were saved became the godly seed.

❖ *Moses.* Remember that when Moses struck the rock in anger he was refused entry into the Promised Land because his presumptuous action had distorted the glory of God. Smiting rather than speaking to the rock was serious, because the rock represented God and His provision for His people. Moses diverted from God's *Agape* and experienced an *Eros* prison.

❖ *David.* We also remember that King David, representative of God and His government, acted in ungoverned desire when he committed adultery and murder. He, too, disfigured God's glory or character, diverted from God's *Agape*, and discovered himself in an *Eros* prison. David's prison is easier to understand than Moses' because we are far more accustomed to loss attributed to adultery than to disobedience to the Word of the Lord. David was so trapped in his *Eros* prison that it took the prophet Nathan to extract him. In the midst of his *Eros* prison and as a result of being set free, David wrote Psalm 32 and Psalm 51.

v *Jeremiah and Old Testament Israel.* Jeremiah is called to identify and resist the velocity and momentum of the *Eros* shift as it envelopes the entire society of Israel (Jeremiah 9:3-6). Jeremiah, as a prophet to this nation, sees his entire people swept up in an *Eros* agenda rather than walking in the *Agape* demands of Jehovah and His Law. Note how Jeremiah states the reason for this *Eros* shift in Jeremiah 2:11, "Has a nation changed gods when they were not gods? But My people have *changed* their glory for that which does not profit."

❖ *New Testament Israel.* The people in Jesus' day were in consummate denial of their imprisonment. Many were in a religious *Eros* prison thinking that by keeping Moses' law they were free. With Roman soldiers all around, Jesus said the truth would set them free and they made this statement, "We are Abraham's descendants and have never yet been enslaved to anyone; how is it that You say, 'You will become free'?" (John 8:33). Total religious unreality causes spiritual blindness, deafness, and a heart that is unable to respond. Soon after this statement regarding their freedom they said, "we have no king but Caesar!"

❖ *The Rich Young Ruler.* This young man (Luke 18:18-34) desired to walk the *Agape* Road, but when Jesus approached him with the cost, he was trapped in his *Eros* prison of material possessions. This may not have been the end of the story, however. Hopefully, after understanding what the issues were, he returned and opened himself to Christ and His Kingdom.

❖ *The Prodigal and the Elder Brother.* The opposite of a worldly prison is a religious prison, consisting of a legalistic approach to life and godliness. The religious road increasingly strives to please God by obeying the laws and rules. The story of the prodigal son's elder brother (Luke 15:11-32) illustrates this. The prodigal ran off, lived a worldly lifestyle, repented, and found a relationship with his father again. But, the elder brother was captured in a legalistic prison of works that would not allow him to open himself to the father. Both of them left the *Agape* Road, and both found themselves in a dead-end *Eros* prison. Scripture never reveals whether the legalistic elder brother ever broke free, but at least we know that the worldly prodigal was restored to intimacy with his father.

❖ *Demas*. Demas was part of Paul's apostolic team, but he was trapped in a worldly *Eros* prison. Timothy shows the strength of the prison when he said, "Demas, having loved (*Agaped*) this present world, has deserted me" (2 Timothy 4:10). Demas set his love on this world. Jesus offered a spiritual freedom; Demas chose a natural one. This may be one of the clearest biblical examples of the fact that no one can set us free from that which we still love.

The *Agape* Conversion

The radical change from an *Eros* shift to an *Agape* conversion means a complete change in the direction in which our lives are moving. This may be in direct contrast to everyone else (1 Peter 4:4). Remember, the *Eros* shift is more than personal; it is also cultural. For an *Agape* conversion to take place, the Lord needs to make us starkly aware that the direction society is headed is *not* the way in which God wants His people to go. When this awareness occurs, we can no longer rest in our comfortable place—we will be on the battle line. We must be concerned not just about eternity, but about the manner in which we are living our lives today, "known and read by all men" (2 Corinthians 3:2).

The only dynamic that will act as an antidote to the *Eros* shift is a full dose of the Kingdom accompanied by a full-blown reformation. Consider whether another 60 million of the same kind of Christians we already have will change the world. With a few exceptions, the whole

Chapter 3 Glossary

Agape **Conversion:** Release from the power of *Eros* and our self-referential human nature. It is the decisive adoption of *Agape* as a lifestyle.

Area of Conflict: The area where the human will and life's choices come together and force us to make a decision. We are presented with three choices: We can seek fulfillment on the religion road, the worldly road, or abide on the *Agape* Road.

Eros **Prison:** The end result of detouring off the *Agape* Road because *Eros* is at the center of our life. Cyclical behavior causes us to spiral downward until the walls become thicker and the bars become stronger than iron.

Eros **Shift:** A move toward man-centered, ungoverned desires, individualism, anarchy, and entitlement. The *Eros* shift involves all levels and units of society–individual, family, church, and government. The five steps of an *Eros* shift are: 1. *Religious Passion; 2. Religion nourished in self-righteousness; 3. Religious violence; 4. Training in skills of intrigue and suspicion; 5. Buried in disgrace.*

Eros **Symbol:** The snake eating his tail. Being convoluted and turned in on ourselves.

Religion: Religion, in the negative sense of the word, is man's effort to replicate what only God can do.

Religious Road: A detour off the *Agape* Road due to a rule-keeping, legalistic focus that captures and controls. The end of the road is a prison is constructed from a self-referential perspective that is the result of refusing God's righteousness and seeking to create a righteousness of our own (Rom. 10:3).

Revival vs. Reformation: Revival is the act of reviving after a decline or discontinuance. Reformation is a visitation of the Holy Spirit accompanied by radical and permanent change in political, religious, and social affairs.

Spiral Downward: Once we are trapped in the *Eros* prison, we begin a downward, ever-tightening spiral. There are three stages in this *Eros* prison: alone, mean, rage.

Worldly Road: A detour off the *Agape* Road in an attempt to *get something* we believe God has been withholding from us. It is rooted in a desire to use God for one's own personal success or advantage.

Chapter 4
The Eros Payoff

Agape is the only good in the world; selfishness is the one thing hateful.[1]
— George MacDonald

Years ago I went on a three-day fast. No one outside of my family knew about it and I really needed others to know how spiritual I really was. During a meeting with several other pastors, I said with dignity and false humility, "Well, this is the third day of my fast. I have been only on water." Quietly, I heard a stern Fatherly voice say, *"You have just received your reward.* Their recognition has just cost you nine wonderful meals." That is an *Eros* payoff. All of a sudden, I understood what Jesus meant when He told us not to pray, fast, or give to be seen of men, or we would have our reward—man's recognition as compared to Father's secret and intimate response (Matthew 6). When religious activity is accomplished for the purpose of being seen, the *Eros* payoff *is* the reward. There *is* nothing more. You have chosen what you esteem as most important.

Agape, we have learned, does not seek its own while *Eros* is the opposite. The *Eros* payoff is a serious and vicious activity that injures and destroys in ways we cannot imagine. The accusation of standing and praying as hypocrites for the simple reason of wanting to be seen by

---

[1]Rolland Hein, *The Heart of George MacDonald* (Harold Shaw Publishers; Wheaton, Illinois, 1994), 315.

men carries far more significance than we have understood. The *Eros* payoff reveals itself by the use and implementation of the most convoluted and subtle movements one can imagine.

My Dad suffered financially most of his life and had deep internal conflicts about when and how much to give to the Lord's work. He would carefully take out a one dollar bill, meticulously crease it lengthwise, and when the offering plate arrived, he would carefully lay it on the top. He wanted everyone to appreciate the fact that he had given a "quiet offering" of paper money compared to the "noisy offering" of coins. As a child, I knew something was wrong with this, but I could not identify the issue. Once we begin to see the *Eros* payoff for what it really is, we understand why Jesus spoke to this phenomenon so forcibly and directly.

People are trapped, used, manipulated, and mistreated on the basis of the *Eros* payoff. When religious leaders, politicians, and salesmen become more skilled in the use of the *Eros* payoff, we suffer at their hands. Some churches use titles and false recognition (*Eros* payoff) to get you to attend their church instead of another. This can be highly motivating to the person who is lost, confused, or unrecognized. The person who attempts to commit suicide does not usually do it quietly and without fanfare. He uses a twelve gauge shot gun to make sure we all know who he was and that now he is gone. It is a cry for illegal recognition. He may even use the suicide to punish us for failing to recognize him. Similarly, a person jumping from the 12th story window doesn't usually do it at midnight; they wait until there is a crowd. Their final *Eros* payoff is saying, "You *will* recognize my importance." This is a form of slavery.

The *Eros* payoff is a strange, twisted internal desire to be seen and noticed by others. It motivates some more than others. We can see it in young children who demand to be seen or noticed. Long after they have received a parent's undivided attention, they continue insisting, pleading, and clamoring to be watched doing silly things in order to satisfy an illegal desire to be noticed. This ungoverned desire is what makes us vulnerable, easy picking for those who know how to use smooth talk and flattery to take personal advantage (Jude 16).

Manipulative advertising and sales techniques are based on an *Eros* payoff. They go something like this: "You must get *yours* now, for there may not be enough." "*You* should be the very first to own this in your neighborhood." "Imagine what your friends will think when you drive this car." Appealing to the *Eros* payoff is one of the reasons these techniques are successful rather than seen as a rip-off.

The *Eros* payoff is one of the motivations of man's cruelty to others. For someone to put you down with criticism, verbal abuse, or humiliation seems to directly contribute to his or her own sense of superiority. Abusing others by an ugly, condescending attitude allows him or her to be somebody. Thus, making a show of our religion before men for the purpose of a payoff has serious and far-reaching repercussions.

Changing the Rules

On the roof-top, Peter was given a vision and told to "rise and eat" (Acts 11). Paul tells us in Romans 14:17, "for the kingdom of God is not eating and drinking, but righteousness and peace and joy in the Holy Spirit." We can see from both Peter and Paul that Jesus is *changing the rules*. God's favor no longer depends on what we eat or drink; He wants us to understand the internal reality of the Kingdom of God. This is very clear in Mark 7:14-23 (AMP):

> [14]And He called the people to [Him] again and said to them, Listen to Me, all of you, and understand [what I say]. [15]There is not [even] one thing outside a man which by going into him can pollute and defile him; but the things which come out of a man are what defile him and make him unhallowed and unclean. [16]If any man has ears to hear, let him be listening [and let him perceive and comprehend by hearing]. [17]And when He had left the crowd and had gone into the house, His disciples began asking Him about the parable. [18]And He said to them, Then are you also unintelligent and dull and without understanding? Do you not discern and see that whatever goes into a man from the outside cannot make

him unhallowed or unclean, [19]Since it does not reach and enter his heart but [only his] digestive tract, and so passes on [into the place designed to receive waste]? Thus He was making and declaring all foods [ceremonially] clean [that is, abolishing the ceremonial distinctions of the Levitical Law]. [20]And He said, What comes out of a man is what makes a man unclean and renders [him] unhallowed. [21]For from within, [that is] out of the hearts of men, come base and wicked thoughts, sexual immorality, stealing, murder, adultery, [22]Coveting (a greedy desire to have more wealth), dangerous and destructive wickedness, deceit; unrestrained (indecent) conduct; an evil eye (envy), slander (evil speaking, malicious misrepresentation, abusiveness), pride (the sin of an uplifted heart against God and man), foolishness (folly, lack of sense, recklessness, thoughtlessness). [23]All these evil [purposes and desires] come from within, and they make the man unclean and render him unhallowed.

When Peter presented this teaching, it was so revolutionary that all of the disciples began to struggle much like we do. It is difficult to change from an outward *Eros* payoff to inward reality. When Paul declared all foods ceremonially clean, it was a termination of all religious externals that destroy the very *source* of our self-congratulation. The old rules do not apply any more. It is not what comes into us, but what comes out of us that causes us to injure others. These things are the source and motivation of the *Eros* payoff. Until and unless we can identify an *Eros* payoff, we will never know freedom as Jesus promised it.

Childhood "Tapes"

Childhood "tapes" are memories of events from childhood that continue to play in our minds and control our behavior long after we have reached adulthood. They are strongholds, untruths, or forms of deception that we hold in a fortified place of defense within our mind. When childhood "tapes" play, unexpected emotions from past hurts are released. We may know intellectually that they are no longer valid, but they still have the power to control us. These strongholds stem from our failure to understand the power of *Eros* and result in self-defeating lifestyles such as manipulation, passive/apathetic, dependent, hostile, sexually seductive, controlling, handicapped/entitlement, despair, power-seeker, entertainer/joker, irresponsible dreamer, and the ever-present workaholic. If we think about it, each of these is severely self-referential. They become *Eros* prisons in our life with bars stronger than iron. The good news is that the mental and emotional strongholds of both pain and pleasure that seek to usurp the Lordship of Jesus in our lives can be broken, but it takes more than psychological excavation. Someone observed that childhood is that time we spend the rest of our lives getting over.

The "tapes" of childhood can also be self-defeating. They play in our ears in such a way that they control our behavior. My father's rejection of me as a young teenager was a "tape" that has played back in my mind for years. These "tapes" are *autonomic* in nature and are usually not consciously chosen, but they have the ability to effectively displace our will and choice in setting our affection on loved ones or even the Lord. They are called hedonic responses because they seek to motivate us toward preservation of our pleasure and avoid further pain by running, hiding, and shifting blame. Running from pain and ultimate reality is the name of the game in our western society.

Agape has a remarkable degree of power to release us from being too concerned about what is or is not healthy. It effectively prevents our childhood "tapes" from playing. *Agape* at the center of our being exposes all our *Eros* crazies, restricting or containing that illegal desire from being the center of attention. This whole bundle of mixture is then pushed to the periphery of our being, effectively stripping temptation of its strength and power. This will be examined in more depth in another chapter and could be a needed and therapeutic insight for our confused and overly psychoanalyzed generation.

Eros and Murder: Poisoned Love

With the strength and seriousness of the *Eros* payoff beginning to make sense, we are now ready to make another important transition into an understanding of James 4:1-5:

> ¹What leads to strife (discord and feuds) and how do conflicts (quarrels and fighting) originate among you? Do they not arise from your sensual desires that are ever warring in your bodily members? ²You are jealous and covet [what others have] and your desires go unfulfilled; [so] you become murderers. [To hate is to murder as far as your hearts are concerned.] You burn with envy and anger and are not able to obtain [the gratification, the contentment, and the happiness that you seek], so you fight and war. You do not have, because you do not ask. [1 Jn. 3:15.] ³[Or] you do ask [God for them] and yet fail to receive, because you ask with wrong purpose and evil, selfish motives. Your intention is [when you get what you desire] to spend it in sensual pleasures. ⁴You [are like] unfaithful wives [having illicit love affairs with the world and breaking your marriage vow to God]! Do you not know that being the world's friend is being God's enemy? So whoever chooses to be a friend of the world takes his stand as an enemy of God. ⁵Or do you suppose that the Scripture is speaking to no purpose that says, The Spirit Whom He has caused to dwell in us yearns over us and He yearns for the Spirit [to be welcome] with a jealous love? [Jer. 3:14; Hos. 2:19 ff.] AMP

James, with great shock to the biblical interpreters, says, "You become *murderers.*" Careful examination of this text gives clear evidence that James means murder in the physical sense of taking another's life. This shows us the power and strength of the *Eros* payoff in language we can understand. You will note that even the Amplified Bible, in our quote above, seeks to modify the implication of murder, by inserting the phrase "when you hate...." Some might think that a Christian would not commit murder, but the sources say it is *real murder*. What we are dealing with is poisoned love: I am so in love with myself, that I am determined not to let you interfere with my satisfaction. This determination will go to the point of eliminating you if that becomes necessary. This is an *Eros* payoff and history is full of such stories.

The Old Testament story of Naboth's vineyard (1 Kings 21:1-16) is a graphic illustration of *Eros* controlling someone to the point of murder. King Ahab wanted Naboth's vineyard for his own use, however Naboth refused to part with it because it was his inheritance from his father. Jezebel, Ahab's wicked wife, under the control of *Eros*, arranged for Naboth to be falsely accused in order that he might be taken out and stoned to death. He was murdered because of a *desire* that controlled both Ahab and Jezebel. People, including Christians, are capable of murder when they are governed by *Eros*.

We have all heard of good Christian leaders, male and female, who have lost it all over an illicit encounter with another person. Many powerful men of God have fallen because of *ungoverned desire*. When King David, the author of so many beautiful Psalms, saw Bathsheba, ungoverned desire (*Eros*) took over (2 Samuel 11, 12). The sexual encounter was the *Eros* payoff; the murder was the consequence of the *Eros* payoff. Being "a man after God's own heart," David was the most unlikely murderer. If *Eros* can drive a man like David to murder, the rest of us are certainly capable of this as well. Although David's intimacy with God was broken, he was still God's anointed. God's prophet, Nathan, confronted him with his crimes and David confessed his sin. The Lord took away David's sin, but the inevitable consequences came in the death of his son.

The mixture in us that James identifies as the double-soul personality is directly due to the *Eros* and *Agape* conflict within ourselves. When we give way to ungoverned desires in the form of *Eros*, the fact that we can be pressed to the point of murder should be no surprise to anyone. The media tells the story every day.

Consider Susan Smith of South Carolina who, in 1995, drove her car into a lake with her two sons strapped in their car seats and drowned them. Whether or not she had an effective relationship with the Lord which she claimed, what occurred was a perfect example of an *Eros* payoff. In order to "free" herself from what she felt was hindering her relationship with her boyfriend, she strapped her two little boys in their car seats and drove the car into a lake drowning them. *Eros* is a powerful force; do not underestimate it. In this case, it overpowered both decency and the strength of a mother's love. Perhaps the Church is more plague-ridden with *Eros* today than it was in New Testament times. This is evidence of the *Eros* shift.

We can also "murder" in ways other than actually killing the body. Through self-serving manipulation, we can destroy people economically or destroy their reputation. Through our tongue—gossip, falsehoods, half-truths and innuendoes—we can devastate a person's name. Our name, like God's Name, is a representation of our character and person. To destroy a person's name is to destroy the person.

Suicide: Self-Murder

Murder must include self-murder or suicide. This is increasing in our own *Eros*-ridden society. Very simply, it is the result of being convinced that the world and those around us would be much better off if we were not here to complicate things and cause trouble. Strange as it may seem, *Eros* in its self-referential delusion would rather see our lives destroyed than for us to give them to God for His Kingdom purposes.

We will deal more with suicide in a later chapter, but if you or someone you know is considering suicide, you need to consider some things: God gave you *value* when you were still a sinner. He put His own love into your very person. By considering suicide, it is evident that you do not grasp the kind of relationship God the Father wants to have with you. There is no doubt that you are in spiritual confusion and the walls are thickening, but carefully consider the following suggestions:

1. Get serious. Get serious with God, Who is your Father, and with yourself. People have failed you. You have failed yourself. The Church may have failed you, but God, as a Father, has not done so. Your life may be messed up, but believe that God has the power to make good of it.

2. Get truthful. Speak clearly to God, your Father and tell Him you are seriously thinking about taking your life. Ask Him to help you give your life to Him rather than destroy it. Ask Him to help you see more clearly what the issues are. Ask yourself who you are trying to impress; what *Eros* payoff are you looking for? Is your contemplation of suicide an attempt to punish someone else?

3. Get help. There is someone, somewhere you can trust even if you have to look for them in unconventional places. However difficult, costly, or self-conscious you may feel, open yourself and your *Eros* prison to someone you can trust. Ask for and expect them to keep your personal secrets. Take it to the bone; do not withhold anything, no matter how embarrassing. Read what David wrote after he recovered from adultery and murder in Psalm 32 and 51.

4. Get real. Stop the pity party and kick the mood swings. Find out who and what is real and learn to stand in that. Seek *first* God and His Kingdom at any cost or personal discomfort. Life in the Kingdom is the only life there is. Your only hope is the righteousness, peace, and joy that is in the Holy Spirit.

5. Get clear. Stop playing games with yourself, with God, and with others. Cease running, hiding, and shifting blame. Take a stand to come clean knowing that God loves you and has given you value. Intentionally and consciously begin transferring the twisted love you are now demonstrating for yourself and give it as your gift to the Lord Jesus Christ. He, alone, is worthy of your absolute affection.

Addiction and the *Eros* Payoff

The addictive substance, whether it is pornography, drugs, or alcohol, is what we turn to when we feel put down by an uncaring world. The root of addiction is that which is self-referential; our love for the feelings the substance gives us is the *Eros* payoff. The following suggestions are not intended to deal with the pandemic presence of *Eros*, but rather to contribute something to those heroes of the faith who have been called of God to minister the Kingdom to those caught in the downward spiral of addictive and compulsive behavior. The following observations were learned in the school of hard knocks.

1. *Watch a person's actions, not their words.* Fruit is the measure of reality, never words or appearance (1 John 1:6). The commitment to the *Eros* payoff is revealed in action, not words. Mature self-referential love is what makes the con artist so professional.

2. *Addiction is achieved disability.* Perversely, it is a twisted form of "engineered incompetence" in the form of an *Eros* payoff that is designed to prevent us from assuming normal responsibilities. Addiction is one of the *Eros* movements that enable us to run, hide, and shift blame. A modified form of this is to do the task someone asked us so poorly, that they will never ask us again.

3. *The addict defends and protects his/her addiction,* creatively *inventing* ways to defeat all efforts to help him or her. No one can set us free from that which we still love. It is the payoff that captures our affection and holds it in an *Eros* prison. Addiction becomes a "stronghold" in the truest sense of the word. It is impregnable and the key is on the inside.

4. *An addict gets more attention* (an *Eros* payoff) than he or she ever would receive as a normal, functioning person. Self-sabotage is exceedingly effective in helping us grab and control center-stage, preserving ourselves as the center of attention. This is the squeaky wheel theory. All of our attention and efforts are captured and focused on this "poor addict." They manage to remain in the limelight, all the while destroying themselves, their family, and their care-givers.

5. *By hiding within the addiction, the addict remains in control.* There they can make their own rules, escape, avoid, and exploit everything and everyone to their own advantage. They use addiction to get their needs met. "*I am a victim,* therefore, you must cater to me, help me, visit me, give to me, pray for me," etc. Brought to full maturity, a victim emerges into a predator who is cruel and uncaring or into a parasite who has become so smooth and efficient at conning people that he begins to believe the deception himself. (We will talk more about predators and parasites in the next chapter.)

6. *Addicts "feed" on the appeal to "please stop, you are killing yourself."* As perverted as it may sound, the addict, by his personal choice, insists

on death on the installment plan. They use their illness as an *Eros* payoff in order to be noticed, catered to, and centered on. No one can truly be free until they see and refuse the *Eros* payoff. We need to ask ourselves and those we are attempting to help the straight question: "What do you intend to gain by defending your addiction?" There comes a time when we must release them to their own choices, stop all appeals, deny the *Eros* payoff, but continue to pray and express *Agape* to them.

7. *In true Eros fashion, he or she becomes skilled at using their apparent weakness* as strength and often as a weapon. This comes in the form of their heart-rending "cover-story" used to evoke the attention and sympathy upon which the addict illegally feeds. Amazingly enough, I have witnessed people altering their personal testimony for the express purpose of eliciting some desired response, i.e. sympathy, money, recognition, etc. That is an *Eros* payoff.

Christians today are no less guilty of these manifestations of *Eros* than were the Christians to whom James wrote his letter. Fortunately, James tells us how God desires to release the body of Christ from the strength and power of *Eros*. If we count the italicized words in James' instruction, we will discover seven aspects of taking up our daily cross:

> [7]*Submit* therefore to God. *Resist* the devil and he will flee from you. [8]*Draw near* to God and He will draw near to you. *Cleanse* your hands, you sinners; and purify your hearts, you double minded. [9]*Be miserable and mourn and weep*; let your laughter be turned into mourning, and your joy to gloom. [10]*Humble* yourselves in the presence of the Lord, and He will exalt you. [11]*Do not speak against one another*, brethren.
>
> James 4:7-11

Boundaries of *Eros*

Matthew 24:12 says, "And because lawlessness is increased, most people's love for one another will grow cold." When lawlessness (doing my own thing—*Eros*) is ruling in someone, the love of God is forced out to the periphery. As we become filled with *Agape* (1 John 4:8-12),

Eros is forced out to the periphery of our lives. However, *Eros* is always on the perimeter waiting for us to provide an occasion for it to express itself.

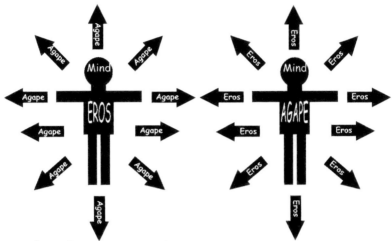

Perfect fear casts out love.   Perfect love casts out fear.
Agape* displaced by *Eros*   *Eros* displaced by *Agape

"For the love of Christ controls us" (2 Corinthians 5:14). When *Agape* controls us, nothing else can. The Kingdom has come and *governed desire* is the result. The reason we do not cheat on our spouse when we have the opportunity or desire is *not* because it's against Moses' law, but because God's *Agape* rules us internally. The power of temptation almost always hits us hardest when we are by ourselves. Love for God is the only thing that will enable us to walk alone in the presence of an Audience of One.

When love (*Agape*) and intimacy break in a marriage, there is little to hold the relationship in faithfulness. Temptations to get emotional or physical needs met illegally (the *Eros* payoff) become almost insurmountable. "Blessed is a man who perseveres under trial; for once he has been approved, he will receive the crown of life, which the Lord has promised to those who *Agape* Him" (James 1:12). *Agape* is the only motivation to stay pure. It is the *Agape* of God that controls us. As *Agape* is formed within, we are able to recognize when an *Eros* payoff is coming toward us. Gradually, the degree in which the Kingdom functions internally becomes increasingly clear, making the *Agape* Road journey exciting and challenging.

Eros and Forgiveness

Eros, by its very nature, refuses to forgive unless it is for self-referential purposes. God, on the other hand, is always insisting that we forgive others without qualification. "For if you forgive others for their transgressions, your heavenly Father will also forgive you. But if you do not forgive others, then your Father will not forgive your transgressions" (Matthew 6:14-15). Remember, one of the easiest ways to get in trouble with God is to receive forgiveness but refuse or fail to give it. To receive mercy and fail or refuse to give it because it is personally demanding and disruptive to our comfort level, is what lay behind our Lord's instruction, "I desire mercy and not sacrifice" (Matthew 12:7). Can you see the refusal to give needed forgiveness as a clear expression of an *Eros* payoff? It feels good to reminisce on how badly we were treated. Forgive you and lose the joy of revenge? Never.

Freedom From the *Eros* Payoff

The freedom[2] which Christ promised in John 8:29-32 *must* consist of the same attitude toward life and God that Christ Himself possessed. Without this freedom, we become drones, doing things not because we choose to, but because we *must.* It is normal to have seasons of feeling unmotivated to do anything, but in those seasons we must not choose an *Eros* payoff. In redemption God created us to be His very own children and we become this by our conscious intention. The ultimate purpose of the entire redemptive process is that of restoring God's image and dominion. If freedom consisted of anything other than this, Christ would not be the One to set us free. Freedom, as Christ interpreted and imparted it, was designed to correct our spiritual ignorance so that we were not completely unaware of our Father's intentions.

---

[2]This section on freedom was influenced by *An Exposition of The Bible* (Hartford: S.S. Scranton, Vol. 5, 1907), 237.

If we could see ourselves as participators rather than being used for the purpose of another, most of us would be willing to embrace difficulty and deprivation. Utilitarianism robs us of all that constitutes personhood. Slavery is real, whether secular or religious. To labor without the consciousness that our work is part of a greater plan and really does matter is to be deprived of our *share in the common cause*. As redeemed human beings, to be embraced in Father's purpose and called "God's fellow-worker" is to be allowed the cosmic privilege of participating in God's purpose for the universe (Romans 8:19-21). This intimacy is most clearly defined in John 15:13-17:

> [13]Greater love has no one than this, that one lay down his life for his friends. [14]You are My friends if you do what I command you. [15]No longer do I call you slaves, for the slave does not know what his master is doing; but I have called you friends, for all things that I have heard from My Father I have made known to you. [16]You did not choose Me but I chose you, and appointed you that you would go and bear fruit, and that your fruit would remain, so that whatever you ask of the Father in My name He may give to you. [17]This I command you, that you love one another.

This carefully worded statement contains the *reasons* for which we are being set free. These incentives are carefully and unmistakably held within the context of *Agape* (John 15:13, 17). *Friend* is the same offer made to Moses in Exodus 33:11, except that now it has been opened, universally, to all men and women. This offer of friendship, accompanied with His determination to respond to us with answered prayer, must not be overlooked. Thus, His *command* for us to "love one another" is to be interpreted by John 15:9-10, "Just as the Father has loved Me, I have also loved you; abide in My love. If you keep *My commandments*, you will abide in My love; just as I have kept *My Father's commandments*, and abide in His love."

Be No

When I was Dean of men and Professor of New Testament at Elim Bible Institute years ago, I had written 21 different "there will be no..." rules for the students. Essentially I was saying that there would be no happiness in the school and they soon began calling me "Beno." As I was laying out these rules, one of the braver students raised his hand and said, "Mr. Mumford, even God only had Ten Commandments!" I realized that I was trying to accomplish by law what God designed to happen by affection.

Scripture says that the whole world sat in darkness, waiting for a great light (Matthew 4:16). The darkness was a direct result of people taking the Law of God and turning it into forms of bondage that not even the most sincere of people could bear. Jesus states this clearly in Matthew 23:4-6 Amplified:

> ⁴They tie up heavy loads, hard to bear, and place them on men's shoulders, but *they themselves will not lift a finger to help bear them.* ⁵ *They do all their works to be seen of men*; for they make wide their phylacteries (small cases enclosing certain Scripture passages, worn during prayer on the left arm and forehead) and make long their fringes [worn by all male Israelites, according to the command]. [Ex. 13:9; Nu. 15:38; Dt. 6:8.] ⁶And they take pleasure in and [thus] *love the place of honor at feasts and the best seats in the synagogues.*

This is not an accusation, but a needed observation to allow us to understand the terrible cost and the ugliness of the *Eros* payoff. The words, "They do all of their works to be seen of men" is *not* a side issue. This is the darkness from which Jesus came to set us free. He does so by the shedding of the light of His Person into this darkness.

The following diagram of Christ fulfilling the law illustrates the strength of the darkness from which Jesus intends to deliver us. It goes like this: God originally gave us His Ten Commandments. The *content* of those Ten Words reveal the necessity of loving God with all of our heart, soul, mind, and strength for our own well-being. God, as a Father, adds that which will guard His children from injuring one another, instructing us to love others in such a manner that we would never injure or encroach upon another's person or their property.

Strangely, and yet, predictably, religious man begins to improve on God's method and His intent. In the Old Testament religious activity, eventually increased the 10 Commands to an unbelievable total of 613 laws: 248 of these rules were positive (things we should do); and 365 were negative (Be No's—things we should not do). The one who keeps the most rules emerges with the reward of an *Eros* payoff. Eventually, it became impossible for the people to enjoy God or life because of the presence and imposition of these rules. Jesus refers to this as darkness that is based on human merit— keeping or not keeping the 613 rules. No one could possibly know spiritual intimacy with God on this basis.

Into this darkness, which Isaiah calls "dry ground" (Isaiah 53:2), comes Jesus as the Messiah. He came to bring light and release us from the darkness of the law so that we could reflect God's glory and light to the darkened world (Isaiah 6:3). Jesus came to fulfill every one of the Father's commands on our behalf.

In John 15:10, the distinction between the Father's commandments and Jesus' commandments are clear, "If you keep My commandments [if you continue to obey My instructions], you will abide in My love and live on in it, just as I have obeyed My Father's commandments and live on in His love" (AMP). Jesus, in John 13:34-35 has already issued us the new commandment. It has to do with an increased capacity for us to love people in the same manner He loves them. Oh, how we have missed it! Release from the external demands of the Law (Galatians 2:21) releases us to love without continually laying heavy loads of false and religious expectations on others. Jesus came to bring the Light of God into this darkness. The Kingdom of Christ offers freedom:

Freedom from *barrenness* due to religious striving and merit
Freedom from *religious games* surrounding an *Eros* payoff
Freedom to pursue God's ultimate *purpose* for our life
Freedom from *trading our inheritance* for immediate reward
Freedom to *know God*

Should our Lord Jesus now be seen as a new "code of rules?" Is He seeking to restore Moses' Law? Or, is *Agape*–Christ's form of freedom–taking us into intimacy with the Father? Is Christ determined that we grow up, or is He, like so much of institutional Christianity, committed to the eternal childhood of the believer? Does He want us to play in the little puddle of the *Eros* payoff or begin to see the Niagra Falls of His Kingdom *Agape* pouring out on hurting people worldwide?

Learning to live for the Audience of One is totally satisfying. It has the ability to strip the *Eros* payoff of its appetite and strength. Ungoverned desires are increasingly recognized for what they are and summarily dismissed. Temptation has been exposed for what it really is, an *Eros* payoff coming to us in some unusual and deceptive attire. The Kingdom principle of standing before the Audience of One can be defined as *never doing or saying anything for the purpose of being seen nor refusing to do anything because we are being seen.* This is freedom from the *Eros* payoff.

Chapter 4 Glossary

Audience of One: The consciousness of becoming a Father-pleaser. Learning to be totally satisfied that the Father alone knows what we are doing and why we are doing it. Never doing or saying anything for the purpose of being seen nor refusing to do anything because we are being seen.

Changing the Rules: God's favor no longer depends on external behavior; He wants us to focus on the internal reality of the Kingdom of God. Jesus changed the rules stating that it is not what goes into us that is important, but what comes out of us that matters. (Matt. 15:11-20).

Childhood Tapes: Memories of events from childhood that continue to play in our minds and control our behavior long after we have reached adulthood. They are strongholds, untruths, or forms of deception that we hold in a fortified place of defense within our mind.

***Eros* Payoff:** The reward we receive for seeking to influence or be seen doing things to impress people. Jesus spoke of that as having our reward (Matt. 6:1-6). That reward is an *Eros* payoff. The opposite is acting and responding for the Audience of One—God, as a Father. (See 1 Kings 21:25).

Poisoned Love: Being so in love with oneself that we are determined not to let anything interfere with our satisfaction. This determination will go to the point of eliminating another if that becomes necessary. Poisoned love is an *Eros* payoff.

Bob Mumford

The Man Who Knew
By Robert Service

The Dreamer visioned Life as it might be,
And from his dream forthright a picture grew
A painting all the people thronged to see,
And joked therein—till came the Man Who Knew,
Saying: "This bad! Why do ye gape, ye fools!
He painteth not according to the schools."

The Dreamer probed life's mystery of woe,
And in a book he sought to give the clue;
The people read, and saw that it was so,
And read again—then came the Man Who Knew,
Saying: "Ye witless ones! This book is vile:
It hath not got the rudiments of style."

Love smote the Dreamer's lips, and silver clear
He sang a song so sweet, so tender true,
That all the market-place was thrilled to hear,
And listened rapt—till came the Man Who Knew,
Saying: "His technique's wrong; he singeth ill,
Waste not your time." The singer's voice was still.

And then the people roused as if from sleep,
Crying: "What care we if it be not Art!
Hath he not charmed us, made us laugh and weep?
Come, let us crown him where he sits apart."
Then, with his picture spurned, his book unread,
His song unsung, they found their Dreamer—dead.

Chapter 5
The Seven Giants: the Real Cause of Failure

Hateful! to me as the gates of Hell is he that hideth one thing in his heart and uttereth another. — Achilles *Iliad* by Homer

God led the people of Israel out of the bondage of Egypt to the border of the Promised Land. Upon their arrival at the border, Moses sent 12 spies into the land to explore it and report back to him. Joshua and Caleb were the only two who came back with a report that the land could be taken. The others reported how terrified they felt when they saw the *giants* who lived in the land and how they made them feel like grasshoppers. Because the people received the bad report rather than abide in God's promise, He refused to allow the older generation to enter the land (Deuteronomy 1:35). In God's displeasure, their journey became cyclical, wandering around the same mountain in the wilderness for 40 years until the older generation perished. In order to enjoy the land of milk and honey, they were prepared to milk the cows and fight the bees, but facing the giants was another matter. The giants served to obstruct the Israelites from entering into the land God had promised them.

> ...When the Lord your God brings you into the land where you are entering to possess it, and clears away many nations before you, the *Hittites* and the *Girgashites* and the *Amorites* and the *Canaanites* and the *Perizzites*

and the *Hivites* and the *Jebusites*, seven nations greater and stronger than you.

Deuteronomy 7:1

These literal giants, whose job was to keep Israel out of the Promised Land, were the shadow or type of the internal and spiritual giants that oppose us from entering the Land of Promises. The Seven Giants[1] we deal with today are:

1. Look Good
2. Feel Good
3. Be Right
4. Stay in Control
5. Hidden Agenda
6. Personal Advantage
7. Remain Undisturbed

James 4:1-5, you will remember, gives us the most accurate insight into how these Seven Giants are able to confuse, hinder, put us to flight, and create desires and urges that cause conflict and injury within our marriages, families, friendships, and church relationships. After 50 years of ministry, I have seen more than my share of strife, discord, feuds, conflicts, quarrels, fighting, jealousy, coveting, envy, anger, etc. The source was not demonic, but was the result of the presence of the Seven Giants. They are very effective in keeping us from entering and enjoying the milk and honey of the Land of Promises. Each of these Seven Giants is *really* bad. They are exceedingly effective especially when we are forced to face them in various combinations. The Seven Giants are pure *Eros*. They are the instruments by which the *Eros* shift is implemented in a life, a family, a church, and in an entire nation.

We are not discussing alcoholism, sexual misconduct, or other external sins; we are at the root of the problem—ungoverned desire identified as the Seven Giants. It is ungoverned desire that interrupts

[1]The first four Giants were given to me in an encounter with Daniel Tocchini in 1987, the last three I added for additional clarification.

our abiding relationship and intimacy with God the Father, with our own spouse, our dearest friends, and with people in general. If we do not identify and clearly understand the manner in which these Seven Giants operate, we will be forced to remain in the borderland of conflict, like Moses, who saw into the Land but was not allowed the privilege of entering and enjoying it.

Like Medusa in Greek mythology, it does little good to cut off the head of *one* of the Seven Giants. The rapidity of their reproduction and their survival rate is like a deadly virus. In an *Eros* climate, the Seven Giants can operate undiscovered for a lifetime, then suddenly manifest boldly and with great authority. These Giants cannot be taught how to behave, be domesticated, or discipled so that they can pretend do the will of God. They can't just be arrested or subdued; they must be exposed, disabled, and brought to death. It is within the sphere of the Seven Giants that the satanic accuser escapes and hides from the "heel" of the woman (Genesis 3:15). The Lord promises to show us how to expose and defeat these Giants so that we may live in the Land of Promise and receive our Kingdom inheritance (Romans 8:37; 2 Peter 1:5-11).

These Seven Giants can exist quietly and appear subdued, but they are nonetheless very resilient, invasive, and dominant. Each of the Seven Giants functions in a synergistic manner, one adding strength and compulsion to the next. They are illusive and increasingly insidious in their various groupings. The kingpin, Stay in Control, however, is the most dominant of all. The

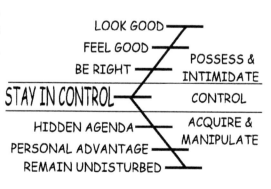

first three Giants are motivations to possess and intimidate. When effectively exposed, the Giant of control will begin to lose its strength. The last three Giants are manifestations of the need to manipulate by acquiring. As we set our love upon God, His love fills our entire person. As a result, we will find that each Giant, with its synergistic companions, begins to lose its grip, freeing us to love God and one another. This is the meaning of *Agape* perfected.

James says that there is no variation or shifting shadow in the Father of lights (1:17). The Lord has called us to freedom and intimacy with Him, but the Giants appear as darkness or shadows between our Father and ourselves. Because of God's covenantal faithfulness, our relationship is still intact, but our quality of intimacy is affected. When the Seven Giants exert their influence in our lives, we are tempted to leave the *Agape* Road. Walking in light rather than in darkness exposes each of the Giants. Because God is light and "in Him there is no darkness at all" (1 John 1:5), if we are walking in His light, God will expose the Giants within us not in guilt or condemnation, but lovingly in order to set us free. God is *Agape* at all times and under all circumstances. He wants us to walk in His light by responding to our neighbor, our enemy, the righteous, and the unrighteous (Matthew 5:43-48) in the same manner that He would respond.

Understanding the manner in which the Seven Giants reveal themselves and how they use the *Eros* payoff may be one insight that can save our spiritual life from irreparable damage. Remember, it is not what comes at us, but what comes out of us that is most damaging. When I realized that it was *not* Jesus Christ and His Kingdom, but the Seven Giants that were effectively ruling my life and actions, I was shocked and bewildered. Like many others, I was calling Him "Lord, Lord," but due to forces of which I was not even cognizant, I discovered myself captured and effectively controlled by the Seven Giants. It is critical that we understand the characteristics of each of them.

Look Good

Matthew 6:1, "Beware of practicing your righteousness before men to be noticed by them; otherwise you have no reward with your Father who is in heaven." The *Look Good* Giant creates the unresolvable issue of appearance as opposed to reality. It is absorbed in the shadow rather than the substance. *Look Good* is not just concerned with outward appearance, but with creating a reputation that is not established in truth. *Look Good* involves an improper or illegal search for originality, uniqueness in dress, language, automobile, etc. Sometimes it is called "styling" with name brand clothes and designer shoes. Don't underestimate the nature of this Giant; it will pay any price and exerts a tremendous amount of effort to preserve its image, especially in contrast to the biblical view of living in reality. People tend to explode or implode when so much effort is expended toward preserving their image. This Giant is a particular curse on our whole generation because people are more concerned with how they *appear* than who they are.

Pastors and Christian leaders are not immune to the *Look Good* Giant. Pride and personal dignity (1 Samuel 15:30) becomes more important than deliverance from that which has captured us. Pride is everything. This Giant is full of ambition, drive, vows, and promises that cause us to posture and position ourselves in order to keep up appearances. *Look Good* wears a mask that includes misrepresentations, half-truths, and false impressions. Matthew 10:33 says, "But whoever denies Me before men, I will also deny him before My Father who is in heaven." One of the reasons someone would deny Jesus would be to continue to look good with those at the office or the club. If we were subjected to real persecution, we would probably embrace it as long as it did not involve personal shame or embarrassment, which would prevent us from looking good.

Look Good is one of the primary sources of anxiety. It reveals itself as the fear of man and the aberrant search for man's approval. *Look Good* is the motivation behind making sure everyone likes us. Scripture says that this is a snare of the soul (Proverbs 29:25). Looking good may also be the reason we are reluctant or lack the capacity to repent—repentance humbles us. It is difficult to preserve our appearance while apologizing to someone. The *Look Good* Giant is the source of an immeasurable amount of spiritual damage.

Some people will do *anything* to look good. Consider the concept of "saving face." I read an article about a middle-aged Oriental man who was working on a 20-foot stepladder when he fell off, landing on the marble floor in a hotel lobby. He got up, bowed properly, apologized to everyone, went into the janitor's closet, and died. He was personally embarrassed and could not humble himself to ask for help.

Bob Mumford

A question that will help discern the presence and strength of this Giant is: Would you rather be a coward with the reputation of a courageous person or be an authentically brave person perceived of as a coward? Our whole society is moving away from true heroes who live free of others' opinions, toward celebrities whose very existence hinges on what others think. This is an *Eros* shift.

Analogous conduct of *Look Good:* search for position; overly concerned with titles—Doctor, Reverend, Bishop, Elder, etc.; an insatiable drive for fame and recognition; inordinate concern for reputation and image; and paralysis when asked to go against the tide of public opinion.

Feel Good

James 4:3, "You ask and do not receive, because you ask with wrong motives, so that you may spend it on your pleasures." The *Feel Good* Giant wants to control our emotions, mind, and heart. This Giant has kept more people from freedom than we can imagine. *Feel Good* involves avoiding pain and discomfort at any cost, is committed to personal pleasure or gain, and is given to the senses or is sensual. This Giant is the epitome of what Scripture identifies as sensuality, causing us to seek gratification of the senses in such a manner that it controls us, effectively becoming our governing force. *Feel Good* operates on the pure pleasure principle. It is the source or first cause of all compulsive and addictive behavior. Due to the *Eros* shift, our whole society is quickly moving toward addictive and compulsive behaviors that eventually will touch all of us directly or indirectly. In psychology it is called the *hedonic response* from the Greek word *hedone* (hedone) (Strong's #2237) meaning related to pleasure. The individual has trained himself to respond to whatever gives him pleasure. Anyone controlled by substance abuse understands both the authority and the power of *Feel Good*.

Modern psychology and cultural preoccupation with feeling good are the source of much of our anxiety. Our society is rooted in feeling good in one way or another. This Giant is why we sit in front of the television like "couch potatoes"—we want to escape reality and feel good. Feeling good must be guarded and protected; it cannot be disturbed.

We do not want to hear what God may be saying because, not only will it bother us, but, it may not feel good. Entire churches and doctrinal emphases are constructed on the premise of feeling good. The *Feel Good* Giant gives us the sense of actually ceasing to exist if we do not feel good. It may be okay to be wrong if we can just continue to feel good. We may even consider that impossible choice of refusing to look good in preference to feeling good because feelings have now become the ruling force. Preservation of *Feel Good* is worth risking anything, because immediate gratification is the insatiable goal. Eventually, however, feeling good stops working because there are not enough drugs, alcohol, attention, or sex to meet the ungoverned desires that keep expanding. This is called the universal law of reduced return: the more that is used, the less results are produced, leaving us in pain and frustration. The frightening truth is that God has not designed us to feel good all the time.

Feel Good is enhanced, enabled, and seems centered on sex, drugs, alcohol, shopping, etc. while the real and deeper problem is that feeling good has become the ruling force. Repeatedly, I have watched powerful men and women of God lose their ministry and marriage for a sexual encounter with someone else's spouse. Someone once said, "The chase is long, the expectation great, the pleasure momentary." These are descriptions of an immature personality, ruled and directed by the pleasure principle. We all know that sometimes our feelings lie to us. When we are in a situation that makes us uncomfortable, we move toward freedom in the Kingdom of God by opposing the demand of the Giant *Feel Good*.

Analogous conduct of *Feel Good:* happiness, entertainment, fun, comfortable, pleased, pleasurable, gratification, satisfaction, diversion, and recreation.

Be Right

Job 40:8, "Will you really annul My judgment? Will you condemn Me that you may be justified?" *Be Right* is directly related to the biblical reality of the fall of man. Original sin left us with an innate longing to enter God's sphere where we have assumed that we possess the needed knowledge of both good and evil. This Giant leaves us insecure, anxious, and unable to admit being wrong. The "know it all" is paralyzed by the domino theory—if we are wrong once, how can we be sure we have ever been right? Since the mind rules our emotions, we are focused, controlled, and overly committed to our own evaluations, ideas, and concepts. The *Be Right* Giant is fearful of being wrong or challenged, making us increasingly rigid—a form of stubbornness and rebellion. This Giant has a perverted "gift of omniscience," feeling he knows everything, but living with the shame and fear of being exposed. *Be Right* often uses anger as protective mechanism to prevent being discovered.

Be Right may be a primary cause of divorce, because each spouse *knows* he or she is right and demands special treatment. Neither have the capacity to admit the possibility of error. I know a married couple who almost came to blows over a ripe banana! They seriously fought over whether the black banana was rotten or just right for making banana bread. *Eros* needs to be "right" at all costs. Our minds become so made up that we will not, or cannot, bend. This Giant is so strong that it refuses to accept reality. It pushes us toward denial, making it very difficult to admit when we are wrong. It says, "My mind is made up, do not confuse me with the facts!" A parent should not fear admitting a mistake or apologizing to a child; however, many parents simply cannot do this. The need to be right may even be used as a source of parental authority: "Because I am your Dad, that's why!"

Be Right has been a curse in my own life since childhood. Many times I have traumatized my dear Judith with the need to be right. This is a terrible Giant who has caused more destruction, division, and injury to individuals, marriages, families, churches, businesses, and social groups than anyone could imagine or measure. Think of how many churches have split because of the demanding and controlling presence of this Giant. I've been called into situations where there were two factions in the church and neither of them had enough *Agape* to yield or compromise over something that was essentially irrelevant. The presence of *Be Right* could actually be felt and measured.

To be right, unchallenged, and face life and the future with an unbowed attitude leads to a form of self-righteousness that turns our light into darkness (Matthew 6:23). Many of us controlled by the Be Right Giant may have traded God's grace for the bizarre privilege (*Eros* payoff) of maintaining a facade of being right, even in the face of God Himself. God asks Job directly, "Are you going to discredit my justice and condemn me so that you can say you are right?" (Job 40:8 TLB). I recommend rereading the book of Job with the Seven Giants in mind—it will provide new insights into the Giants God exposed in Job and his friends.

I have never met anyone controlled by the *Be Right* Giant who was very joyful. We are incapable of enjoying community when we cannot be wrong. This is partially due to the fact that the person who must be right approaches every relationship with a determination to win. If I have eight of something, this person must increase theirs to nine. It is called one-up-man-ship: "I may not be first, but at least I am ahead of you."

Be Right injures our ability to exegete the Scriptures, respond to prophetic direction, or obey some specific instruction from the Lord Jesus. It signifies our commitment to our tradition or system, i.e. Calvinism, Lutheranism, Catholicism, etc., above the over-all authority of God's Kingdom. Conversely, *Be Right* may be the source of our anger and alienation from the main stream of Christian doctrine called the "tenor of faith." There is a particular danger in personal revelation when we think something is "of the Lord"—it has the power to capture us. Have you ever experienced the joy of an *Eros* payoff when you eventually have been proven right in an argument, a conflict, or a difference of opinion? The urge to say, "I told you so," is more than addictive; it borders on obsession. The other extreme is the sheer despair of being proven wrong, to have gambled and lost, or to have put ourselves on the line only to have been mistaken, misled, or deceived. *Be Right* seems to be one of the more difficult Giants to identify, expose, and slay because it is so defensible and insidious. Getting free from the *Be Right* Giant requires grace, space, liberty, and understanding from others; *Eros* demands grace, but refuses to give it.

Analogous conduct of *Be Right:* justice, duty, obligation, prerogative, privilege, responsibility, unyielding, obstinate, self-righteous, self-justified, and implacable.

Stay In Control

And the devil said to Him, "To You I will give all this power and authority and their glory (all their magnificence, excellence, preeminence, dignity, and grace), for it has been turned over to me, and I give it to whomever I will" (Luke 4:6 AMP). Desire to control is a major issue–it is also set forth in Isaiah 14:13-14 in the five "I will's" of Satan. *Stay in Control* demands to have his hands on the steering wheel— he *always* wants to be in control. He believes that if he is in control, everyone is safe and the results are guaranteed. Because he thinks he is god, *Stay in Control* must determine the outcome of everything for everyone. There is always anxiety regarding the future, because it may be just beyond their control, questioning or challenging their self-confidence. *Stay in Control* simply freaks out when control is relinquished to God.

Attempting to stay in control is one of the greatest traps of the Christian life. We are afraid that if we really let go, Jesus will ask something of us that is more than we can give. *Stay in Control* exceeds the normal pace of life that leads to crash and burn cycles.

Stay in Control refuses to take *no* for an answer. This Giant refuses the biblical limitation that says we must live within God's assigned sphere, walk in our limitation, and not encroach upon the measure of others. *Stay in Control* determines to have everything and everyone within their sphere of life in their power and subject to their influence. This even includes anesthesia. In missionary medical school I experienced several occasions where people flatly refused to be anaesthetized for necessary surgery because of an irrational fear of being out of control. People who control will use and consume those who love them. They use the need for human intimacy as the instrument to maintain their control.

Stay in Control believes in the humanistic myth "I can be anything I *want* to be." When we get saved, this can reappear under the Bible verse, "I can do all things" (Philippians 4:13). We leave out the "through Christ which strengthens me" phrase. Because of the *Stay in Control* Giant, we cannot participate in anything *with a whole heart* that we are not leading. We deceive ourselves into thinking that we are the only ones who know how to correctly do the project.

Agape Road

Anxiety is a major symptom for anyone who has the fear of losing control. If a person is given to anxiety and lack of rest, chances are this Giant is roaming freely in their life. Anxiety is the sin of our culture. Lie detectors function on the principle of our fear of losing control and consequently being discovered.

Being a loner is one way to stay in control. We intentionally remain isolated from people because we don't want to lose control. We think that if we really get to love someone, they are going to hurt us. It is true that we become what we focus on. Loss of control, with its accompanying rage, violence, defiance, and self-hate, is the first cause of suicide. Loss of control leads to the heart-breaking discovery that you are *not* God.

My mother was very controlling, increasingly so after her divorce. After my father left, my responsibility as the surrogate father for my five sisters began to emerge. All of us loved our mother deeply, yet we suffered under her control, the effects of which continued long after we were married adults. Our childhood tapes played for years. One day the Lord encouraged me to go and confront her. I flatly refused, but He kept prodding me until finally, I knew I had to go. I said, "Mother, you have ruled my life and ruled the girls' lives long enough. We are releasing ourselves from your control. As your only son, I am telling you that the umbilical cord is cut, and your rule and control over us is broken." She threw herself on the floor and her eyes rolled back in her head. I just stood there grieving for a few minutes and then I said, "When it's all over, you can get up." That day the control Giant was broken off of me and my five sisters. When we are called upon to confront the *Eros* prisons of this world and encounter the Giants that guard those prisons, we must do so with grace, mercy, and forgiveness. However, we cannot confront *Eros* and continue to look good, feel good, be right, or stay in control.

Analogous conduct of *Stay in Control:* arbitrary, arrogant, autocratic, better idea, despotic, exacting, overbearing, dictatorial, fussy, determined, and dominant.

Hidden Agenda

Jude 12 refers to a *Hidden Agenda* when it says, "these men are hidden reefs in your love feasts." *Hidden Agenda* is covert with words of peace and a heart of criticism. It is like a snowball with a rock in it. It appears to be one thing, but when it unexpectedly hits someone, they are devastated. With this Giant in operation, we lie in ambush with undisclosed motives, watching for weakness and vulnerability, ready to spring the trap, which has been disguised and then set with lies or half truths. We hide one thing in our hearts while proclaiming another. This Giant is a user; it seeks to use life, people, and every event for the express purpose of advancement of our own interests.

In our day, hidden agendas can be found everywhere–in social relationships, in politics, on television, and in the pulpit. *Hidden Agenda* may be the most *destructive* of the Seven Giants to relationships. A hidden agenda is making up your mind before you go into a council meeting, then sitting through the whole meeting *creating the impression* that there is unity in the decision-making process. This is dishonoring to others. If we are only seeking someone's approval for what we have already decided, we have a hidden agenda. Often the agenda itself is cloaked in Bible verses. This helps us see the ubiquitous nature of *Eros* reappearing in ways that only God Himself can detect and destroy (Hebrews 4:12). *Hidden Agendas* destroy the unity and joy of the Church.

Some hidden agendas are overt, short term, and obvious; others are subtle, complex, elaborate, and may require years to play out. Sayings like "all that glitters is not gold" show the prevalence of *Hidden Agenda.* When I was teaching at San Quentin Prison, an inmate once referred to *Hidden Agenda* as "sub-tile trickeration." Judas Iscariot had a hidden agenda.

The apostle Paul isolates three hidden agendas in 2 Corinthians 4:1-2: "Therefore, since we have this ministry, as we received mercy, we do not lose heart, but we have *renounced the things hidden because of shame, not walking in craftiness* or *adulterating the word of God,* but by the manifestation of truth commending ourselves to every man's conscience in the sight of God." *Hidden agendas* are maneuvered, cultivated, and nourished in secret, clandestine and often self-deceiving ways. Once engaged, we cannot rest until and unless our hidden agenda has been accomplished.

Analogous conduct of *Hidden Agenda:* subterfuge, wile, fraud, conniving, cunning, guile, crooked, perverse, twisted, calculating, devious, crafty, manipulative, shrewd, trickery, and double-minded.

Personal Advantage

Jude 16, "These are grumblers, finding fault, following after their own lusts; they speak arrogantly, flattering people for the sake of gaining an advantage." With *Personal Advantage* in operation, we are constantly maneuvering for title, position, or recognition. The original Greek word for *Personal Advantage* is translated "selfish ambition" (Strong's #2052). This Giant uses others for its own purposes. When we are not the center of attention, we suffer envy and pain. We will help others only if it directly benefits us. This Giant troubled even the disciples. Jesus was going to Gethsemane and the disciples were asking each other who was going to run things when He was gone. They said, "We've given up everything to follow you. What will we get out of it?" (Matthew 19:27 NLT). At the Lord's Table they were arguing about who was going to be the leader. *Personal Advantage* is the most obviously self-referential of the Seven Giants. It is purely utilitarian in every relationship. People are used for self-promotion or self-advantage. Every opportunity, friendship, or event is evaluated by "what is in it for me." This Giant of *Personal Advantage* has the capacity to transform our call to be a dream-enabler of others—one called of God to help others reach their destiny—into a dream-stealer (John 10:10). We possess, acquire, and control others in an utilitarian manner so that we can be successful. We are not concerned about their dream, but only about how they can help us bring our vision to pass.

An original idea behind the word *parasite* in ancient Greek was one who arranged to have all of their meals in other people's homes and then paid for these meals by flattering their host or hostess. The Church is full of people who will take personal advantage of another. Remember, the Seven Giants operate in groups, several working together synergistically. Note the innocent sounding statement in 3 John 9, "I wrote something to the church; but Diotrephes, who loves to be first, does not accept what we say." His efforts to gain personal advantage hindered the apostolic words of John, himself.

Eros appears in biblical clothes when we use crowds, churches, mailing lists, fund-raising, church-growth, and even evangelism to work the system to our own advantage. Once *Personal Advantage* is wrapped in biblical clothing, it is very difficult to challenge and can even be encouraged and assisted. Working the system then takes on the wrappings of success, and no one can argue with success.

Analogous conduct of *Personal Advantage:* expedience, benefit, reward, usefulness to me, profit, success, self-reliance, narcissism, egocentricity.

Remain Undisturbed

Jeremiah 48:11, "Moab has been at ease since his youth; he has also been undisturbed, like wine on its dregs, and he has not been emptied from vessel to vessel, nor has he gone into exile. Therefore he retains his flavor, and his aroma has not changed." *Undisturbed* may be the most insidious, secretive, and difficult to expose of all. Subtle and sophisticated, his presence is not as blatant as the other six. He is far more ominous and demanding than he first appears. This Giant disguises himself as the need for stability, or the need to preserve his reputation or honor of respectability when more is asked of him than he wants to give. Becoming Father-pleasers requires that we deal with being undisturbed. Kingdom rule may cause serious disruption and/or interference with our own plans, desires, and comfort levels. Undisturbed says, "I will follow you, but I cannot follow you *that* far!" Undisturbed is that subtle difference between admiration for Christ and identification with Him.

What is particularly offensive and needs to be avoided at all costs by this Giant is that any disturbance created by the demands of the Kingdom not become de-centering, troublesome, or course-changing in the possessor's life. When the *Undisturbed* Giant sees drastic or unpredictable change in his life, he sets his face, hardens his will, and determines to deny or avoid all challenges at any cost. Note Jesus' evaluation of the power and strength of the *Undisturbed* Giant in Matthew 13:14-15,

[14]You will keep on hearing, but will not understand; you will keep on seeing, but will not perceive; [15]for the heart of this people has become dull, with their ears they scarcely hear, and they have closed their eyes, otherwise they would see with their eyes, hear with their ears, and understand with their heart and return, and I would heal them.

The most remarkable insight into the power of being undisturbed is that if they *understood* with their hearts, it would demand that they change. If they did so, Jesus says He would heal them. Because disturbance accompanies change, the intentional choice was not to hear.

I have personally experienced *Undisturbed* several times and each time I was faced with a painful choice. A friend of mine accompanied me on a ministry trip one time and when we got in the car after the meeting he said, "You handled that verse in First Peter wrong. That wasn't the proper Greek word." It has always been very important to me to use the original language of Scripture accurately, so when he said this, pride and self-righteousness indignation surged through me. Knowing the Lord was using this painful experience to deal with something in me, I asked my friend, "What is the right Greek text?" Of course, my friend was prepared and proceeded to correct me. He said things I did not want to hear and I was forced to either close my ears or choose to listen. Not only was I wrong, I was shocked and bewildered to watch my complacency shatter. It wasn't until after all the emotions subsided that I recognized that the Lord was trying to expose and slay the *Undisturbed Giant*. Please do not underestimate the strength of this Giant.

Because of this Giant, we seek to avoid or manipulate anything that could result in inconvenience or discomfort. *Undisturbed* requires more assurance and confirmation than is reasonably available, consequently we allow *inconvenience* to become a barrier to our helping others. The real problem is that we simply can't be bothered, "Don't ask me to get involved, it's my day off!" It is too inconvenient to feed the hungry, give drink to the thirsty, invite the stranger in, clothe the naked, or visit the prisoner (Matthew 25:35-36). As someone once observed, those with modern home entertainment centers do not rise up in revolt.

Undisturbed reared its ugly influence and control when the priest and the Levite passed by the victim of crime who lay stripped and beaten in the road (Luke 10:30-35). It wasn't that the Levite and the priest were not concerned about the man; they just did not want to be disturbed. The Samaritan was willing to have his day, journey, and pocketbook disturbed in order to act in mercy and compassion. *Undisturbed* is a life-style so guarded and protected that we don't let anybody or anything touch it. Every one of us has experienced this.

After years of being hurt and injured by Christians, I began to seriously seek an undisturbed life-style. I said to my wife, "I'm going to buy five acres, get a German shepherd, and teach him to bite anyone who carries a Bible." This may sound humorous, but it is very revealing!

When we set ourselves to remain undisturbed, we calcify and soon become undisturbable. "Ephraim is joined to idols; let him alone" (Hosea 4:17). Jesus said of the people about to be judged in the fall of Jerusalem that He made music and they wouldn't dance, He played the funeral songs and they wouldn't mourn (Matthew 11:17). Their unwillingness and inability to be disturbed and respond to Christ and His purpose was symptomatic of what it means to be ruled by this Giant.

Undisturbed can describe a powerful and potentially useful person wrapped in spiritual sloth, apathy, and self-preservation. We can lose our life because of the refusal to embrace the adventure and take the risk.

Analogous conduct of *Remain Undisturbed:* unruffled, unchanged, uninvolved, apathy, disengaged, self-preserving, overly cautious, placid.

The Giants' Triggers

The Seven Giants can be seen throughout Scripture. Here is just one reference:

> Cleanse your hands, you sinners (*Personal Advantage*); and purify your hearts (*Hidden Agenda*), you double-minded. Be miserable and mourn and weep; let your

laughter be turned into mourning, and your joy into gloom. Humble yourselves (*Look Good/Feel Good*) in the presence of the Lord and He will exalt you.

James 4:8-10

Look Good
Feel Good
Be Right
Stay in Control
Hidden Agenda
Personal Advantage
Remain Undisturbed

They are activated, revealed, and engaged by the following five things:

1. Feeling Slighted. Feeling slighted or overlooked does not have to be real, only perceived to be real. It includes feelings that we were not received correctly, given the proper seat, honored in the appropriate sequence, or spoken to at the proper time or in an acceptable manner. Others were put ahead of us, promoted, or honored before us. This list could go on until eventually we see ourselves and our responses. Some years ago, a friend visited me at a large meeting where I was teaching. He said that he did not want to be recognized because he came just as my friend. In my ignorance of the Seven Giants, I took him at his word and did not introduce him at the meeting. He was so offended that he did not speak to me for several years. This experience helped me understand the illusive strength of the Giants and the manner in which they attack and destroy Kingdom tranquility.

2. Being Questioned. Because the Seven Giants have successfully convinced us that we are right and need to be in control, for anyone to dare question, challenge, or even think differently than us becomes a major source of conflict. There is an increasing type of false leadership that demands total loyalty. We must sell our soul to the company store for the privilege of being in the inner circle. Everyone I have known who has failed sexually, financially, or doctrinally surrounded themselves with people they thought were "loyal" to them—"yes-men" who would not or could not disagree or question the status quo. The Seven Giants thrive in such a climate. The Hebrew word for loyalty is faithfulness. The Seven Giants want loyalty; *Agape* wants faithfulness. Our faithfulness to the Lord and to one another comes in the form of support, which sometimes includes confrontation and disagreement when the issue is various interpretations of the plain meaning of Scripture. Pity the leader who does not have anyone with the strength and character to question their impulses and inclinations.

3. *Revealed Prejudice.* Prejudice is a strange manifestation of the Seven Giants. It has a strength that will defy God Himself. In place of the spiritual Kingship of Jesus Christ, color, social standing, education, reputation, occupation, denomination, geographical origin, etc. (John 4:9) seek to control the Kingdom of God. The Seven Giants gather themselves in synergistic force, bringing pressure to bear on the harmony and intent of the Kingdom itself. They seek to displace the rule of Christ with cultural values, academic excellence, or denominational preference. Challenge the Giants in the area of prejudice, and you are dead. My pastor friend lost his position for daring to feed homeless, migrant workers using cookware from the church kitchen. They were offended because he contaminated what had been dedicated to the Lord. They chose their prejudice against the migrant workers rather than the *Agape* of God.

4. *Demand for Repentance.* It does not take long to realize that the call to authentic, effective, and Kingdom-type repentance does not leave room to look good or to maintain reputations. The Seven Giants will often challenge the bona fide presence of repentance. Asking others to forgive us makes us uncomfortable; it embarrasses us in the community and strips away our *Look Good* image that must, at all costs, be preserved. We cannot have Kingdom humility without humiliation.

5. *Unmet Needs.* Only God can reveal to us the manner, degree, and depth that our needs—whether real or perceived—effectively guide, pull, demand, dictate, and govern our human behavior. When we are experiencing a perceived need, even one in our imagination, everything and everyone must stop until that need has been satisfied. Awakened and ungoverned desire has a strength and motivational force many of us do not understand. Real and perceived needs are easily taken hold of by the Seven Giants and used to create havoc in marriages, churches, and social structures. *Eros* and the Seven Giants can easily diagnose and identify the needs that our mate is not supplying. If allowed, these will be exaggerated until they become grounds for divorce. *Agape*, on the

other hand, can see the needs that *are* being met, even the ones that are met quietly and without fanfare. Many feel that because it is *my need,* others cannot possibly understand. When our desire, in the form of an unmet need, has been awakened, the Seven Giants rape, pillage, and plunder until that need has been supplied. This is the psychological basis for all advertising. Awaken the desire, and then the strength of the Seven Giants take over. We *want* what we want; affording it is hardly even a consideration because it can be accomplished by 36 easy payments that are hard to make.

Reciprocal Lawlessness

Under the auspices of the Seven Giants, *Eros* uses a most clever form of subterfuge that I call *reciprocal lawlessness:* I give you permission to annul or change what the Bible says, if you, in turn, will do the same for me. Matthew 5:19-20 says,

> Whoever then annuls one of the least of these commandments, and teaches others to do the same, shall be called least in the kingdom of heaven; but whoever keeps and teaches them, he shall be called great in the kingdom of heaven. For I say to you that unless your righteousness surpasses that of the scribes and Pharisees, you will not enter the kingdom of heaven.

Suppose we are both trying to lose weight and, with a *hidden agenda,* I suggest we go out for ice cream. I ask, "Why don't you go ahead and have one of those special chocolate sundaes?" I am setting you up to say something like, "Okay, if you'll have one too." Once you see *Hidden Agenda* and understand how he operates, he is not so hidden. Reciprocal lawlessness is one of the sources of the increase in velocity and strength of the *Eros* shift. After all, who can argue with the majority?

The *Eros* shift has been intensified and accelerated by the phenomenon of adjusting truth to desire. This is especially easy to rationalize when Scripture is asking for a response which will cause personal discomfort, expose what we hoped to keep hidden, or force into view motivations which we ourselves did not think were present. It is easier to keep the Giants hidden, allowing them to control and govern in secrecy. This is what the Bible identifies as *darkness*. Walking in Light is exposes the Seven Giants and brings about their demise.

Governed and Ungoverned Desires

There is a degree of mystery in the resolve and strength of mind that is revealed in human desire once it has been awakened. A missionary doctor once described the Good News to several abandoned and desperate orphans within the darkened nation of China in these words:

> There was a home where the Father, Creator, Provider, and Sustainer placed us in perfect care. Yet our earliest relatives rebelled against Him and scorned the provision and the Provider. From that point on, we have, each of us in turn, raised the fist, run away from home, and preferred to live as orphans, masters of our own destinies, planners of our own tomorrows, and rulers of our own worlds.

It is enough for us to know that ungoverned desire is "good for food; a delight to the eyes and desirable to make one wise" (Genesis 3:6). This desire, awakened in the fall, caused us to raise the fist (stubbornness/rebellion), run away from home (run, hide, shift blame), prefer to live as orphans (denying God's Fatherhood), be masters of our own destinies (little gods), planners of our own tomorrows (all we like sheep have gone astray each to our own way), and rulers of our own worlds (be right, stay in control).

The Seven Giants utilize the power of ungoverned desire to implement their *Eros* agenda. It is important to see that the issues are deeper than having our sins forgiven. "He shall save His people from their sins" (Matthew 1:21) means eliminating both the act and the root cause which are the result of the Seven Giants.

Desire, both governed and ungoverned, has more direct influence upon human behavior than we could possibly imagine. Ungoverned desire directly affects the manner in which the Scriptures themselves are understood. Attempting to take refuge in what we innocently call "the plain meaning of Scripture" is no longer possible. It is not that the Scriptures have changed, but those who interpret them have. Figures don't lie, but liars figure. E. Michael Jones, a Catholic scholar, helped me understand the real issue. Desire, both governed and ungoverned, has the ability to change the way the Scripture is understood and explained. He essentially says the choice is two-fold:[2]

Conform desire to the truth, or
Conform truth to desire.

This is a very important distinction because we are now facing post-modernism and some of the most difficult conflict awaits those of us who believe that Scripture is the very foundation of society and freedom. In the *Eros* shift, ungoverned desire increases until society itself is influenced and controlled. This is evidence that the *vox populi*, the voice of the people, can become a controlling factor. We have all seen how easy it is for people to become an angry mob, insisting and demanding to the point of death or incarceration that the will of the people be done (Exodus 32:22-23). When the majority of experts (*vox populi*) interpret the Scriptures according to their ungoverned desire, the possibility emerges to make it say anything their desire demands. When something is not in accord with their desire, it is considered radical fundamentalism and should be discarded or oppressed. The Seven Giants often are the source of the ungoverned desires that controls how the Bible is understood. When the voices are sufficiently confused, no one knows who to believe or who to trust.

Truth is capable of disturbing that which insists on remaining undisturbed. When our ungoverned desires (Seven Giants) are faced with a biblical challenge to yield to Christ's government and be conformed to the Image of God's Son, our response is two-fold: Recognize that we must conform our desires to the Truth if we are to be free to move into intimacy with the Father; or seek another teacher,

---

[2]E. Michael Jones, *Degenerate Moderns* (San Francisco: Ignatius Press, 1993), 11.

another church, or another interpretation of that same verse that will tell us what we want to hear. This is similar to searching for a doctor who will tell us what we have already determined is wrong. The *Eros* payoff may cost us, but many people decide it is more than worth it. We are now effectively conforming God's Truth to our ungoverned desire (Revelation 22:18-19; 2 Peter 2:1-3).

We can hardly understand why Esau would trade his inheritance for lentils—a pittance of an *Eros* payoff (Genesis 25:29-34)—apart from understanding the nature of ungoverned desire. Ungoverned desire is why successful and wealthy people are arrested for shoplifting. It is why people are ruled by the iron yoke of addictive substances including pornography and gambling. Ungoverned desires are deeper than they appear on the surface. To be *ruled by desire* is very real and exceedingly difficult to change. We seldom realize how controlled we are until someone asks us to cease doing something we do not *want to stop doing*. Remember that no one can set us free from that which we still desire.

Ungoverned desires make us enemies of the Cross (Philippians 3:18-19). Note that we are not enemies of Jesus, because ungoverned desires still need the good things He can do for us, i.e., salvation and healing. It is when He asks us to adjust our desires to His truth that we want to avoid or circumvent (deny, avoid, endure) the demands of the Cross. This is Cross-less Christianity. It is only by embracing the Cross of Christ that our human behavior can be changed.

For many years, I could not understand the need for a daily Cross. My idea was that I could call upon the Cross in times of crisis, personal need, or failure. However, the more I understood the pervasiveness of the Seven Giants and the *Eros* payoff, the more I understood why the Cross must be ever present rather than something we simply call upon. The daily need for the Cross will appear and reappear as we discover these Seven Giants operating in our own life and in the lives of others whom we know and love.

The strength and function of *Eros* as expressed in pleasure is severely underestimated. Once we decide to move toward something we want, the awakened desire becomes lust taking on a momentum and acquiring a *possessiveness* of its own. This explains how *Eros* can attempt to acquire and control, capturing something or someone for its own use or pleasure. If that motion or momentum toward anticipated pleasure and satisfaction is disturbed or denied, the result is anger.

Suppose a woman flirts with a man, but then denies the satisfaction that she alluded to in the flirting. More powerful than the arousal of desire is the force of his consequent anger. This explains the motivation behind rape, which is most often not sexual, but awakened desire to possess, acquire, and control that cannot or will not be denied.

Eros, awakened but unsatisfied, is also the primary source of *depression*. Almost every person sulks when denied access to what they were going after, whether the goal was real or imagined. King Ahab had everything at his disposal, but when denied the purchase of Naboth's vineyard, he sulked like a spoiled child (1 Kings 21).

Have you ever really desired a certain make or type of automobile that seemed just out of your reach? Or, perhaps you felt deeply that you deserved a certain position in your company or the lead role in a project? Have you ever vowed to be unhappy until you got what you wanted from someone? How did you respond? The forces of darkness, aware of something that we have *set our affections* upon, offers desire to us in illegal ways, wrong timing, or injurious circumstances. The fact is, what is being offered may, indeed, be something God has already promised, but the setting or the timing may not be right. Understanding ungoverned desire helps us see the *strength of temptation*. *Eros* uses desire for its advantage, twists and distorts it so that it is no longer wrapped in God's *Agape*. Because the nature of *Eros* is to possess, acquire, and control, the desire itself gains a momentum and takes on a life of its own for which we may be unprepared. Once that momentum is interrupted or denied, anger, rage, depression, even suicide are among the responses that follow.

The force of ungoverned desire happened to Jesus in John 6 when the crowd tried to take Him by force and make Him King. Father had already declared Him King, and the popular movement was appealing to the awareness of that Kingship in an illegal manner. They were seeking to awaken an ungoverned desire in Him to fulfill His destiny at the wrong time and under the wrong circumstances. If Jesus had yielded to this, it would have twisted or distorted the larger purpose of His Father. Most errors in guidance have to do with timing, rather than direction, because we are so eager to help God out.

Two things can ultimately defeat *Eros*: waiting for Father's initiative (John 5:19) rather than attempting to control, and waiting for Father's timing to add something to us (Matthew 6:33). Governed desire yields to Father's government. Many times I found myself sulking when something that was legal and clearly the will of God for me was being denied or eluded my grasp due to some human failure, capricious event, or wrong timing. A sense of depression swept over me when I was denied the pleasure or satisfaction at the time it was expected. This depression was a form of anger toward God for not only failing to do what I thought He promised, but for not doing it in the manner and time span I expected. To put it bluntly, God disappointed my pleasure principle. Who does He think He is, God? God uses even disappointments to expose and disable the Giants.

Predator or Parasite

When the Seven Giants mature, they produce two forms of human behavior: predators or parasites. Jude 12-13 describes them accurately,

These are *hidden reefs* (elements of danger) [*predators, Hidden Agenda*] in your love feasts, where they boldly feast sumptuously [carousing together in your midst], without scruples *providing for themselves* [alone] [*parasites*]. They are clouds without water, swept along by the winds; trees, without fruit at the late autumn gathering time — twice (doubly) dead, [lifeless and] plucked up by the roots; wild waves of the sea, flinging up the foam of their own shame and disgrace; wandering stars, for whom the gloom of eternal darkness has been reserved forever. AMP

A predator (Jude 12) is the consummate user. They are out to get anything or use anyone to their personal advantage. They are determined to stop at absolutely nothing to satisfy ungoverned desire, including murder. Predators force their will on everyone and everything around them. At San Quentin prison, we learned that a predator is a very violent type of person who will do anything and say anything to acquire what he wants. In prison, this is very ugly. It is also ugly in society. There are predators in business, medicine, law, education, and ministry. Every pastor knows what it is like to have a predator within the congregation.

A parasite, on the other hand, takes advantage of the generosity of others while refusing to make any useful contribution in return. Jude 16 describes them as "inveterate murmurers (grumblers) who complain [of their lot in life], going after their own desires [controlled by their passions]; their talk is boastful and arrogant, [and they claim to] admire men's persons and pay people flattering compliments to gain advantage." Parasites are becoming more prevalent in the body of Christ. A parasite uses everyone and everything for their own advantage. They are like leeches. They get on you, around you, and among you. They use you, refusing to produce anything. They con, whine, and plead to have their own way. Parasites are also discovered in business, medicine, law, education, and ministry.

Both predators and parasites feel they are entitled. *Entitlement* is the attitude that we *expect* others to provide for us. We have the "right" to claim these things. A few years ago, a lady came up to me after I finished teaching on this subject, and she appeared visibly shaken. She told me she had been a social worker for 17 years and that the sense of entitlement she was seeing within the system deeply troubled her. People would lie, falsify documents, intimidate, and cheat in order to get services. On one occasion an enraged middle-aged man drew a small hatchet out of his coat and embedded it in her desk yelling that she better not stop his government checks!

When predators and parasites increased in early Rome, they significantly contributed to the *Eros* shift, encouraging those who had already broken loose to become out of control. Ungoverned desire resulted in the inevitable fall of Rome.

Entitlement has "broken loose" in our western society. It is one of the explanations for a staggering national debt that is about to push our nation toward the inevitable and consequential effects of ungoverned desire.

Self-Willed Determination to be Godly

Oswald Chambers[3] gives us a valuable insight into how the Seven Giants operate:

> But it is hardly credible that one could so persecute Jesus! "Saul, Saul, why persecutest thou Me?" Acts 26:14. Am I set on my own way for God? We are never free from this snare until we are brought into the experience of the baptism of the Holy Ghost and fire. Obstinacy and self-will will always stab Jesus Christ. It may hurt no one else, but it wounds His Spirit. Whenever we are obstinate and self-willed and set upon our own ambitions, we are hurting Jesus. Every time we stand on our rights and insist that this is what we intend to do, we are persecuting Jesus. Whenever we stand on our dignity we systematically vex and grieve His Spirit; and when the knowledge comes home that it is Jesus Whom we have been persecuting all the time, it is the most crushing revelation there could be. Is the word of God tremendously keen to me as I hand it on to you, or does my life give the lie to the things I profess to teach? I may teach sanctification and yet exhibit the spirit of Satan, the spirit that persecutes Jesus Christ. The Spirit of Jesus is conscious of one thing only—a perfect oneness with the Father, and He says "Learn of Me, for I am meek and lowly in heart." All I do ought to be founded on a perfect oneness with Him, not on a self-willed determination to be godly. This will mean that I can be easily put upon, easily over-reached, easily ignored; but if I submit to it for His sake, I prevent Jesus Christ being persecuted.

---

[3]Oswald Chambers, *My Utmost for His Highest* (Grand Rapids: Discovery House Publishers, 1993, 1935), January 28.

Agape Road

Oswald Chambers has done us an enormous service in setting out the Seven Giants in the *Eros/Agape* paradigm in a way that significantly affects our Christian life-style:

1. Look Good   Standing upon our dignity
2. Feel Good   Easily put upon, over-reached, ignored
3. Be Right   Obstinate and self-willed
4. Stay in Control   Self-willed determination to be godly
5. Personal Advantage   Set upon my own ambitions
6. Hidden Agenda   Set in my own way for God
7. Undisturbed   Self-willed determination to be godly

The only manner in which the Seven Giants can be exposed, destroyed, and replaced with *Agape* is by an invasive understanding of the Cross and the Kingdom. When the Kingdom comes, it requires repentance and acceptance. We are admonished in Scripture not to think we know others' reasons or judge obscure and hidden motives; we are instructed and encouraged to look for the fruit of *Agape*, which causes the exposure of the Seven Giants. Only you and God know if your dress, hairstyle, body piercing, tattoos, etc., are for the purpose of impressing others, and are motivated by an *Eros* payoff. For every new and fresh discovery of the human *Eros* predicament, we must have a fresh baptism of *Agape*.

All conflict is internal, manifesting as external attitudes or behavior (Matthew 15:10-20). The only *possible* motive for us to embrace the truth of the *Eros* prison, the *Eros* payoff, the Seven Giants, and its consequential *Eros* shift is our shared commitment to reflecting God's glory. The Kingdom is invasive and demanding. It requires us to conform our desires to the truth. Are we committed to our own spirituality in a self-willed determination to be godly? Or, are we committed to seeing the glory of God revealed in the Church (Ephesians 3:21)? God, as a Father, has committed Himself to those to whom He has given His glory, His name, and His purpose. He is waiting for the Church to reveal His glory in the earth.

Bob Mumford

Chapter 5 Glossary

Be Right: One of the Seven Giants. The inability to admit that we are wrong. A "know-it-all" paralyzed by the domino theory—if wrong once, how can we be sure we have ever been right? Because the mind rules the emotions, *Be Right* is focused, controlled, and overly committed to his or her own evaluations, ideas, and concepts. The fear of being wrong or challenged makes them increasingly rigid—a form of stubbornness and rebellion. *Be Right* often uses anger and rage as protective mechanism to prevent being discovered. (Job 40:8).

Cross-less Christianity: Being an enemy of the Cross of Christ due to ungoverned desires (Phil. 3:18-19). Note that we are not enemies of Jesus, because ungoverned desires still need the good things He can do for us, i.e., salvation and healing. Adjusting our desires to Truth causes us to deny, avoid, or endure the demands of the Cross. Embracing the Cross of Christ is the only way our human behavior can be changed. The daily need for the Cross will appear and reappear as we discover these Seven Giants operating in our own life and in the lives of others whom we know and love.

Feel Good: One of the Seven Giants. The pure pleasure principle. *Feel Good* avoids pain and discomfort at any cost, is committed to personal pleasure or gain, and is given to the senses or is sensual. *It* controls the emotions, mind, and heart and is the source or first cause of all compulsive and addictive behavior. (Jam. 4:3).

Governed Desires: Christ's love controls me; therefore I am able to govern my desires under the Lordship of Christ (2 Cor. 5:14). This is the essence of the Kingdom of God.

Hidden Agenda: One of the Seven Giants. He is covert with words of peace and a heart of criticism. *Hidden Agenda* is like a snowball with a rock in it. With this Giant in operation, we lie in ambush with undisclosed motives, watching for weakness and vulnerability, ready to spring the trap, which has been disguised and then set with lies or half truths. We hide one thing in our hearts while proclaiming another. This Giant is a user; it seeks to use life, people, and every situation to advance his own interests (Matt. 10:26-27).

Land of Promises: The New Testament fulfillment of the Promised Land. In the New Testament, all that was type and shadow (Col. 2:17) is brought to spiritual reality in the Person of Christ. Rom. 8:1-39 is the most succinct description of the Land of Promises which speak of intimacy and usefulness.

Look Good: One of the Seven Giants. Over-concern for appearance or image rather than character. *Look Good* is not just concerned with outward appearance, but with creating a reputation that is not established in truth. It involves an improper or illegal search for originality, uniqueness in dress, language, automobile, skills, etc. It will pay any price and exerts a tremendous amount of effort to preserve its image. (Matt. 6:1).

Parasite: One who habitually takes advantage of the generosity of others without making any useful contribution in return; it is the result of entitlement. Early description of a person who continually seeks invitations to meals, rewarding his host with flattery (Jude 12-13).

Personal Advantage: One of the Seven Giants. This Giant uses others to accomplish its own agenda. It is constantly maneuvering for title, position, or recognition. When not the center of attention, it suffers envy and pain. We ask, "what's in it for me?" and will help others only if it directly benefits us. Selfish ambition. (See Jude 1:16).

Predator: (Jude 12-13 AMP) One who victimizes, plunders, or destroys, particularly for one's own gain or personal agenda. There are predators in business, law, medicine, ministry, etc.

Reciprocal Lawlessness: I give you permission to annul or change what the Bible says, if you, in turn, will do the same for me (Matt. 5:19-20). Reciprocal lawlessness has hidden agendas and is one source of the increase in velocity and strength of the *Eros* shift.

Remain Undisturbed: One of the Seven Giants. Unwilling to be inconvenienced. *Undisturbed* is not as blatant as the other six—he is insidious, secretive, subtle, and sophisticated. This Giant disguises himself as the need for stability, perhaps as the need to preserve his reputation or the honor of respectability when more is asked of him than he wants to give. *Undisturbed* says "I will follow you, but I cannot follow you *that* far!" It is that subtle difference between admiration for Christ and identification with Him. (Jer. 48:11).

Seven Giants: Manifestations of *Eros*; behavioral patterns which hinder us from coming into intimacy with God: Look Good / Feel Good / Be Right / Stay in Control / Hidden Agenda / Personal Advantage / Remain Undisturbed. Slaying these Giants is essential to maturity.

Stay in Control: *Stay in Control* demands to have his hands on the steering wheel—he always wants to be in control because then everyone is safe and the results are guaranteed. Because he thinks he is god, *Stay in Control* must determine the outcome of everything for everyone. He experiences anxiety regarding the future because it may be just beyond his control. *Stay in Control* refuses to take *no* for an answer. He is a control freak determined to have everything and everyone that touches his sphere of life within his power and subject to his influence. (Esth. 1:12).

Ungoverned Desires: Ungoverned desire, awakened in the fall (Gen. 3:6), caused us to raise the fist (stubbornness/rebellion), run away from home (run, hide, shift blame), prefer to live as orphans (denying God's Fatherhood), masters of our own destinies (little gods), planners of our own tomorrows (all we like sheep have gone astray each to our own way), and rulers of our own worlds (be right, stay in control). The Seven Giants utilize the power of ungoverned desire to implement their *Eros* agenda.

Chapter 6
The Right Road Home

God puts the sanctification of his Name, the doing of his will, and hence the coming of his kingdom in the hands of men and women. He waits for his glorification through the people of his choice.

Jürgen Moltmann[1]

Have you ever felt despair over failing the same problem eight times? This reminds me of the man who said he had to marry the teacher to get out of the ninth grade! There is a particular kind of discouragement that appears when circumstances require us to come back to the same problem over and over again, whether it is financial, sexual, mental, or marital. Sometimes it's almost more than we can stand, and goes beyond despair into depression and hopelessness. In our human frailty, we inevitably stumble along the way, missing the road, and falling into one of six patterns of failure: projection, cyclical, right and left swings, or mountains and valleys.

Linear Progress

Linear movement is living life as God intended it—always moving forward in measurable growth or progression. Everything that God does on the earth has a beginning and an end. We are designed to move incrementally in a linear direction

Linear Progress

---

[1]Jürgen Moltmann, *The Coming of God* (Minneapolis: Fortress Press, 1996), 332.

towards the planned unfolding of His purpose in our lives. This is the freedom that Paul describes in Romans 8:21.

As we make our spiritual journey, we should be able to measure personal spiritual growth in some discernible, incremental way[2]—from D to E and from E to F all the way to Z until we comprehend and embrace more perfectly what it means to be experientially conformed to the likeness of His Son (Romans 8:29).

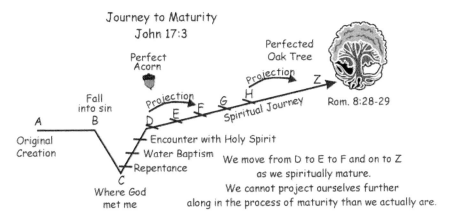

Projection

In our spiritual knowledge, growth, and maturity, we are at E, but for the purpose of looking good, we do religious things to create the *impression* that we are at H. In a deep voice we say "Gawd" rather than God. Projection is using a multitude of actions and religious behavior, seeking to create the impression that we are much more spiritual, advanced, and mature than we really are. We give the impression that we are just waiting to be called on to explain deep biblical complexities and solve perplexing spiritual problems. The difficulty is that once we have created an image based in spiritual unreality, we are forced to create another one to maintain that impression.

---

[2]The basic A-Z diagram is from DeVerne Fromke, *Ultimate Intentions* (Indianapolis: Sure Foundation Publishers, 1998), 84; additions to diagram were added to clarify *Agape* Road concepts.

I have been given two honorary doctorates, but I have never been comfortable using a title. As a guest speaker, I was once introduced as "Dr. Mumford." I jokingly replied, "Dr. Mumford!? I'm not even a nurse!" If your title is real, however, do not be ashamed to use it. We need to examine our own behavior to discover if there is an *Eros* payoff. If we are seeking to mature spiritually, we must cease and desist creating religious impressions, however expensive it may seem at the time.

Cyclical Patterns

If the journey to Philadelphia takes an hour and a half and we have been driving for three hours and see a sign that says, "Philadelphia 60 miles," it does not take a rocket scientist to know that something needs to be corrected; we are traveling in circles. Unfortunately, many of us are trapped in cyclical patterns that Paul identifies as "slavery to corruption" which is a result of the sin of Adam and Eve (Romans 8:21). This cyclical diagram illustrates how we do *not* want to proceed because going around in circles and ending up at the same place results in spiritual exhaustion. This is one of the main reasons why people backslide. We find ourselves in cyclical behavior, so in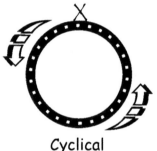

Cyclical

despair we say, "I quit." Cyclical behavior, however, has an inexorable ability to force us into God.

When God exercises resistance toward anything or anyone, He allows it to go in circles. He has a weapon in His arsenal that we often underestimate—time. He just waits us out. If, on our journey, we miss God and head in the wrong direction, God in His mercy, brings us back around to the issue again and again, giving us as many opportunities as possible to get it right. This is what it means to take another lap around the mountain.

Some years ago I wrote a book entitled *The Purpose of Temptation* about the Israelites taking another lap around the mountain. We become like the children of Israel, going around and around Mt. Sinai making the trip last 40 years instead of 14 days. God used the cyclical principle to discipline and teach them. It is important to remember that His resistance is a manifestation of His *Agape* love. God's resistance is one of the most valuable gifts a Father can give. God can resist an individual, a family, a denomination, or a nation. Whenever the scenery is too familiar to you, it might be wise to begin recognizing a cyclical pattern. If God isn't leading you on into some new challenges, something may be out of line.

Right and Left Swings

The third and fourth patterns consists of repeated, never ending, swings from left to right and right to left—always swerving across the *Agape* Road but never stopping on it. "Your ears will hear a word *behind* you, 'This is the way, walk in it,' whenever you turn to the right or to the left" (Isaiah 30:21). When we hear God's voice *behind* us, we know

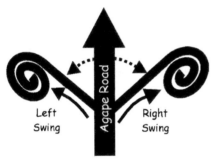

we have missed the way, because He is the Leader. As we read the Scriptures, we see that Jesus turned neither to the right nor to the left; He walked straight up the middle of the *Agape* Road toward His Father. There are many verses that instruct us to avoid right and left swings. Proverbs 3:5-6 says, "Trust in the Lord with all your heart, and do not lean on your own understanding. In all your ways acknowledge Him, and He will make your paths straight." As Oswald Chambers puts it, when we fail to abide or wrongly react to Father's discipline, we "run away from home" by taking one road or the other.

Mountains and Valleys

Finally, there are the fifth and sixth patterns which are the mountain and valley models. This is the path that we, as Yo-Yo Christians, tend to follow. We find ourselves on the mountain top of spiritual experience. If we attempt to stay up there too long, we become puffed up in pride that inevitably causes us to be cast down into the valley of despair. The

Agape Road

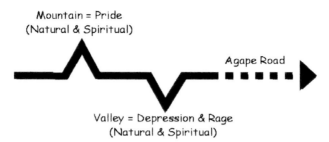

Yo-Yo Christian is full of these up and down experiences. One day we are going to charge hell with a water pistol, the next day we are so depressed that we are contemplating suicide. Pride (the mountain top) and rage (the valley of despair) are Satan's twin arsenals used to beat up and wear down the unsuspecting believer. He loves to jerk us up in pride and push us down in rage, preventing us from achieving any observable stability in our Christian walk.

Jesus, on the other hand, humbles us when we are full of pride, and lifts us up when we are sinking in despair and depression. "Let every valley be lifted up, and every mountain and hill be made low; and let the rough ground become a plain, and the rugged terrain a broad valley; then the *glory of the Lord* will be revealed, and all flesh will see it together; for the mouth of the Lord has spoken" (Isaiah 40:4-5). He brings the mountains down and the valleys up, leveling things out. He is carefully and methodically teaching us to abide in His own Person.

The minute we step into a realm where the Lord begins to reveal Himself to us, the number one danger is pride. Pride and depression are very serious because we can become conceited and fall into the same temptation the devil once did–that of wanting or trying to act like God (1 Timothy 3:6). Pride and rage, represented by the mountain top experience and the valley of despair, are both rooted in a purely *Eros* phenomena. Pride and rage can best be diagnosed and treated by a simple phrase: "If you pout when you are left out, it is certain that you will be puffed up when you are let in" (source unknown). This has been one of the foundational principles and Kingdom absolutes of my spiritual walk. When we are in pride on the mountain top, we are *unable* to hear correction or adjustment. When we are in rage, we do not *want* to hear correction or adjustment. Our safety lies in applying this simple, but profound lesson: deal with the mountains and valleys of pride and rage. Anger, pouting, and pity-parties that seem inexorable and so very predictable when we are neglected or overlooked are not the normal Christian life. Neither is a life lived on a spiritual mountain top. Our goal is steady progress on the *Agape* Road to intimacy with the Father.

Injured Expectations

The broken spirit, who can bear? (Proverbs 18:14). Injured expectancy is the result of broken promises, unfulfilled prophecy, or failed words of "encouragement" from well-meaning people, false brothers, or selfish desire. When expectation has been injured, it turns into *resignation*. Resignation, if we are not careful, can turn into subtle forms of fatalism or suppressed anger, especially if we are too religious to admit that we are angry. To lose our expectancy is to lose our childlike relationship to the Father.

Many churches do not pray for the sick because they have injured expectations and do not *expect* anyone to get healed. Many Episcopalian and Roman Catholic churches do not give altar calls to receive Christ because they are not expecting anyone to come to Christ in that manner. Why is it that you may no longer expect God to do what He has promised for you? Perhaps you have lost your own expectancy.

Expectancy can be seen in the anticipation of children who still believe in Santa Claus. I remember preparing for Santa to come with our oldest son, Bernard, who was three at the time. We filled a glass with milk, put some cookies on a plate, and then tucked him into bed to wait for Santa. A while later, I went outside, walked in the snow, stomped across the porch, leaving huge Santa boot prints, slammed the door loudly, and cried out in my most Santa-like voice, "HO, HO, HO, I have come to visit Bernard's house tonight!" I drank half the glass of milk and took a huge bite from the cookie, then went outside, slammed the door again, and made more Santa prints in the snow to make it look like he was leaving. Meanwhile, Judith put some presents under the tree, I quickly changed and we called him to come downstairs to see the evidence of Santa's visit. He dashed down stairs to see the snow on the kitchen floor, the milk half gone and a bite out of the cookie. The tracks led out into the snow again, and we could hardly contain ourselves because we had just barely missed seeing the man himself. While the older girls enjoyed it, Bernard was so ecstatic that Judith and I have never forgotten it. Even as an adult, Bernard still has an expectancy for all that God has in store for his life. Santa has come and gone, failure and disappointments have visited his house, but he lives with the knowledge that God is able to do all that He has promised.

True, Bible-based expectancy is a vital part of our journey toward intimacy. We are instructed to continue in child-like anticipation (Matthew 18:3), looking for all God has intended for those who love Him. As a result of knowing His goodness, we can look forward to all Father is wanting to reveal at 'F' and 'G'. We must not permit expectancy to be lost (Hebrews 9:28), even when that which was expected has been injured by human failure or disappointing circumstances.

We do not need to lose Bible-based expectancy even when our expectations have been injured by failure and disappointment. I am not asking that we grow up still thinking that Santa is real, but we *can* walk in biblical reality, knowing God and His hidden attributes. God, as a Father, has the ability to *preserve* our expectation and maintain our resiliency. Maturity is expressed by governing our desires, embracing disappointments, and learning to wait for Father's initiative and timing.

This diagram explains the concept of expectancy. Once we have come to 'D' on our spiritual journey we can expect that we will get to 'F' and be a little more spiritually mature. Many denominations say

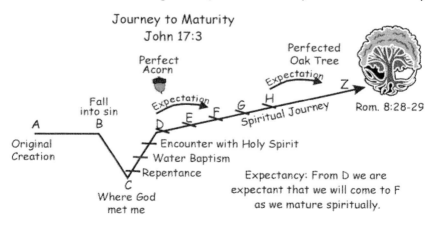

that God has nothing more for us beyond that point. Some of us, dissatisfied with 'E', have doggedly arrived at 'F' and we adjust to our new maturity by assuming that we are now fully educated and no longer have to believe in Kingdom dreams. In our self-satisfaction, we consider all of these other movements as children playing spiritual games—*our* mature group thinks we know better. Now, our expectancy has been deeply injured, future spontaneity and risk with all of the adventure has been removed and we are dead in the water. Our understanding of God's Kingdom is that it is a creed or liturgy demanding that we be good and not do anything wrong.

Injured expectations leave us like professional Christians—amazingly enough, still anointed, making some progress, and by grace, still useful in Christ's Kingdom; but not happy because the joy is missing. We find ourselves seeking to draw our sustenance from *past* successes and victories, i.e., the times when God did what we were expecting. With injured expectations, we often cease rejoicing in the Person of the Father, becoming increasingly petulant because He has not done what *we* expected (see Philippians 3:13).

It is not that God can not and will not do things for us; *it is that we have lost our expectancy that He will do something more. Agape* has done something very special for Judith and me even after 50 years in ministry—He has restored our expectancy. *Our Father can do anything!* We have returned to a point in our walk with God, like our three-year-old son at Christmas, where we are wide-eyed and thrilled at all He has planned. We are willing to embrace disappointments, time delays, and even injuries as part of the package. Our prayer is that Father would heal all of us from injured expectancy and restore us to the delight and anticipation of His Kingdom.

Regressive Paradigm

1 Corinthians 13:11, "When I was a child, I used to speak as a child, think as a child, reason as a child; when I became a man, I did away with childish things." Childishness is not wrong; it is simply insufficient. Child-like must be carefully distinguished from childish. The Seven Giants, moving toward the *Eros* shift, yield a revolt against

maturity. We simply do not *want* to grow up because it hurts. There are a lot of advantages to remaining young and stupid. Continuing to claim that we are "new here" and, therefore, cannot be held responsible allows us to run, hide, and shift blame. Growing up involves response-ability, cultivating our ability to properly respond to the demands and expectations of life.

When we cast away our *confidence*, there is a regression in every aspect of human behavior—projection, missing the road to the right or the left, going up and down in pride and rage, or being trapped in cyclical behavior. "³⁵Therefore, do not throw away your *confidence*, which has a great reward. ³⁶For you have need of endurance, so that when you have done the will of God, you may receive what was promised" (Hebrews 10:35-36).

The Greek word translated "confidence" (Strong's #3954) is used 31 times; it means openness, boldness, freely, plainly. I would encourage you to study this word in your Strong's Concordance; you will gain great spiritual value. Confidence can be seen from these references in Hebrews:

1. "...if we hold fast our *confidence...*" (Hebrews 3:6).
2. "Let us draw near with *confidence* (*boldly)* to the throne of grace" (Hebrews 4:16).
3. "Do not throw away your *confidence*" (Hebrews 10:35).

As the result of *repeated* attempts at projection, cyclical behavior, right and left turns, and yo-yo experiences of pride and rage, we are so pressed out of shape that we are sorely tempted to "throw away our confidence." This perfectly describes the phenomenon of backsliding. If we do not have confidence in the Person of Christ, we are in serious trouble.

Where, then, does our confidence lay? In ourselves? In other people? God forbid! In science, philosophy, or psychology? Hardly. In religion? May it never be! Christianity is following Jesus—placing our love and confidence in His Person. We must never misplace that confidence or cast it aside. There isn't any one or any thing worthy of receiving our confidence besides the Person of Christ.

Loss of confidence in the linear progression of God's intention for us results in the determination to "eat, drink, and be merry." This is the essence of hedonism, the fruit of which is irresponsible behavior. Paul unpacks God's *Agape* for us "while we were yet sinners," in Romans 8:32-39 describing the fact that "nothing can separate us from the *Agape* of God that was given to us in Christ Jesus our Lord." If we understood this, we would never, ever "throw away our confidence" no matter how many times we have taken the wrong road or discovered ourselves in cyclical behavior. It is to each of us personally that the words are written, "My grace is sufficient for you." It is more likely that the bird singing on a tree limb will run out of oxygen, than you will run out of grace.

The Wrong Road Home

Wisdom says: "If a dog bites you once, that is the dog's fault. If the dog bites you twice, that is your fault." We do not learn much from the second kick of a mule. If we find ourselves on the wrong road for the third or even the fifth time, we must get radical and discover what is wrong.

The apostle Paul's concern in many of his letters was to restore the Church to an abiding relationship on the *Agape* Road—one that leads to the Father and intimacy. Only God Himself can correct man's failures. Following are three biblical examples of the manner in which the Scripture seeks to restore us to the *Agape* Road. In these examples, my intention is to try to demonstrate how Paul uses *Agape* as both the motivation and the goal of the New Testament believer, seeking to correct us and prevent us from taking the wrong road home: "Men *loved* darkness, rather than light because their deeds were evil" (John 3:19); "Demas *loved* this present world" (2 Timothy 4:10); and "Let *love* be without hypocrisy" (Romans 12:9). These negative references allow us to see that what we love ignites our desire to take the wrong road home.

The Right Road Home

There are three compelling reasons to take the right road home: First, *Agape* (is used 319 times in various forms in the New Testament) is the translation of the concept of love in the Old Testament and the

Septuagint. Second, *Agape is* God. Most of us are comfortable with the phrase "God is love" but not so comfortable reversing this phrase. God is not faith or hope. God *is Agape*. Third, *Agape* is God Himself, coming into the human predicament as *Agape* Incarnate in the Person of His Son (John 14:9).

Paul uses *Agape* to correct and adjust five New Testament churches in their journey toward God.

1. The Corinthians had taken a wrong turn to the right, moving rapidly in an *Eros* shift toward worldliness. Paul corrected and adjusted this church with *Agape* in 1 Corinthians 13:4-8:

> ⁴Love is patient, love is kind and is not jealous; love does not brag and is not arrogant, ⁵does not act unbecomingly; it does not seek its own, is not provoked, does not take into account a wrong suffered, ⁶does not rejoice in unrighteousness, but rejoices with the truth; ⁷bears all things, believes all things, hopes all things, endures all things. ⁸Love never fails.

In chapter 12 he explains the gifts of the Holy Spirit and by chapter 14 he has to correct the selfish *Eros* payoff that had been attached to the supernatural manifestations of the Holy Spirit. Paul uses *Agape* 36 times in his letters to the Corinthians.

2. The Galatians had taken the wrong road home by attempting to go back to Moses' law (2:18). They had wandered off to the left of the *Agape* Road, attracted and captured by *religious* activity (Galatians 3:3-4) and were struggling with ungoverned desires (Galatians 5:19-21). Paul corrected and adjusted them to govern their desires by saying, "the fruit of the Spirit is love, joy, peace, patience, kindness, goodness, faithfulness, gentleness, self-control; against such things there is no law" (Galatians 5:22-23). *Agape* was so important to Paul that he used the word four times in Galatians 5:6, 13, 14, and 22. He saw the fruit of the Spirit coming out from or being the result of *Agape*.

3. In Ephesians, Paul uses *Agape* 21 times. It is the exegetical key to the Epistle. He seeks to keep the Ephesian believers on the right road

that leads to the Father by saying, "Therefore, be imitators of God, as beloved children; and walk in love, just as Christ also loved you and gave Himself up for us, an offering and a sacrifice to God as a fragrant aroma" (Ephesians 5:1-2). His *Agape* for us is evidenced by the fact that He did not give us "things," He gave us Himself—no greater gift is possible. Our sacrifice to God in refusing *Eros* and embracing *Agape* is a sweet-smelling aroma to God as a Father. This is the *Agape* Road.

4. To the Colossians Paul says something about *Agape* that is most compelling, using the word 11 times. We want to see Paul's correction and adjustment in 3:14: "Beyond all these things *put on* love, which is the perfect bond of unity." Above or beyond *Agape* there isn't anything else because God *is Agape*. *Agape* is the demonstration of the Christian life for the simple reason that *Agape* is God's glory. When God's glory is being seen, the intent of God the Father has been fulfilled (Numbers 14:21).

5. The Thessalonians were about to miss the *Agape* Road due to an overemphasis on the coming of the Lord. Paul uses *Agape* 13 times in this book; his correction and adjustment is gentle and somewhat unusual.

> [11]Now may our God and Father Himself and Jesus our Lord direct our way to you; [12]and may the Lord cause you to *increase and abound in love for one another*, and for all people, just as we also do for you; [13]so that He may establish your hearts without blame in holiness before our God and Father at the coming of our Lord Jesus with all His saints.
>
> 1 Thessalonians 3:11-13

Paul was adjusting the Thessalonians back toward the *Agape* Road by encouraging them to increase in love for one another. There is a different kind of holiness that really does prepare us for the coming of the Lord—that holiness is increased *Agape*. When we love, fear of judgment subsides. If we are seeking to know the Father, it really does matter what road we take. Jesus, who is *Agape* Incarnate, is the road, "...no man comes to the Father, except by Me."

Agape Road

Imagine yourself as a brand new Christian looking at your life as a spiritual journey up the *Agape* Road. Think about how many times you wandered to the right into worldly behavior and to the left into legalistic or religious behavior. After 50 years of my own spiritual journey, I have taken many excursions and could give you a guided tour! Occasionally we find ourselves on both sides of the road at the same time, wondering why we feel spiritually bipolar, mumbling, "what I do not want to do, that's what I do; what I do want to do, that I don't do" (Romans 7:15). In this same chapter, Paul states that it is Christ Who shall deliver us from our *Eros* prison (7:24). In Romans 8:28-29, this same Apostle tells us that God will use anything and everything for the purpose of taking our hook out so that the image of God, and consequently God's glory, can be restored to the earth (Romans 8:19; Matthew 5:16).

Area of Conflict

The scene of action where every challenge and temptation occurs is the area of conflict depicted by the dotted line on this diagram. We are tempted to either turn right toward worldly, sensual things; or left, toward religious activity and *Eros* payoffs, seeking to get something from God or prove something to Him. Satan tempts us with *Eros* just as he tempted Jesus in the wilderness with bread, power, and possessions. What Satan met in the Person of our Lord was Christ's *love* for the Father. He was unwilling to share or trade that love for anything that was being offered. It was an issue of *Agape*, not willpower. He quoted 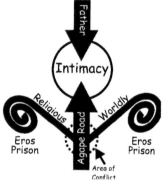 Deuteronomy 6:5, "You shall love the Lord your God with all your heart and with all your soul and with all your might." Jesus knew that "Love is as strong as death" (Song of Solomon 8:6) and that it would hold Him. This is what it means to take the yoke in Matthew 11:28-30,

> [28]Come to Me, all who are weary and heavy-laden, and I will give you rest. [29]Take My yoke upon you and learn

from Me, for I am gentle and humble in heart, and you will find rest for your souls. [30]For My yoke is easy and My burden is light.

Our love for God is what protects us. It keeps us from making wrong choices in the area of conflict. When we take His yoke upon us, He will be bearing *more* than the other half of it. He will walk with us through the same temptations He already conquered. If we seem to journey up either of the side roads, He will resist us until we choose to come back to the right road home. He is determined and unrelenting to bring us into the freedom of Agape and He will remain faithful even if we are not. Preferentially choosing the Father breaks the power and force of temptation. It is at the point of conflict that what and who we love is revealed. Temptation reveals whether we love ourselves and our own

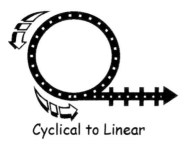

Cyclical to Linear

way more than God and His Kingdom. To stop cyclical behavior and begin moving in a more linear direction, we must set our affection on God as our Father. Jesus proves that our love for God can protect us from all temptations, revealing that it is unnecessary for us to project, travel in circles, turn to the right or to the left, or repeatedly demonstrate pride and rage. God's love shields us and allows us to successfully defeat temptations so that we can find rest and abide on the *Agape* Road.

While in a barbershop, I looked down at a magazine rack. As I'm sure you know, some magazines in men's barbershops are not all that great. I could not see the whole cover, just the title of one of the articles that read, "How to Recognize a Love-Starved Wife." I thought about how powerful the temptations would be for someone who was love starved. If our love for God is real and flowing, the temptations seem to increasingly lose their strength and power. The forces of evil recognize that the majority of believers are essentially love-starved; we are separated from God and one another and desperately seeking to maintain intimacy with God the Father. *Eros* uses our need for intimacy against us.

Agape Road

Once the Lord's yoke is firmly in place and our responses are secure, the area of conflict loses its power, and the *Eros* hook can be straightened. We are then able to proceed to intimacy with God because His *Agape* meets our *Agape*. This is the inheritance for which God, as a Father, waits (Ephesians 1:18).

The area of conflict reveals that intimacy is not so much a question of a deeper understanding of the Bible as it is simply getting to know God and learning to love Him for Who He is, not what He does (1 Corinthians 8:3). God wants an intimate relationship with each of us. Jesus Himself prayed this in John 17:3, "And this is eternal life, that they may know Thee, the only true God, and Jesus Christ whom Thou hast sent." Paul beautifully expressed our choice in the area of conflict in his letter to the church at Philippi:

> [10]That I may know Him, and the power of His resurrection and the fellowship of His sufferings, being conformed to His death; [11]in order that I may attain to the resurrection from the dead. [12]Not that I have already obtained it or have already become perfect, but I press on in order that I may lay hold of that for which also I was laid hold of by Christ Jesus. [13]Brethren, I do not regard myself as having laid hold of it yet; but one thing I do forgetting what lies behind and reaching forward to what lies ahead, [14]I press on toward the goal for the prize of the upward call of God in Christ Jesus.
>
> Philippians 3:10-14

These are mainstream, orthodox, biblical, and trans-denominational goals for every Christian. If we, like Paul, will lay aside those things which are behind and stretch forward to what lies ahead, Jesus, as *Agape* Incarnate, will lead us along the *Agape* Road because He has walked it Himself.

Acorns and Oak Trees

Jesus invites us to follow Him along the *Agape* Road when He says, "I am the way, and the truth, and the life; no one comes to the Father, but through Me" (John 14:6). Amazingly, the words "follow/following" are used 83 times in the New Testament. If we seriously follow Him and He forms Himself in our very being (Galatians 4:19), what will we look like? How would we act? Following Jesus involves a close relationship with Him on the *Agape* Road. Such intimacy should be the goal of every Christian. This is the normal Christian life!

Remember, every acorn has in it the DNA potential to become a mighty oak. However, of the thousands of acorns that fall from an oak tree each year, only a few take root, and even fewer develop into full-grown oaks. Some fall on barren ground, some are never properly watered or nourished, and many begin to grow but are prevented from coming to a full maturity for various reasons.

Once the acorn is properly planted and watered (Water Baptism), it is fed and nourished by the Holy Spirit. It is then hedged about and protected by the yoke that God has provided (Deuteronomy 6:4-5; Matthew 11:28-30; Galatians 5:13-15). A few, with proper care and nourishment, develop to their full potential—"For many are called, but few are chosen" (Matthew 22:14). All Christians are called to journey along the *Agape* Road toward intimacy with the Father, but not all finish the race. The pressures of life seek to destabilize and uproot us, so that our journey to intimacy with the Father, like the growth of the acorn, is interrupted or irreparably damaged.

Walking Against the Light

Religious

Worldly

Agape Road

Area of Conflict

Rationalizing or biblicizing the choice of alternate roads

We must walk against what we thought true to get back on the Agape Road

Some Christians have rationalized and biblicized their way up either the religious or worldly road. In order to return to the *Agape* Road, they may experience a steep *un-learning* curve and the strange sensation that they are walking against the light. Those of us who have traveled these alternate roads know that there is a painful period of having to go against everything humanism or religion may have taught us was the right way home. Only our love for God will allow us to follow Christ, when, like Peter on the rooftop, we are being asked to respond in freedom to that which has kept us bound. *Agape* was determined and unrelenting in its effort to set Peter free from that which held him in legalistic bondage. Love really is stronger than death.

Sabbath Rest

Once we get past the area of conflict or temptation, we enter a sphere of rest resulting in the cessation of works, human merit, and self-conscious effort that leads to death. God wants us to rest, in confidence, in His *Agape*.

> [9]There remains therefore a Sabbath rest for the people of God. [10]For the one who has entered His rest has himself also rested from his works, as God did from His. [11]Let us therefore be diligent to enter that rest, lest anyone fall through following the same example of disobedience.
>
> Hebrews 4:9-11

In this supernatural rest of God, we will find ourselves at peace, not trying to get anything or prove anything to ourselves or to anyone else. We are free in the Presence of an Audience of One. As we abide in this place of rest, the oak tree of God's eternal purpose begins to emerge; we are able to enter into a sphere of intimacy with Father God. Consistent and unbroken intimacy can only be found on the *Agape* Road.

Chapter 6 Glossary

Area of Conflict: The area where the human will and life's choices come together and force us to make a decision. We are presented with three choices: We can seek fulfillment on the religion road, the worldly road, or abide on the *Agape* Road.

Cyclical Patterns: Traveling in circles and ending up at the same place (Rom. 8:20). If we miss God and head in the wrong direction, God, in His love and mercy, sends us in a circle, bringing us back around to the issue again and again, giving us as many opportunities as possible to get it right.

Injured Expectations: The result of broken promises, misconceptions, illusions, unfulfilled prophecy, or failed words of "encouragement" from well-meaning people, false brothers, or selfish desire (Prov. 18:14). Injured expectancy can turn into resignation, subtle forms of fatalism, or suppressed anger, especially if we are too religious to admit we are angry.

Linear Progress: Linear movement is life as God intended it—always moving forward in measurable growth or progression. Everything that God does has a beginning and an end. We are designed to be moving incrementally in a linear direction towards the planned unfolding of His purpose in our lives (Rom. 8:21).

Mountains and Valleys: This is the path that Yo-Yo Christians tend to follow. Alternating between being puffed up in pride on the mountaintop of spiritual experience and cast down in rage in the valley of despair. Pride (the mountain top) and rage (the valley of despair) are Satan's twin arsenals used to beat up and wear down the unsuspecting believer.

Projection: Seeking to create the impression that we are more spiritual, advanced, and mature than we really are. Once we have created an image based in unreality, we are forced to create another one to maintain that impression.

Regressive Paradigm: Not wanting to grow up; acting childish (1 Cor. 13:11). Child-like must be carefully distinguished from childish. Growing up involves response-ability, cultivating our ability to properly respond to the demands and expectations of life.

Right and Left Swings: Repeated, never ending swings from left to right and right to left–always swerving across the *Agape* Road but never stopping on it. (See Is. 30:21).

Chapter 7
A Word From God

It is Agape that seeks, that knocks, that finds ... and is faithful to what it finds.
–St. Augustine

Jesus' temptations in the wilderness give us insight into how to respond to the Seven Giants and *Eros* circumstances that want to move us in a direction off the *Agape* Road. In all three temptations, Jesus countered with "It is written...." When tempted in the wilderness to turn the stones into physical bread, He replied, "It has been written, Man shall not live and be upheld and sustained by bread alone" (Matthew 4:4 AMP). He knew that "in order to really live, man needs every word from God. Food alone is not enough to sustain him" (UBS).

Tempted by Good

George MacDonald[1] gives us additional insight into Christ's temptation:

> How could the Son of God be tempted with evil—with that which must to Him appear in its true colors of discord, its true shapes of deformity? Or how could He

---

[1] George McDonald, *Creation in Christ* (Wheaton: Harold Shaw Publishers, 1976), 271.

then be the Son of His Father who cannot be tempted with evil? In the answer to this lies the center, the essential germ of the whole interpretation: He was not tempted with evil but with the good; with inferior forms of good, that is, pressing in upon Him, while the higher forms of good held themselves aloof, biding their time, that is, God's time. I do not believe that the Son of God could be tempted with evil, but I do believe that He could be tempted with good—to yield to which temptation would have been evil in Him—ruin to the universe.

There is nothing sinful or illegal about being hungry and wanting nourishment, particularly after a forty day fast. However, if giving into that hunger is a result of provocation from the forces of darkness (Seven Giants), to do our own thing ahead of and apart from Father's intervention in our behalf is sin. That is ungoverned desire. Jesus was strategically offered the bread of man—the opportunity to do His own thing (*Eros*) rather than keeping Himself in the *Agape* of God. He simply chose to abide—that is governed desire. He did not argue, rebuke, or strive. He never sought to possess, acquire, or control anything to His own advantage. He quoted from Deuteronomy, stating quietly and without equivocation what it was that God, as His Father, had intended and requested: "You shall not put the Lord your God to the test" and "You shall worship the Lord your God, and Him only shall you serve" (Matthew 4:7, 10). These Scriptures are what effectively governed His own personal desires. The apostle Paul said it plainly: "The *Agape* of Christ controls me" (2 Corinthians 5:14). Paul, like Christ, is saying that the Bread of God brings life, while the bread of man brings death. Jesus actually lived by every word that proceeded from the mouth of God. He simply had no doubt that His Father would take care of the issues in His way and in His time.

It requires a paradigm shift to understand the difference between being tempted to do evil and being tempted to do something that is good, but outside Father's purpose for us. Jesus understood the difference, and even after 40 days without food He exhibited governed desire by remaining in a posture of abiding. His preference was to listen for and depend upon a word from God rather than the sheer pleasure of turning the stones into bread.

Bread of Man or Bread of God

The *bread of man* is sustenance that originates from us; the *Bread of God* is sustenance that originates from God Who is spiritual, eternal, and uncreated. It takes more than natural bread to keep a man alive. *Every word that proceeds from the mouth of God* is *Agape* for the simple reason that God is *Agape*. As a Father, He has spoken into the human predicament with His Word—Christ as *Agape* Incarnate. He comes to bring a word from God to those of us who are poor, in captivity, spiritually blind, and oppressed (Luke 4:18). Jesus, as the Bread of God, comes to break the walls of the thickened *Eros* prison, pluck us out of our religious fixations and denominational narrowness, as well as our addictions and ungoverned desires. He seeks to provide a way of escape from our spiritual poverty by granting us insights into the riches of His grace. He came to pour wine and oil into our broken hearts and injured expectations.

Failure to understand and apply every word that proceeds from the mouth of God has the frightening capacity to consign us to a certain kind of death. Not a death where we cease to exist, but what 1 Timothy 5:6 refers to: "she who lives in pleasure and self-gratification [giving herself up to luxury and self-indulgence] is dead even while she [still] lives" (AMP). This kind of living death can only be dispersed and transformed by the life of God. Living death can be seen in inauthentic spirituality on the religious road or in the law of reduced return that plagues the worldly, hedonistic road. The more we expect or demand from the bread of man, the less it has to offer us. Living by bread alone assumes that we can do it ourselves: "Just give me the rules and I will show you how they work." "I can be spiritual if *I* decide to do so." "I will be a millionaire before I am 40." Living by bread alone describes the legalistic and materialistic existence of life in an *Eros* prison. This is the living dead. Because of the *Eros* shift, our generation is experiencing this culture of death in movies, music, and philosophies that exalt death as a means of escape from cyclical and compulsive life-styles.

Walking in the Light

There are two pivotal issues in being able to receive a word from God: learning to walk in the Light, and understanding preferential choice. The following Scriptures from the Amplified Bible help us see the context of walking in the light and understanding grace and the wedding garment:

> 1 John 1:5, And *this is the message* [the message of promise] which we have heard from Him and now are reporting to you: God is Light, and there is no darkness in Him at all [no, not in any way].

> John 3:19, *The [basis of the] judgment* (indictment, the test by which men are judged, the ground for the sentence) lies in this: the Light has come into the world, and people have loved the darkness rather than and more than the Light, for their works (deeds) were evil.

> 1 John 1:7, But if we [really] are *living and walking in the Light*, as He [Himself] is in the Light, we have [true, unbroken] fellowship with one another, and the blood of Jesus Christ His Son cleanses (removes) us from all sin and guilt [keeps us cleansed from sin in all its forms and manifestations].

James reinforces this idea by saying that God is the Father of Lights and in Him there is no shadow or variableness that would even *cause* a shadow (James 1:17). We are released to find a relationship of intimacy with Him without fear or reservation because we know that His very Being is Light.

Although as human beings we love darkness (for it is in line with our nature which is darkness), Father God cannot and will not permit us to persist in our love and movement *toward* darkness. Darkness enables, even encourages us to run, hide, and shift blame. In the new birth, Light has come. He is invading our life-style and thought life for the purpose of releasing us from the darkness that holds us captive. Our Father, by means of the Person of Jesus Christ, is determined to bring us to that Light which is freedom and Truth. Walking in Light and keeping ourselves in the love of God are synonymous terms. This is the *Agape* Road.

Our degree of commitment to walk in that which God shows us (Philippians 3:16) is what exposes the Seven Giants and defeats the purposes of darkness. What we have to deal with is the mixture: I do love God, but I also love my own agenda with its personal advantage. Mixture is what creates the inner tension and conflict. Mixture can only be sorted out by the presence of the Cross (1 Corinthians 2:2).

A Response of Faith

The moment we hear a word from God, it always requires a faith response. God is more concerned for our freedom than our comfort levels.

When I began understanding the value of a faith response, it started with my hunting boots. My passion is spending time in the woods, but I don't like cold feet. I literally began to save my pennies and nickels to buy a pair of insulated hunting boots. Like a child, the expectancy of these new boots brought me joy. When the L.L. Bean box arrived I was thrilled. It was not quite idolatrous, but close. They were insulated to a temperature of 10 below zero and that made me happy. To break in these brand new hunting boots, I would walk up and down the living room in them.

The day after the boots arrived my pastoral visits took me to see a man who worked in a chicken yard. He was extremely poor. The weather was below zero and I immediately noticed that he was working in the cold, mud, and chicken muck in canvas running shoes. Without warning, I suddenly became angry, knowing what God was going to say, even before I had received a "word from the Lord." Immediately, resistance and refusal set in: "I won't do it! No, Sir! Let him freeze!" Finally,

Father's voice said, "When you are all done with your reactions, give the man your boots!" All day and the rest of that night the Lord kept urging me to give him the boots. My arguments seemed futile and finally, I responded properly, got the brand new, unworn boots down from the shelf, kissed them good-bye, and drove over to the man's farm. I handed them to him rather abruptly and through clenched teeth and a fake smile I said, "Here are the boots. I hope you enjoy them!"

Although I didn't know it at the time, Father God put His finger on the boots because He could see the walls of my *Eros* prison thickening and gave me the word, the Bread of God, which enabled me to break out. Was I forced to give the man the boots? No. But I certainly didn't want my personal *Eros* prison to get any tighter or the walls to get any thicker. When I responded, amazing things happened. As I walked away from the man, I was still angry, but by the time I got back to the car I began to experience the joy of the Lord. Something deeply self-referential had been broken. My own pity-party was over and I had been set free! If I had known this was the end result, I'd have given the man my boots with greater freedom.

A similar request was made of the rich young ruler, "But when he had heard these things, he became very sad, for he was extremely rich" (Luke 18:22-23). Have you ever had the Lord ask you to give away your last $50? The request is not because He needs the money; we are the ones needing to give it so we can break free from the *Eros* prison.

When we hear a word from God requiring a faith response, there are five simple steps that can be difficult to take. They are:

1. *Believe.* Believing penetrates and supersedes all human emotion and reaction. Our confidence is in God, not in our feelings. Ezekiel 3:14 shows us that God can and does set His love upon us even when we are full of rage, "So the Spirit lifted me up and took me away; and I went embittered in the rage of my spirit, and the hand of the Lord was strong on me." Ezekiel's anger did not lessen God's demand upon him.

2. *Receive.* We cannot earn God's love or make Him love us more; we can only receive it by faith. "We have come to know and have believed the love which God has for us. God is love, and the one who abides in love abides in God, and God abides in him" (1 John 4:16).

3. Speak. Hosea 14:1-2, "Return, O Israel, to the Lord your God, for you have stumbled because of your iniquity. *Take words with you* and return to the Lord. Say to Him, 'Take away all iniquity, and receive us graciously, that we may present the fruit of our lips.'" The words that I am asking us to take to the Lord are "Abba Father, I love You with all my heart, soul, mind, and strength" (Deuteronomy 6:5; Luke 10:27). This may not strike us as being very important, however, Paul says, "If anyone loves (*Agape*) God, he is known by Him" (1 Corinthians 8:3). Words are important for us to know God and allow Him to know us. Talk to God; He is our Father. Tell Him what the issues are. Be assured that nothing you say will be a surprise.

Recently, a friend of mine took these points seriously and really let God know what he actually thought and felt. He let fly a string of complaints, anger, and expressions of frustration, occasionally peppered with a few choice words. When he stopped to get his breath, Father said, "Are you finished?" He said, "Yes," and God's liquid love flowed down upon him until he melted. Suddenly, he understood that his relationship is dependent upon God's love for us, not our love for Him.

One hot summer day I was working in the back yard and took a drink out of the hose and nearly gagged. The hose had been sitting in the sun all day and it was hot, plastic-tasting water. After I let the water run through the hose for a few minutes, out came cold, clear water. When we first start verbalizing our words to God, they may come out like hot plastic hose water because we are not used to verbalizing them. However, the more you verbalize to the Lord, the more natural it becomes.

4. Respond. Respond in love to whatever the Father is asking of you. If He asks you to write a letter to your Dad and tell him you're sorry for the way you conducted yourself, do it out of a loving response to God. When I was a new Christian, I was speaking love words to the Lord. He said to me, "Were you a medic in the Navy?" I said, "Yes, Lord, I was." He said quietly, in a strong Fatherly impression upon my spirit, "I'd like you to gather up all the instruments and medicines you stole from the Navy and take them back." My first alarmed response was, "If I even try to return that stuff, I will wind up in the federal penitentiary at Leavenworth!" However, everything in me wanted to respond properly to the Lord's request. Reluctantly, I gathered up all the equipment and supplies in two shopping bags and walked up to the gate of the Naval station with my heart pounding and anxiety controlling my every thought. The officer at the gate allowed me to walk right through without asking questions or inspecting the content of my two shopping bags. That was the first miracle. Inside the medical dispensary was a civilian employee whom I had known prior to my conversion. He said, "Bob, I can put all of that back into inventory. You get yourself out of here before they know what's happening." That was the second miracle. I literally felt clean and alive as I walked back out those gates.

5. *Redemption.* Redemption is another word for freedom. We must come to a deep recognition that each word from God is redemptive. Cease being afraid of what God may say to you, and know that His purpose is to reveal to you the strength of your *Eros* prison and through "every word that proceeds from the mouth of God," provide the only means of escape. When He speaks, it is *Agape* exposing the *Eros* Giants. Of course, it is demanding to obey, but it is also exciting and liberating.

The Eternal Seed

Our human predicament demanded that God, Himself, had to come to us here on earth because *all* human beings—including popes, priests, pastors, and saints—had been infected with *Eros* (Romans 3:23). Our help came in the form of an Eternal Seed, implanted in the womb of a young virgin resulting in the sinless Son of God Who was capable of living a *governed life* on our behalf (John 1:14). This same Eternal Seed is implanted in us when we believe in Jesus and the result is the new birth or being born from above. "But

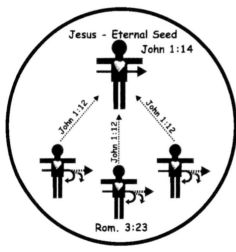

as many as *received* Him, to them He (God) gave the authority to become the children of God, even to those who *believe* in His name" (John 1:12).

Other than the dialogue between Jesus and Nicodemus, Peter gives the clearest understanding of the new birth:

> [20]For He was foreknown before the foundation of the world, but has appeared in these last times for the sake of you who through him are believers in God, [21]who raised Him from the dead and gave Him glory, so that your faith and hope are in God. [22]Since you have in obedience to the truth purified your souls for a sincere love of the brethren, fervently love one another from the heart, [23]for you have been born again not of seed which is perishable but imperishable, that is, through the living and abiding word of God. [24]For, 'all flesh is like grass, and all its glory like the flower of grass. The grass withers, and the flower falls off, [25]but the word of the Lord abides forever.' And this is the word which was preached to you.
>
> 1 Peter 1:20-25

1. (vs. 20) The New Birth was implemented *before the foundation of the world.* It came into being prior to the entrance of original sin and the *Eros* phenomenon. Because all humanity was in the same self-centered condition we were in, *our help had to come from the outside.*

2. (vs. 21) *Christ is both our example and enabler.* When God raised Jesus, the Eternal Seed, from the dead, it was for the purpose of Him dwelling in our hearts by faith (Ephesians 3:17). In order to do this, He had to first become an individual person and then take on the spiritual form of the cosmic Christ.

3. (vs. 22) *This Eternal Seed is Agape Incarnate.* According to God's creation mandate the Eternal Seed must bring forth "fruit after its own kind." The issue of the universe is the fruit of Father's love (DNA) being replicated. Jesus loved us and commanded that we "love one another."

4. (vs. 23) *The Eternal Seed* is *incorruptible* and *imperishable*. This seed is pure *Agape* and as such, is God's incorruptible and imperishable nature in you and me.

5. (vs 24) *All flesh is grass*. Attempting to live by bread alone is man's bread—religious and/or worldly flesh. Our only hope is in the Eternal Seed that is the bread of God.

6. (vs. 25) *The Eternal Seed abides forever*. This Eternal Seed produces eternal life because it is God's own DNA in the Person of His Son so "that we might have life and that more abundantly" (John 10:10).

7. *Summary*. When we take the focus off ourselves, with all of its self-referential, self-righteous, narrow, and religiously critical attitudes, it releases us from *Eros* prisons and cyclical behaviors which dominate this world system. Our freedom can only be found in the Eternal and Incorruptible Seed. Our confidence now lies in the possibilities and potential of that mysterious and supernatural Eternal Seed. This is the only known antidote from becoming religious, cynical, or yielding to the tendency to throw away our confidence. God sent forth His seed with the prophetic declaration that it would not return to Him empty (Isaiah 55:11). It will produce that for which it was intended. We can believe in the Eternal Seed even while observing the most gross and evil human behavior.

Consider how a seed can fall between the cracks in a sidewalk. As the seed takes root and grows, it can break up the concrete. This Eternal Seed is explained beautifully in Mark 4:26-29:

> [26]And he was saying, The kingdom of God is like a man who casts seed upon the soil; [27]and goes to bed at night and gets up by day, and the seed sprouts up and grows—how, he himself does not know [mystery]. [28]The soil produces crops by itself [no human assistance]; first the blade, then the head, then the mature grain in the head [a fruitful kingdom that is supernatural and universal]. [29]But when the crop permits, he immediately puts in the sickle, because the harvest has come.

This is the mystery of the Kingdom coming to us from the outside. "God was in Christ reconciling the world to Himself" (2 Corinthians 5:19).

Peter's *Agape* Conversion

We have described the *Eros* shift as a pendulum swinging inexorably toward consummate *Eros*. This shift can only be resisted and reversed by an *Agape* conversion that the Scripture defines as the coming 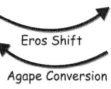 of the Kingdom of God. When I use the word conversion I mean being experientially conformed to the image of Christ (Romans 8:29) not only being born again.

We all know of Peter's failure and his denial of the Lord three times before the cock crowed (Luke 22:34, 54-62). The Lord warned him about what Satan intended to do to him and He used the experience to bring about an *Agape* conversion in his life. "[31]Simon, Simon, behold, Satan has demanded permission to sift you like wheat; [32]but I have *prayed for you*, that your faith may not fail; and you, when once you have *turned again* [Strongs G1994, converted], *strengthen your brothers*" (Luke 22:31-32). Why did Jesus pray for Peter? Because he was, consciously and unconsciously, governed by all Seven Giants. Peter was not primarily concerned about the things of the Father; he was all wrapped up in man's interests (Matthew 16:23). Jesus carefully and intentionally spoke of what Peter was to do after he went through the breaking of the *Eros* prison—he was to release God's *Agape* toward the other eleven apostles. The Father wanted His love replicated in Peter. After he was converted (not born again), Peter was able to give himself to others. Some *Agape* conversions come on the installment plan, but Peter's conversion involved Jesus exposing and releasing him from the power of all Seven Giants in one mega-crisis. Peter's three-time failure was a terrible experience because he did not look good, he certainly didn't feel good, he wasn't right, and he could not remain undisturbed! But, it was the process God used to set him free. He was restored to fellowship with the Lord in the beautiful scene at the seashore when

17). *Agape* turned Peter into a rock that could be built upon. *Agape* will turn any person who is an unstable, wishy-washy Simon into a Peter upon whom the Lord Jesus can depend.

Our Healing Words

If the Eternal Seed is working in us, it produces God's DNA, and the DNA produces words that heal. Our words bring healing when they line up with God's Word. James 3:2 says, "We get it wrong nearly every time we open our mouths. If you could find someone whose speech was perfectly true, you'd have a perfect person, in perfect control of life" (MSG). *Eros* produces injurious words; *Agape* produces healing words. We can see in this verse that James was not looking for works, but the presence or absence of *Agape*. If *Agape* is present, it changes our behavior and brings freedom. Imagine being in an argument and never saying anything that would injure. The word 'mouth' is used 76 times in Scripture; it is an important issue. Let's look at a few of the uses:

❖ "For out of the abundance of the heart the *mouth* speaks" (Matthew 12:34 NKJ).

❖ "It is not what enters into the mouth that defiles the man, but what proceeds out of the mouth, this defiles the man" (Matthew 15:11).

❖ "...Whose *mouth* is full of cursing and bitterness" (Romans 3:14)

❖ Jesus "Who did no sin, neither was any deceit found in His *mouth*" (1 Peter 2:22).

James continues to explain that the *Eros* and *Agape* mixture is *revealed* by what comes out of our hearts through our *speech*. He insists that our tongue will tell us in which direction we are moving and where we are caught in the *Eros-Agape* conflict:

> ⁹With it (our mouth) we bless our Lord and Father; and with it (our mouth) we curse men, who have been made in the likeness of God; ¹⁰from the same *mouth* come both blessing and cursing. Does a fountain send out from the same opening both fresh and bitter water?
>
> James 3:9-10

James wants us to understand, without guilt or condemnation, that mixture comes from the Seven Giants, *in the believer.* These Seven Giants are motivated, energized, and revealed by selfish ambition:

> [14]But if you have bitter jealousy and selfish ambition in your heart, do not be arrogant and so lie against the truth. [15]This wisdom is not that which comes down from above, but is earthly, natural, demonic (*Eros*). [16]For where jealousy and selfish ambition exist, there is disorder and every evil thing.
>
> James 3:14-16

Agape, because of its origin in the nature of God, is the Eternal Seed, and will yield a fruit which is *righteousness.* The conflict is not external sin, such as substance abuse, sexual misconduct, or violence, but internal *Eros,* revealed as:

> Bitter jealousy
> Selfish ambition
> Arrogance
> Lying against truth

These issues are far more important than we have been taught in church. James knows that if *Eros* is not identified, revealed, and broken by the power of the Cross of Christ, disorder and evil will result.

Our tongue does reveal our inner person. Whatever is in our heart just comes out because speech lies at the very center of our personality. When someone is under the influence of alcohol or anesthesia they are likely to say strange, embarrassing, or revealing things; what is in the heart comes out. When we discover that we are controlled by *Eros,* we are *unable* to choose to speak or not to speak. Joseph's brothers *"hated him and could not speak to him on friendly terms"* (Genesis 37:4). This is why praying in the Holy Spirit (1 Corinthians 14:1-2) is so important—it allows the Person of the Holy Spirit to cleanse and release the very center of our personality. When we are controlled by *Agape* (2 Corinthians 5:14) and have made a preferential choice to be in proper alignment in the yoke of Christ's Kingdom. This yoke, though "light and easy," serves to expose the presence of the Seven Giants. This is James' argument as to why we will see "good works" follow new birth.

Freedom in Preferential Choice

Eros always costs us our capacity and freedom to choose. The only way our freedom to choose can be restored is through Christ and His redemptive act. This loss makes us increasingly predictable because we tend to choose whatever is in our own self-interest. Paul describes this loss of choice in Roman 6:16: "[16]Do you not know that when you present yourselves to someone *as* slaves for obedience, you are slaves of the one whom you obey, either of sin (*Eros*) resulting in death, or of obedience resulting in righteousness (*Agape*)?" Peter repeats this loss of choice by saying, "...[19]promising them freedom while they themselves are slaves of corruption; for by what a man is overcome, by this he is *enslaved*" (2 Peter 2:19).

When Paul says, "the *Agape* of Christ controls (governs) me" (2 Corinthians 5:14), he is not describing willpower, conscious self-effort, or religious striving. Self-control, as one of the nine fruits of Holy Spirit, is God's restoration of our freedom to give Him, by faith and in gratitude and affection, our love in the form of preferential choice. God makes the restoration of our choice possible by first choosing us so that we can have the capacity to choose Him.

Being controlled by *Agape* does not mean that we are exempt from feelings of hatred or envy, but we choose to yield to the indwelling Christ and watch Him bring them into subjection. Once God frees me from the bondage to myself, I am then free to choose things that really matter—this is governed desires. One of the reasons we can know that we are controlled by *Agape* is that our *Eros* responses begin to diminish. The loss of our ability to choose, results in the loss of our response-ability. If I desire to hurt you, my responses are motivated by *Eros*. Essentially, I am being controlled or governed by the Seven Giants. Preferential choice involves choosing to keep ourselves in the *Agape* of

God and asking the Father to help us with our response. This is not works nor self-help; it is the *Agape* of God restoring to us self-control (Galatians 5:22-23).

Jesus preferentially chose the "cup which the Father has given Him" and He asks us to do the same. In the following encounters we can more clearly understand what our choice involves:

"Are you able to drink the cup that I am about to drink?"

"My cup you shall drink ...."

"My Father, if it is possible, let this cup pass away from Me..."

"The cup which My Father has given Me, shall I not drink it?"

"And when He had taken a cup and given thanks, He gave it to them, saying, 'Drink from it, all of you; for this is My blood of the covenant, which is poured out for many for forgiveness of sins.'"

Our following Jesus must be transformed from infatuation and appreciation to that which involves our embrace of Him and His purpose. We must continually *choose His cup*. Following Jesus involves preferential choice. He loved His Father and sought to choose His Father's will preferentially above His own. The preferential choice can be defined as loving what the Father loves. It is His cup that we prefer when we could have chosen to run, hide, or shift blame. This choice is a simple demonstration of our affection that allows a Kingdom life-style to emerge. Preferential choice unfolds something like this:

1. *Caught in the Eros Prison*. My self-referential nature has me imprisoned within myself. Being totally predictable, I will choose that which contributes to my own personal advantage. My life is material; I am seeking to live by man's bread alone which is absent of the Kingdom dimension.

2. *Conflict within*. When Jesus comes with a transformational Word from God, He speaks His Light and Life to my prison, poverty, blindness and broken heart. Now, I really am in conflict. I love my own darkness *and* I love His Light.

3. *Responding to spiritual conflict*. The end result of mixture and temptation at the area of conflict seek to cause us to choose the wrong road. Whether religious or secular, that road does not take us to the Father.

4. *Making a preferential choice.* The reality of my new freedom can be demonstrated by choosing God in a preferential manner. I am now free to regard others as more important than myself. I can testify that God's compassion is now seeking to flow through me to others.

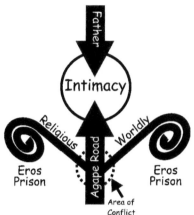

Preferential choice does not mean making some big, willful decision like "I will never be angry again." We all know this does not work. There will be occasions when we will feel that we have no choice. Preferential choice is difficult even after the Lord restores our freedom for two reasons. First, because we love darkness—our own way, pleasures, and plans—more than Light. It is to this love that all temptation is addressed. Preferential choice is also difficult because of the cultural influences of the *Eros* shift—everyone, it seems, is moving toward darkness. This causes us to want to go there, too. I am asking each of you who are seeking to make this journey on the *Agape* Road to become more aware of the issue of mixture and more intentional in choosing the cup which the Father is offering rather than yield to the strong temptation to run, hide, and shift blame.

Proper Use of Freedom

In light of *Eros* and *Agape*, we must learn to properly use our freedom that Christ has purchased for us in His redemptive act. This is such an important concept in the New Testament that Jesus, Paul, and Peter all describe the suitable manner in which we should use the freedom that God has given us.

1. Jesus says, "If you continue in My word, [follow Me] then you are truly disciples of Mine; and you will know the truth, and the truth will make you free" (John 8:31-32).

2. Paul says, "For you were called to freedom, brethren; only do not turn your freedom into an opportunity for the flesh, [self-referential] but through *Agape* serve one another" (Galatians 5:13).

3. Peter says, "Act as free men, and do not use your freedom as a covering for evil, but use it as bondslaves of God" (1 Peter 2:16). We are not to use our freedom as a covering for malicious and injurious behavior, but as God's servant we are to surrender our illegal and self-referential rights.

The plain meaning of the three statements regarding the use of our freedom by Jesus, Paul, and Peter reveal our *choice* in how we implement and utilize that freedom—either in a selfish and *Eros* controlled behavior, or by setting our affections on God, His Kingdom, and Father's Glory. It is possible to use redemption itself in an *Eros* manner. The alternative is an *Agape* response of concern for others, resulting in release from an *Eros* prison.

However weak, frail, and inadequate our choices may be, our freedom in Christ reinforces our ability to set our affection upon God as our Father. If, for any reason, we refuse or deny the reality of that choice, we have effectively injured the moral structure of God's creation in man (Hebrews 1:9). It is preferential choice that allows us to become who we already are. Note how carefully this is stated in John 1:12, "To as many as received Him, to them He gave the authority to *become* children of God." Our proper response allows us to *become* that which Christ has already made us: sons and daughters of the Father.

God wants to be wanted. See His lament in Jeremiah 2:2, "I *remember* when you were deeply devoted, when you expressed your love to Me, when you were eagerly following after Me...." Our salvation in the Person of Christ provides the redemptive freedom to break all forces, passions, and illegal and compulsive desires so it can be said that we have regained our freedom to choose. This is the Kingdom of God and the manner in which governed desires function.

There have been times when deep inside I have felt the Holy Spirit saying, "Choose Me." There also have been multiple times when I heard Him say just as clearly, "You will live to regret that choice." These choices were only possible because God, through Christ, restored our capacity to choose. Before Jesus broke the power of evil (Colossians 2:15), we had very limited capacity to choose—we were dead in trespass and sin! It is often painful to discover how much damage the effect of ungoverned desires have had on us. They have caused the walls of our *Eros* prisons to thicken. The deeper we are in the habits of sin, the greater our personal conflict in preferentially choosing Christ because desire rules our freedom of choice. As Jesus sets us free, our ability to choose is restored. As we set our love (*Agape*) on God, our preferential choice releases the power of God and brings us to freedom (1 Corinthians 2:5).

Simply stated, preferentially choosing Christ is the evidence of our love for God, the Father. Our choices, we must remember, are rooted more in our love and affection than they are in human willpower.

Summary

For the Word that God speaks is alive and full of power [making it active, operative, energizing, and effective]; it is sharper than any two-edged sword, penetrating to the dividing line of the breath of life (soul) and [the immortal] spirit, and of joints and marrow [of the deepest parts of our nature], exposing and sifting and analyzing and judging the very thoughts and purposes of the heart.

Hebrews 4:12 AMP

Every word from God is a two-edged sword. As a living force, God's Word pierces deeply into our person—between soul and spirit—revealing the distinction between *Agape* and *Eros*, judging even the *thoughts of our hearts*. Love for Light as compared to love for darkness (John 3:19), as well as our response of faith to a word from God, are demonstrated in Peter's *Agape* conversion when Christ restored him after his failure. All of these ingredients give us increased insight into the two vital concepts we have called preferential choice and proper use of our restored personal freedom and are important for our journey on the *Agape* Road.

Chapter 7 Glossary

Bread of God: "In order to really live, man needs every word from God. Food alone is not enough to sustain him" (Matt. 4:4 UBS). The Bread of God is sustenance that originates from God Who is spiritual, eternal, and uncreated. Every word that proceeds from the mouth of God is *Agape* because God is *Agape*. Father spoke into the human predicament with His Word–Christ as *Agape* Incarnate.

Bread of Man: Bread of man is sustenance that originates from us. It is doing our own thing (*Eros*) rather than keeping ourselves in the *Agape* of God. The bread of man brings death (1 Tim. 5:6).

Choose the Cup: Symbolism for preferentially chosing the Father's will above our own. By choosing the cup, we follow Jesus' example even at great personal expense. (See Preferential Choice).

Eternal Seed: The sinless Son of God, *Agape* Incarnate, Who is implanted in us when we believe in Him. The result is the new birth or being born from above. The Seed is incorruptible and imperishible (1 Pet. 1:23); it abides forever.

Law of Reduced Return: The more we expect or demand from the bread of man or living in our own strength, the less benefit we receive.

Preferential Choice: Loving what the Father loves. God restored our freedom of choice through the redemptive act of Christ. He first chose us so that we can have the capacity to choose Him.

Temptation: Opportunities, suggestions, or pressures to yield to desires which are self-serving. Temptation is something we want more than our freedom. Tempted to do good is activity that is good, but outside of Father's purpose for us at the time.

Chapter 8
The Healing Power of Agape

Now the whole power of Christ's instruction was directed to this point... I say unto you, love (*Agape*) your enemies...the necessary result will grow out of these exercises; happiness, or life, will be added as a consequence. –James B. Walker[1]

Many of us have come too far in our walk with the Lord to try to present or even infer that the concept of *Agape* is some kind of cure-all. The fundamental concern of the New Testament is the preservation of the absolute Who is Christ, our foundation. Nothing can be added below this foundation. "For no man can lay a foundation other than the one which is laid, which is Jesus Christ" (1 Corinthians 3:11). Jesus Christ, *Agape* Incarnate, is the foundation. It was God, Who came to us in the Person of His Son, to reconcile the alienated world to Himself. We now need to see that *Agape* is also the *very highest* concept of the New Testament—nothing can be added above it. This is stated clearly in Colossians 3:12-15:

> [12]Put on therefore, as [the] elect of God, holy and beloved, bowels of compassion, kindness, lowliness, meekness, longsuffering; [13]forbearing one another, and forgiving one another, if any should have a complaint against any; even as the Christ has forgiven you, so also

---

[1]James Walker, *Philosophy of the Plan of Salvation* (New York, Chautauqua Press, 1887), 130.

[do] ye. [14]And to all these [add] love, (*Agape*) which is the bond of perfectness. [15]And let the peace of Christ preside in your hearts, to which also ye have been called in one body, and be thankful. (Darby)

We see several life-changing insights regarding God's Own Person in this portion of Paul's letter:

1. (vs. 12) First, Paul meticulously restates the seven hidden attributes of God. This is a New Testament re-statement of Exodus 34:6-7, God's self-disclosure of His Own Person. (These restatements occur 11 times in the entire Bible.)

2. (vs. 13-14) Paul asks that these seven attributes be present in our relationships; they are the vital content of *Agape*, God's very Presence, and His Glory. Paul says that *beyond Agape* or *above Agape*, there isn't anything else, because God, Himself, *is Agape*. So, what brings healing to us personally, to others, and to a hurting world is walking in *Agape*, the perfect bond of unity. *Agape* holds the Christian community together (Ephesians 4:15-16).

3. (vs. 15) Let the *peace* of Christ act as umpire—call the plays and interpret the rules—in our hearts and show us how the Kingdom works.

By making *Agape* to be both our foundation below and our highest good above, God has set the parameters for His Bride to function in this fallen world. God uses *Agape* to heal us and place us in right relationship with Himself. He gives us value and worth and insists that we love ourselves as He loves us. This is healing from all internal conflict. Then, He asks that we take the same healing that we received from Him and pour it on those He allows to touch our life. These He calls our neighbors. This is the healing power of *Agape* in three basic steps.

Without an extensive word study on *Agape*, my hope is that the following diagram will give you insight into the complexity and wonder of the word love. It is important to see how the translators have chosen to represent and explain God's very being and nature both in the Hebrew Old Testament and the Greek New Testament.

The healing power of *Agape* can be assessed and observed by the way the word *Agape* has been translated into English[2]. To know that we

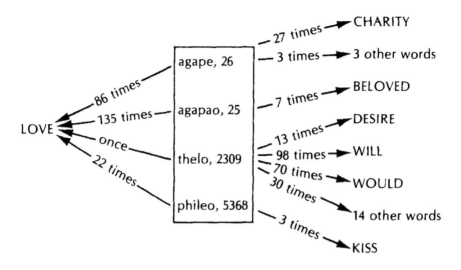

are loved, that we are His beloved, and that love is what causes us to want to do the will of God, contributes to our wholeness and sense of well-being.

The Wedding Feast

The story of the wedding feast (Matthew 22:2-14; Luke 14:13-24) could also be entitled, "Two Idiots and a Hen Pecked Husband" because those who were invited to this special occasion created illogical, if not down-right inane, excuses as to why they would not be able to attend the wedding celebration. Matthew and Luke give us a beautiful picture of who actually accepted the invitation to the wedding—the poor, crippled, blind, and lame. After the king's slaves gathered people off the streets and the wedding hall was filled with dinner guests, the king came in to look over the dinner guests. "He saw a man there who was not dressed in wedding clothes, and he said to him, 'Friend, how did you come in here without wedding clothes?'" (Matthew 22:11-12). Those who came were not skilled in the social graces of using three forks and two spoons set at their place. The issue was not their social

---

[2]George Wigram, Ralph Winter, *The Word Study Concordance* (Wheaton: Tyndale House Publishers, 1972, 1978), xvi.

skills, but their wedding garment—the host of the dinner wanted to be sure everyone who came had on the right clothing. The primary reason someone would not be allowed to enter was failure or refusal to put on the wedding garment freely provided by the host of the wedding feast.

As a socially inept teenager, I was invited to a celebration dinner at the home of one of my school friends. I had never been in such a beautiful home and I felt uncomfortable. As the roast lamb was being passed, some green jelly followed. I eagerly placed a spoonful of the green jelly on my bread since, in my world, bread and jelly always went together. The people at the table were all amused and I remember being puzzled about what was so entertaining. When I tasted the mint jelly on my bread I wondered why anyone would serve something like that. This, and many similar experiences, enabled me to understand and identify with the poor, ignorant, and socially inept who have been invited to the fancy wedding, but never had opportunity to be taught how to properly behave. They, like myself, do not know how to do the Church thing. It is difficult to explain to many who are blind, crippled, poor, and marginalized why the Church is not ready for them and they are not ready for the Church.

This parable is amazing in that the poor, crippled, blind, and lame were the only ones who accepted the invitation. These four categories identify every one of us in one way or another. The *poor* are those without means with which to pay back. They could not even reciprocate with a dinner invitation. The *crippled* are those struggling with physical, moral, or spiritual weaknesses, hardly able to keep up with the pressures of life. The *blind,* which describes most of us, are incapable of seeing spiritual things; we have eyes, but see so very little. The *lame* are simply unable to walk out all of the teaching on how to live a Christian life; they struggle with internal conflicts and habit patterns that seem to impair their very walk with the Lord. If Jesus invites these people to the wedding, He had to have made some kind of provision for them because He always knew what was in man.

The people who refused His invitation were governed and controlled by the Seven Giants and considered themselves in need of nothing. As a direct result of this attitude, Jesus said that the publicans and harlots would enter His Kingdom before religious pretenders (Matthew 21:31). The Father wants us, the Church, to demonstrate His *Agape* to those who are hurting and teach them how to behave (Matthew 28:20) at the Marriage Supper of the Lamb (Revelation 19:9). Remember that Jesus does not clean His fish until after they are caught. They, too, need to know not to put mint jelly on bread.

The Wedding Garment–Our Robe of Righteousness

The prophet Isaiah speaks of the robe of righteousness and describes prophetically the wedding feast and the wedding garment. If possible, read this Scripture aloud:

> I am overwhelmed with joy in the Lord my God! For he
> has dressed me with the clothing of salvation and draped
> me in a robe of righteousness. I am like a bridegroom in
> his wedding suit or a bride with her jewels.
> Isaiah 61:10 (NLT)

Isaiah is giving us an important prophetic insight into God and His Kingdom. He was preparing us for the day when Jesus would come and we could embrace Christ alone for our righteousness. Christ, *Agape* Incarnate, coming as our wedding garment is *the* pivotal point of the whole New Testament. Martin Luther re-discovered this when he said "the just shall live by faith" and it caused a world-shaking reformation, disrupting the foundations of society at political, economic, and geographic levels. The importance and centrality of faith righteousness cannot be over-stated or over-emphasized. The freedom and spiritual intimacy that we seek comes *only* as a result of full and undivided faith in what Christ has done in our behalf, *not* what we do for Him.

In the letter to the Romans, Paul carefully reasoned for nine chapters how God's righteousness is *revealed*. Peace with God cannot be bought, coerced, or earned by our faithfulness to doctrinal beliefs or denominational distinctives. Finally, in Romans 10, Paul addresses the most subtle and pervasive religious trap—our zeal for God, but not according to correct knowledge. Note how direct and straightforward he states the problem in the following verses in the New Living Testament version:

Romans 10:3, "For they don't understand God's way of making people right with himself. Instead, they are clinging to their own way of getting right with God by trying to keep the law. They won't go along with God's way. For Christ has accomplished the whole purpose of the law. All who believe in him are made right with God." If we do not understand God's gift of righteousness as the wedding garment given to us in the Person of Christ, we will continually attempt to create a righteousness of our own. God's Kingdom does not function on a little of our righteousness mixed with a little of Christ's righteousness. When we attempt to do that, Paul says we do not go along with God's way of making us right with Him. The end result is religion without the Presence of God.

Romans 10:4, "For Christ has accomplished the whole purpose of the law. All who believe in Him are made right with God." Christ, as the sinless Son, without guile (*Eros*) perfectly (Greek *telios*) fulfilled all that God could expect or demand through Moses' law. He then gave that righteousness to us as His gift.

Romans 10:9, "For if you confess with your mouth Jesus as Lord, and believe in your heart that God raised Him from the dead, you will be saved." Our freedom is the result of faith, belief, and confidence that God raised Christ from the dead (Romans 6:4). This is the wedding garment.

Romans 10:11, "As the Scripture tells us, 'Anyone who believes in him will not be disappointed.'" If we have embraced Christ in this manner, Father says we will never be *ashamed*. The strength of this promise is shocking. Nothing can separate us from God's *Agape* given to us in the Person of Christ (Romans 8:31-39).

Romans 10:20, "And later Isaiah spoke boldly for God: 'I was found by people who were not looking for me. I showed myself to those who were not asking for me.'" The lame, the blind, the poor, the weak, the harlot, and the publican have received an invitation to the wedding by means of the Good News of the Gospel and they accepted His invitation. We were not seeking Him; He was seeking us.

Romans 10:21, "But regarding Israel, God said, 'All day long I opened my arms to them, but they kept disobeying me and arguing with me.'" Paul states boldly that there is no distinction between Jew and Greek (Romans 10:12), but those of us who are religious have a frightening propensity to make excuses as to why we cannot receive God's gift of righteousness freely. We have to earn it, work for it, and we feel we *must* be doing something to participate. All God wants us to do is *believe* and *receive.* His request is that the righteous man will live and respond in faith.

Freely we have received from God that righteousness Christ bought for us in His death and resurrection and freely we are able to give that good news to others. A mixture of the two covenants, a little law and a little grace, does not produce the freedom of the gospel, nor does it release God's promise. When we have had to earn our righteousness by religious effort and human works, we are not so eager to freely give grace to our neighbors. We have the sense that because we have earned our righteousness, others should earn theirs as well. God's love, however, is always evidenced by freedom, spontaneity, and risk.

The moment we discover Christ as our righteousness, two things occur. First is the release from guilt and condemnation that comes from Moses' Law (Romans 5:1). Any accusations Satan could direct toward us have already been absorbed in the Person of Christ. The only way we can fail and learn from our mistakes without being buried under guilt and condemnation is by immersing ourselves in *Agape.* This is the healing power of *Agape.* This is the Good News.

Second, we have a deep and personal assurance that we have been accepted and received by God the Father (Hebrews 9:24 AMP). Our confidence increases because we have been invited to the wedding and have been given the proper garment to wear. Christ is the wedding garment. This is what it means to "put on the new self" (Colossians 3:10). It is Christ, *Agape* Incarnate, Who will see to it that we learn how to be pleasing in His sight and know how to behave at the wedding feast. We only have one garment—God's righteousness that was brought to us in the Person of His Son, our Lord Jesus Christ.

When I teach about the wedding garment, I often use a white handkerchief to explain the righteousness of God as the following pictures of my hand illustrate. The first picture represents the Adam Factor–each of us in our sinful state. Then, I completely cover my hand with a handkerchief just as God's righteousness completely covers us– this is imputed righteousness or "putting on the new self." The handkerchief represents the righteousness of Christ given to us as God's gift. We did nothing to deserve or earn it. It is God's righteousness imputed or implanted within us as the Eternal Seed giving us the authority to *become* sons and daughters of God by faith (John 1:12). Third, as Christ's righteousness begins to be worked into us, we

The Wedding Garment

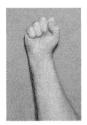  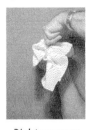 

| Adam Factor Rom. 1:16-17 | Putting on the "New self" Imputed Righteousness Col. 3:10 | Righteousness Worked into us Kingdom Transformation Gal. 4:19 | Being conformed To His Image Imparted Righteousness Rom. 8:28-30 |

experience Kingdom Transformation. Finally, through this process we are being conformed to the image of Christ which is imparted righteousness.

Christ gives us the wedding garment so we will be properly dressed for the wedding. Our job is simply to receive the wedding garment believing that Christ fulfilled all the laws and requirements of the Old Covenant. His careful and loving *impartation* of His righteousness is the cultivation of that Eternal Seed, the growth of which results in being conformed to the Image of God's Son (Galatians 4:19). God's intention is for us to become His mature bride, able to participate both in His provisions and in His purpose as it is being revealed in the earth.

Practical Use of the Wedding Garment

The white handkerchief illustration is very workable especially when pressures, condemnation, and guilt come down on us for no recognizable reason. I have, over the years, literally placed the white handkerchief on my head for the purpose of countering, breaking, and/or releasing the barrage of thoughts, accusations, and unpredictable emotions.

After an impressive and rewarding ministry trip, I was on my way home, but because of airline delays, I missed my connecting flight. With no other flights available, the airline put me up in a hotel room at the airport. I was physically tired, emotionally fragile, and spiritually numb. Everything in me wanted to be home. Upon entering the hotel room, an unexpected and unprovoked barrage of sexual and unclean thoughts immediately swept over me. Bone weary, I tried to sleep, but the mental and emotional attack was unrelenting. I jumped out of bed, opened the drapes, and looked out the window. Then, I took my white handkerchief, the very one that I used some hours earlier to teach this concept of the wedding garment, and carefully and intentionally placed it on my head. Out loud I said, "I belong to Jesus Christ. He is my Bridegroom and I am His bride. He is my righteousness. All mental and emotional conflict must cease in Jesus' name." Without exaggeration, the conscious Presence of God swept over my entire physical person and filled the room. *Agape* brought healing to the torment. My mind and emotions began to settle and I slept the rest of the night without interruption.

Putting the handkerchief over my head was a child-like *faith* response. It was motivated by full confidence in the finished work of Jesus Christ on my behalf. God, as a Father, will respond to each of us in a similar manner when we choose to trust, rely on, and put our confidence in the redemptive provision of God's Son.

The word 'confidence' means trust, reliance, out-spoken, and bold assurance. It suggests the absence of timidity and false or religious expressions of humility. Confidence does not mean more human courage, greater effort, or expended will-power, but boldness in believing what Christ has done for me and in my behalf. Hebrews 3:6 says, "But Christ was faithful as a Son over His house whose house we are, if we hold fast our *confidence* and the boast of our hope firm until the end."

The Greek word for confidence can also imply being unusually forward, almost shameless. The absence of shame for who we are or what we have done can never come from within ourselves. The promise of Romans 10:11, "We shall never be put to shame or be disappointed," (AMP) is totally dependent upon our being able to stand in bold confidence in the presence of God and other people, even when we have failed or missed it, simply because our *confidence* rests in what Christ has done on our behalf.

Confidence in the Garment

In 1517, Martin Luther reemphasized confidence in this wedding garment apart from the works of Moses' law. The entire world was impacted by the freedom and release discovered in this evidence of God's love. Luther's message was simple, he said,

> Now is not this a happy business? Christ, the rich, noble, and holy bridegroom, takes in marriage this poor, contemptible and sinful little prostitute, takes away all of her evil, and bestows all his goodness upon her! It is no longer possible for sin to overwhelm her, for she is now found in Christ and is swallowed up by him, so that she possesses a rich righteousness in her bridegroom.[3]

The apostle Paul especially influenced Luther with his bold statement, "I am not ashamed of the gospel, for it is the power of God for salvation to everyone who believes" (Romans 1:16). This was the basis for Luther's understanding of the wedding garment. This illustration is the essence of the gospel message. It was the Father Who set His love upon us and sent Christ as His gift. We were not seeking Him; He was seeking us. When He sets His love upon us, it is His sovereign declaration. Understanding and receiving that love is the essence of spiritual maturity.

---

[3]Alister McGrath, *Martin Luther on Sin and Grace* (Oxford: Blackwell Publishers, Ltd., 1995), 230.

We must "come to *know* and *believe* the love which God has for us" (1 John 4:16). The ultimate issue is confidence in Christ alone as our righteousness demonstrated by our straightforwardly accepting the wedding garment. This is what enables us to abide on the *Agape* Road in communion and intimacy with the Father. Attempts to please God that do not originate and rest in faith are unacceptable.

God provided the wedding garment so that we would be *comfortable* in His presence. We are astounded that the God of the universe has invited us to be His Bride. We can add to our amazement His promise that with the invitation He gives us the assurance that "He who began a good work in us will perfect it until the day of Jesus Christ" (Philippians 1:21). We can have confidence in God's faithfulness to make us righteous. The wedding garment is *passive righteousness;* meaning Christ provided righteousness on our behalf. Faith is ceasing the struggle to create a righteousness of our own. If God said it, we should believe it and that is the purest form of humility.

Christ has invited us to the Holy Place, but it takes New Testament boldness to enter (Hebrews 10:19). We must rely solely on Christ's sacrifice making us acceptable to God the Father. Once the Holy Spirit illuminates to us how acceptable we are and we actually begin believing it, no one can ever take our confidence from us.

Hebrews 4:16 encourages us to "draw near with *confidence* (boldness) to the throne of grace, that we may receive mercy and find grace to help in time of need." We are always forced to rely on confidence in the wedding garment for free access to God's presence when we do not feel worthy to enter on our own. Knowing God as our Father requires a boldness and confidence to run *into* God's presence instead of away *from* it when we have failed, especially when our mind and emotions accuse and condemn us. The voices seem to demand that we, of all people, should leave the wedding celebration. The accuser (Revelation 12:10) would like for us to leave the wedding and go out and wait in the hall. It is shameless confidence that can say, "No, Christ invited me and provided my wedding garment. He has asked me to stay, regardless of my sin or your accusations."

Romans 10:3 says, "For not knowing about God's righteousness, and seeking to establish their own, they did not subject themselves to the righteousness of God." We have two choices: either accept God's righteousness or create our own. Instead of standing by faith in the righteousness God gave us in the Person of Jesus Christ when we are in trouble, we almost always attempt to create our own righteousness or seek to add something to the wedding garment so that we can feel accepted by God the Father.

We have all been instructed to read more Scripture, witness to more people, repent more deeply, pray more sincerely, etc. We need less repentance, self-condemnation, and guilt and more confidence in the wedding garment. Our confidence rests in what God has done and God rewards those who believe this. The challenge is to honestly and practically lean into God's righteousness every day believing that His righteousness really is *the power of God* for us. When we lay our head on the pillow at the end of the day feeling alone, frustrated, or angry at the world, will the wedding garment work for us? If it doesn't, we have lost or discarded our confidence in the garment, thinking our sin or failure is simply too immense, or that we are just too different and unstable to walk in God's righteousness. Consider the implications of 1 John 5:10, "The one who believes in the Son of God has the testimony in himself; the one who does not believe God has made Him a liar, because he has not believed in the testimony that God has given concerning His Son."

There are many Scriptures on boldness and confidence. Some of these are repeated from our previous section:

❖ Proverbs 3:26, "For the Lord will be your *confidence*, and will keep your foot from being caught."

❖ Isaiah 32:17, "And the work of righteousness will be peace, and the service of righteousness, quietness and *confidence* forever."

❖ Philippians 3:3, "…put no *confidence* in the flesh."

❖ 2 Thessalonians 3:4-5, "And we have *confidence* in the Lord concerning you, that you are doing and will continue to do what we command. And may the Lord direct your hearts into the love (*Agape*) of God and into the steadfastness of Christ."

❖ 1 John 2:28, "…we may have *confidence* and not shrink away from Him in shame at His coming."

❖ 1 John 4:17, "By this, love is perfected with us, that we may have *confidence* in the day of judgment; because as He is, so also are we in this world."

❖ 1 John 5:14, "And this is the *confidence* which we have before Him, that, if we ask anything according to His will, He hears us."

The Scandal of Dismus

Dismus was a hardened thief sentenced to death by Roman law. He was crucified next to Jesus and his encounter on the cross gives us an important insight into the manner in which the wedding garment functions. Both thieves railed against Christ, but something turned inside Dismus. His spiritual perception began to awaken as to who Jesus was and the significance of what was happening. Dismus believed with his heart and confessed with his mouth when he said, "Master, when You come into Your Kingdom, remember me." Surprisingly, Jesus said "Today you shall be with Me in Paradise" (Luke 22:42-43). Apart from water baptism, without taking the Lord's supper, ignorant of the catechism, and never having been confirmed, Dismus, clothed in the righteousness of Christ alone, enters eternity with our Lord Jesus. *Agape* brought immediate healing and release to Dismus.

Imagine the scene in heaven when he arrives, "What are *you* doing here? You've never even been to church!" He missed the whole Christian journey, but could *see* the King and the Kingdom and he *believed.* The Sovereign Lord put His preferential choice upon him. Don't get me wrong; all means of grace are important, but Dismus was God's first illustration to show those of us who are so religious and eager to earn our righteousness how much we're loved and accepted apart from any performance. Like Dismus, we can do nothing to earn our way home.

When God came to us in Christ, He came as a gift that must be received by faith plus nothing. "By grace you are saved not of works lest any man should boast" (Ephesians 2:8-9). If God was able to do that for Dismus, why can't He do that for you? The ultimate battle in our spiritual life is *confidence* in the wedding garment. The good news is that when we lose or desert our confidence, God doesn't (2 Timothy 2:13). We can even say to God, "Leave me alone!" His response is "I will never desert you, nor will I ever forsake you" (Hebrews 13:5).

Hidden Shame

Shame is more than a feeling; it is an *experience*. Hidden shame describes the *Eros* phenomena of being turned in upon ourselves with such a force as to precipitate paralyzing fear, disgust with our own weakness, self-hate, and often, thoughts of suicide. The idea is that the whole world, including our family, would be better off without us! We experience strong urges to run and hide as well as the desperate need to find someone else to blame for our failures. Hidden shame involves feelings of failure that others cannot see. It is a subterranean form of shame flowing deeply in what we think are the most secret regions of our personality. The manifestations of hidden shame are feelings of:

Insecurity

Illegitimacy

Abandonment

When, due to original sin, the entire creation ran away from home, God's intention of creation being in harmony with Himself was shredded. *Eros,* and all that is self-referential, released *insecurity*. The rupture between our Father and us produced anxiety and fear resulting in feelings of *illegitimacy* and self-hate. We were also left with a sense of *abandonment* or worthlessness. Hidden shame often manifests in a quiet anger or rage. Many of us, including outwardly successful and religious people, struggle with insecurity, illegitimacy, and abandonment. Internalizing hidden shame easily turns to self-hate. Self-hate yields its own fruit, which is guilt along with waves of condemnatory thinking that often results in a strong impression that no one really likes you. The process is cyclical and the end result is a prison of rejection. This is a very serious and prevalent issue in the body of Christ. God knew that the only way to break this was to require us to accept the fact that He has given us value and for us to obey His command to love ourselves.

I personally experienced deep, hidden shame when my own Dad rejected and abandoned me as a teenager. Strangely, we can almost rationalize that we deserved it because of the self-deprecation and self-hate that nourishes the injury. Rejection still comes over me in waves sometimes, more than 60 years later. You can see now why I have sought so diligently and dug so deeply to discover the *Agape* Road. We all need to know this. In some mysterious manner, this book was placed in your hands so that, you too, may find the route out of the *Eros* prison.

God gives us *value* when He places "His *own* love (*Agape*) in us while we are yet a sinner" (Romans 5:8) and, then as if He did not know what He was doing, invites *us* to the wedding. Father God knows that we were dead in trespasses and sins, twisted and turned in upon ourselves. Because of His love for us, He implanted the Eternal Seed in us in the New Birth and now asks us to learn to love on three levels: love God, love yourself, and love others. He covered our nakedness and shame with the righteousness of Christ–the wedding garment. In Him, we are accepted and received. *Believe it.* Self-hate, then, is to hate something on which God, as a Father, has set His *own* love. He has given us value. Any thought of disappearing by running, hiding, or shifting blame has been disrupted. Persistent and gnawing thoughts that we have no value or of taking our own life must be understood in light of the Eternal Seed and the wedding garment. Sometimes that which is self-referential is so strong that we would rather destroy our life rather than give it to God and His purpose.

Self-flagellation is a religious addiction. We think that if we are especially hard on ourselves, go on extended fasts, read more Scripture, and witness to more people, that God would love us more. Not so. This may be shocking, but there is *nothing* we can do to make God love us more! *We need less repentance and more faith* expressed as confidence in what Christ has done for us in the wedding garment.

Shame, self-hate, and feeling that our life is not worth saving are often the motivating cause of why we act in self-destructive ways. *Eros* continually seeks to turn us in upon ourselves, then beats us with accusations and guilt because it nourishes all that is injurious and self-destructive. When we continue, even as believers in Christ, to nurse our insecurity, our sense of illegitimacy, and feeling that we do not belong, it drains our joy and decreases the sense of well-being that Father is offering us as His own. Like Adam and Eve, we place our confidence is in the fig leaves to cover our nakedness and shame rather than God's provision. Paul addresses this by saying their "glory is in their shame" (Philippians 3:19).

The absence of love for ourselves often reveals itself in strange and weird ways. I have known quite a few people who would deny themselves *things* in order to punish themselves. That is not what the Scripture is asking. It asks us to deny *ourselves.* The *Eros* prison wants us to suffer because it makes us feel better. We feel we deserve to go the hard way. Christ cannot rescue us, for we are destined to failure, sickness, and poverty. To deny *ourselves* would mean refusing to live by these twisted ideas. It takes confidence and boldness to step out into the purpose of Christ and say "God's will is that I should live and not die. He has given me value and purpose." Our love for Him is what causes us to *believe* in what He has done for us in the Person of Christ. Do not make God a liar. Allow the Father access to you even if you do not completely believe He knew what He was doing when He set His love upon such a failure as you. Father knows that we really are poor, crippled, blind, and lame. It is to each of these that He addresses the invitation to His wedding celebration. Will you come? Or will you, like others, continue to make excuses, avoid the issues, and persist in your stubborn ways? This is a birthing process and the Scripture says, "the whole creation *groans*; we *groan* within ourselves and the Holy Spirit Himself *groans*" (Romans 8:23-26) to bring forth a new creation that is properly related to God the Father. If you will receive God's Son, whom He sent to reveal His love, He will give you the antidote to self-hate and hidden shame and teach you how to love God and yourself.

Security, Identity, and Belonging

God, as a Father, gives us three of the most scarce, expensive, and exceedingly valuable commodities in the earth in place of insecurity, illegitimacy, and abandonment. He gives:

His *security* in place of our insecurity
His *identity* in place of our feeling illegitimate
His *belonging* in place of our feeling abandoned

Failure is inevitable. Whoever says, "I have not sinned" is self-deceived. What we must grasp is *how* to fail and deal with the shame and guilt in that failure without losing the place and relationship that God, as a Father, has given us as His gift. He is the one who initiated this relationship; it is His responsibility to pull us through it if we can stand the pull. It is through condemnation and guilt that we tend to lose our posture of a faith-relationship in God. Remember, the accuser hammers on us until we finally give up convinced that we are that one case for whom the grace of God was not sufficient (2 Corinthians 12:9). If salvation is a gift and it is not earned (Ephesians 2:8-9), holding our *confidence* in what God has done for us in Christ is totally different than building our confidence on what we have or have not done for God. The redemptive cure, given to us through the Person of Jesus Christ is three fold: *security* as acceptance by the Father; *identity* as a member of God's own family; and *belonging* to Him, who is a Father, whose very Nature *is* eternal love. These three things cannot be self-generated. Security, identity, and belonging must come from the Father. This is true naturally and spiritually. Most of us know that security, identity, and belonging do not magically appear when we graduate with honors, take ownership of a successful company, become the celebrated winner of an Oscar, or win the PGA finals. Worldly success does not yield God's approval.

Jesus was tempted in all three of these areas: The temptation to disrupt His *security* and, consequently our own, can be seen in these words, "*If* you are the Son of God, command that these stones become bread" (Matthew 4:3). The Satanic accusation "if You are" comes against the security of Christ's relationship with the Father by challenging its veracity. Christ expresses His own security by dependence on every word from God. Attempts to dislodge Jesus from 'every word' is the essence of this temptation. His acceptance and security in His relationship with His Father took precedence over the anxiety of what to eat and how provision should be made so that He could eat. Christ responded from a place of *security* when He said "man shall not live by bread alone, but by every word that proceeds out of the mouth of God" (Matthew 4:4).

The temptation to disrupt His *identity* can be seen in the temptation to leap from the roof of the Temple. "*If you are the Son of God*, throw Yourself down" (Matthew 4:6). Christ's confidence in His Father did not require Him to "put God to the test" (verse 7). He was able to abide in what God had declared without supernatural accompaniment.

Christ's *belonging* was also challenged when Satan said, "...if You will fall down and worship me." The temptation was to trade His belonging for "all the kingdoms of the world and their glory" (Matthew 4:8-9). Jesus said, "You shall worship the Lord your God, and Him only shall you serve" (Matthew 4:10). The underlying issue had to do with who or what was worthy of worship, a word derived from worthship. Christ came for one reason: to do the will of His Father (Hebrews 10:7). It was to God and His Kingdom that He *belonged*.

The apostle Paul in the well-known text of Galatians 2:20 said, "I have been crucified with Christ; and it is no longer I who live, but Christ lives in me; and the life which I now live in the flesh I live by faith in the Son of God, who loved me and gave Himself up for me." Reading this text in light of security, identity, and belonging helps us see that the very strength of the three temptations can be stripped of their power by the life of Christ living in us. We can also see the love of the Son of God demonstrated in His giving Himself up for us. Jesus chose to embrace the betrayal of Judas, the rejection of His nation Israel, and the whole judicial system of His day so that you and I may never know the loss of security, identity, and belonging. The Father provided a way so that this world—religious or secular—could lose its tempting power. It can no longer *add* anything to us, for we are complete in Christ (Colossians 2:10); it cannot *take* anything from us, for the resurrected Christ dwells in us. He has brought with Him all we will ever possibly need in the form of His security, identity, and belonging. This is Father's gift to us. "For if we could be saved by keeping the law, then there was no need for Christ to die" (Galatians 2:21 NLT).

The Man Who Couldn't Walk

There is a beautiful and powerful story found in 2 Samuel 9 that is especially meaningful for those of us who perceive ourselves as *poor, crippled, blind,* and *lame* when we received the invitation to the wedding celebration. This story is about Mephibosheth, Jonathan's son and king Saul's grandson. After David became the king of Israel, he decided to show kindness to this child for the sake of Saul's family. Mephibosheth was *crippled in both feet* as a result of being dropped by his nurse as an infant while they were escaping their enemies. The lameness was due to a set of circumstances in his life that he could not control. David, taking the initiative, searched out Mephibosheth and had him moved from the city where he lived to Jerusalem where he could eat at the king's table regularly. David also restored to him all the land that belonged to his grandfather, Saul, and put an entire family of 15 sons and 20 servants at Mephibosheth's disposal and instructed them to cultivate his land.

David's love for this young man was strictly vicarious and covenantal. There was nothing in the young man that would *cause* someone to love him; David simply set his *Agape* on him. Mephibosheth's response was to prostrate himself and say to David, "What is your servant that you should regard a dead dog like me?" (2 Samuel 9:8). This is called the condemnation of self-knowledge–he knew what he was like even if no one else did. We do not have to reach far to see this young man wallowing in insecurity, illegitimacy, and abandonment. He knew he was a burden that others had to bear.

Being crippled or lame in both feet represents our inability to *walk* the Christian life. More Bible teaching does not help those who do not have the capacity to walk it out in the first place. However, just because we seem unable to walk this path, does not change the King's desire to invite us to His table. Almost all of us have seen ourselves like a dead dog. Like Peter, we could say, "Lord, depart from me, for I am a sinful man!" (Luke 5:8). Four times David says, "He shall eat at my table," which is suggestive of Revelation 3:20, "Behold, I stand at the door and knock; if anyone hears My voice and opens the door, I will come in to him, and will dine with him, and he with Me." This was not written to unbelievers; it was written to the Church. Eating at the table represents privilege and intimacy. Family involves the freedom to enjoy a cup of coffee with one another at the kitchen table.

The name Mephibosheth means "destroying shame." Because this whole story is vicarious, we can easily and legally substitute ourselves for Mephibosheth and Christ for David. It's not what Mephibosheth did; it's what someone did for him, on his behalf. Jesus sees us lame in both feet and He willingly paid the price for us to eat at the King's table.

Five Questions

There are five questions we want to consider in this story about Mephibosheth. The goal is to strengthen our faith and confidence in the wedding garment and increase our grasp of security, identity, and belonging. Answering these five questions with honesty may help:

1. *Does the King have the right to choose?*

2. *Can He choose you?* Can He choose a person who is "lame in both feet?" That is called election, predestination. You have heard Him call your name. John 5:25 says, "the dead shall hear His voice." I was a twelve-year-old street kid badly in need of a literal bath when I heard Him call me. I did not call Him; He called me. He does the choosing. He chases us down for years, throws us to the ground, puts His foot in our neck and the next morning we say, "Last night I found the Lord!"

3. *Does He have the ability and freedom to set His love and favor on you?* We cannot refuse to let God love us. Often it is not as much refusal as it is sheer incapacity to receive His love. Note how this is stated in 1 John 4:16, "We have come to know and have believed the love which God has for us." We assume that if we let people get too close to us, they will get to know us and, of course, rejection will follow. The question we need to deal with arises from self-hate: how can God love a dead dog like me? We may feel like a dead dog, but God says we *are* going to live! Sometimes it seems as if He chastens us with His love. If He would just give us a good crack instead of covering us with love, we might feel better! After all these years, I often wonder if I didn't reject Christ because I was afraid of His love. Since the time I was 13 years old when my father abandoned me on the streets of Baltimore, Maryland, I have, like thousands of others, struggled with the feeling of being a "dead dog." Once God set His love upon me, He never let up.

"I will never fail you nor forsake you" (Hebrews 13:5) can be more of a threat than a promise.

4. *Can He love someone lame in both feet?* Every tyrannical dictator in history has intended to destroy and kill everything or everyone they considered weak and useless. Think of the events in Hitler or Stalin's regime. God, in a complete reversal of this "choose the best" policy, knows what He is doing by setting His love on the weak to show Himself strong. He, in His wisdom, invited the lame, the poor, the crippled, and the blind (Luke 14:13). Unfortunately, it seems we have successfully turned the church into a place for perfect people with perfect behavior when all the while Jesus said there was an open invitation to all who are trying to find intimacy with God. This includes you and me. We can run, but we cannot hide. This is clear in Psalm 139:7-12.

5. *Can His love heal our incurable wound or offense?* Many of us who love the Scriptures have been in awe at the sheer intensity, brutality, and magnitude of the events that surrounded the death of Christ. Theologians struggle to help us grasp God's own suffering. As one of the desert fathers would say, "God forsaken of God, how can it be?" The more I have understood *run, hide,* and *shift blame,* the deeper my understanding into the depth of the fall of man. Since the redemptive act was before the foundation of the world, my mind kept reaching for some understanding of *why* it was considered necessary for His death to be so passionate and extreme. Every time I read the crucifixion events, it overwhelms me. God reaches to the dregs of man's sin, the deepest transgression, the most calculated betrayal, and the grossest rebellion, so that none of us will ever be excluded or abandoned again. I am ever thankful that the very depth of the sufferings of Christ reached me. It has the capacity to reach you, irrespective of the complexity of your particular problem or the extent of your offense.

God's *Agape* really can heal every incurable wound; it has the capacity to break cyclical behavior and heal lame feet so that in the years that we have left to walk this life, we *can* walk with Jesus in health and wholeness. This is the *Agape* Road and it is this Road that allows us to become a voice of healing for others. One of the early Church Fathers said that the glory of God is man fully alive.

Give Me Or Make Me?

It is not my intention to do the prodigal son thing on you, however, we must briefly examine how *Agape* healed his relationship with his father. The younger son asked his father for his portion of inheritance with intent to leave home. In Jewish custom, asking for his inheritance was in effect wishing his father were dead since the only way he could "inherit" was upon his father's death. His father accommodated him without comment, but not without pain and personal suffering. This son, who thought he knew it all, went away and squandered his entire inheritance. In spite of the fact that he had wished his father dead, injured the intimate relationship between father and son, and created enmity and distance between himself and his family, he never ceased to be his father's son.

Sometime during one of his meals with the swine, it must have occurred to him what his life had become—infected with *Eros*—and he decided to go home. This was the first step in straightening the hook in his life. It was a conscious choice. The prodigal left saying, "*give me* my inheritance," and returned saying "*make me* your slave." The difference between these two statements contains the *Eros/Agape* paradigm. He made a preferential choice, the nature of which reversed the *Eros* shift and caused this young man to begin his *Agape* conversion. He came home; the living dead can know life.

Like the prodigal, we sometimes say, "I am going to get all I can from God. I will take my inheritance and enjoy all that life has to offer." When we discover Father's refusal to retract His offer of security, identity, and belonging, we experience our own *Agape* conversion.

It is important to the Father that His son or daughter not be allowed to *permanently* brand himself or herself as an outsider, one who refuses to release the accusation of rejection. Remember Dismus. The inexorable result of our refusal to get up and go home will be increased isolation and loss of personal worth leading to self-hate. This does not have to come to pass.

When we break intimacy with the Father, we do not cease *belonging* to Him. All three—security, identity, and belonging—have been traumatized, but Father's covenant love is resilient and eternal. When we choose the things of the world, our salvation is not lost, but our intimacy with God, as a Father is essentially out of order. Like the prodigal, we have actually run away from home. When the son returned, it was his father who saw him from a long way off and welcomed him with open arms, just as God stands ready to welcome us as we seek to restore intimacy with Him. This elderly and distinguished father abandoned caution and decorum, and literally ran down the path to find his boy, giving him the robe (security), the ring (identity), and the sandals (belonging). He is not restored to the status of one of his father's slaves, but like Mephibosheth, he is restored to his father's table.

As a father myself, may I invite you Home? Right now, say to the Father, *"I have repeatedly said, 'Give me.' Father, I am now asking that You to 'Make me.' I accept Your robe of security, Your ring of identity, and Your sandals of belonging."*

With the robe, the ring, and the sandals comes the overwhelming sense of the healing and transforming power of *Agape*. This is the beginning of our *Agape* conversion.

Agape Perfected: How the Kingdom Comes

Take time to carefully read the following lines of George MacDonald. Consider the insights of this deeply spiritual man of God, as he explains the way God's Kingdom is brought to manifestation. He does this as only a poet can do, saying so much more than is actually written:

O Christ, who didst appear in Judah land,
Thence by the cross go back to God's right hand,
Plain history, and things our sense beyond,
In thee together come and correspond:
How rulest thou from the undiscovered bourn
The world-wise world that laughs thee still to scorn?
Please, Lord, let thy disciple understand.

'Tis heart on heart thou rulest. Thou art the same
At God's right hand as here exposed to shame,
And therefore workest now as thou didst then—

Feeding the faint divine in humble men.
Through all thy realms from thee goes out heart-power,
Working the holy, satisfying hour,
When all shall love, and all be loved again.

From thine, as then, the healing virtue goes
Into our hearts–that is the Father's plan.
From heart to heart it sinks, it steals, it flows,
From these that know thee still infecting those.
Here is my heart–from thine, Lord, fill it up,
That I may offer it as the holy cup
Of thy communion to my every man.[4]

---

[4]George MacDonald, *Diary of an Old Soul* (Minneapolis: Augsburg Press, 1994), 58-60.

Chapter 8 Glossary

Belonging: One of the three qualities that grow out of intimacy with the Father; replaces the feeling of abandonment, rejection, and worthlessness.

Confidence in the Wedding Garment: Trust, reliance, bold assurance that Christ alone is our righteousness demonstrated by our acceptance of the wedding garment (Heb. 3:6).

Hidden Shame: Feelings of failure that others cannot see. An *Eros* phenomena of being turned in upon ourselves with such a force as to precipitate paralyzing fear, disgust with our own weakness, self-hate, and often, thoughts of suicide. We experience strong urges to run and hide as well as the desperate need to find someone else to blame for our failures. The manifestations of hidden shame are insecurity, illegitimacy, and abandonment.

Identity: One of the three qualities that grow out of intimacy with the Father; realizing my significance or value as God's child; replaces the feeling of illegitimacy.

Imparted Righteousness: Allowing Christ's righteousness to be worked in us; becoming conformed to the image of Christ (Rom. 8:29). Illustrated by the white handkerchief.

Imputed Righteousness: The righteousness of Christ given to us as God's gift which completely covers us. We did nothing to deserve or earn it. It is God's righteousness imputed or implanted within us as the Eternal Seed giving us the authority to *become* sons and daughters of God by faith (John 1:12). Illustrated by the white handkerchief.

Security: One of the qualities that grow out of intimacy with the Father; replaces insecurity. Knowing and accepting that God has chosen me.

Wedding Garment: The white robe of righteousness bought for us by Christ's death for our sins. Illustrated by the white handkerchief. God provided the wedding garment so we would be comfortable in His presence (See Is. 61:10; Rev. 6:11).

Chapter 9
Cultivating the Eternal Seed

The kingdom of God is like a man who casts seed upon the soil; and he goes to bed at night and gets up by day, and the seed sprouts and grows—how, he himself does not know.

Mark 4:26-28

There are two prevailing theories regarding the Christian experience: Jesus has done it all, just believe; and we, alone, are responsible for the outcome of our spiritual journey. Wrongly applied, the first leaves us irresponsible, weakening the moral fiber of God's people; the second leaves us drowning in human effort and religious striving that leads to despair. In this one chapter, I hope to correct some 2000 years of wrong emphasis, setting it all in proper context! While humorous, this is obviously not possible. If we have walked with the Lord long enough, we know that more than balance is needed. Mixture of the Old and New Covenants is very damaging when it comes to our journey on the *Agape* Road.

Nourishing the Eternal Seed

In the New Testament, everything depends upon the Eternal Seed, which, as we know, is *Agape* Incarnate. Jesus gives us the parable of the seed in Mark 4:26-29,

> [26]And He was saying, "The kingdom of God is like a man who casts seed upon the soil; [27]and he goes to bed at night and gets up by day, and the seed sprouts and

grows—how, he himself does not know. ^{28}The soil produces crops by itself; first the blade, then the head, then the mature grain in the head. ^{29}But when the crop permits, he immediately puts in the sickle, because the harvest has come.

There are four important lessons in this passage:

1. The Eternal Seed is the Kingdom of God that comes internally and imperceptibly (Mark 4:27).

2. The Eternal Seed is mysterious; it grows and produces what God intends, but we don't know how. This is a preservation of the mystery of the Kingdom (Romans 16:25).

3. The Eternal Seed determines the time of the harvest. Our responsibility is to water, nourish, care for, and protect the Eternal Seed so it may bring forth fruit 30-, 60-, and 100-fold (Matthew 13:8).

4. The Eternal Seed is what comes to maturity and is responsible for our spiritual progress, not our own effort. "Greater is He Who is in you, than he who is in the world" (1 John 4:4).

The Eternal Seed is the essence of the creation mandate of Genesis 1:28, "be fruitful and multiply." This is repeated in Matthew 28:19, "Go therefore and make disciples of all the nations...." Because Jesus is the true vine and His Father the vinedresser or farmer (John 15:1), it is the Father Who has the responsibility to see to it that the Eternal Seed produces the proper fruit that He is expecting. Because the Father is the vinedresser, He reserves the process of cultivation and pruning for Himself. Isaiah 5:1-6 tells us that the Old Testament Vine failed in its designed intent to reveal the glory of God. When Jesus said "I am the True Vine" it was His guarantee that this failure would not be so the second time.

As believers, we have a responsibility to be *cultivated* and to assist in the *cultivating* process of others. If we are *cultivated* and *cultivatable*, we are able to more fully cooperate with God's intention of cultivating others, our own family, our neighbors, and the nations without *self-conscious effort or human striving*. In cultivating and being cultivated, we need to keep a biblical tension to pray for a good harvest (God's responsibility) while continuing to hoe (our responsibility). Cultivation is not "good works," but the process of protecting and nourishing the Eternal Seed. It is the same responsibility God required of Adam and Eve in the Garden of Eden. The concept of cultivating requires us to focus on nourishing and protecting the Eternal Seed in our own garden. Ministry, then, would be cultivating the Eternal Seed in the lives of others whom God defines as "our neighbor." We *cannot* do God's part; He *will not* do our part.

Paul talks about cultivating the Seed by saying that one plants and waters, but God causes the growth" (1 Corinthians 3:6-9). In his writings, Paul continually seeks to present us all to the Father in a state of maturity. As the Eternal Seed continues to mature in us, we find ourselves indwelt by the Person of Christ (Ephesians 3:17) and manifesting the fruit of the Spirit. As the Seed matures, *Agape* is demonstrated as God's glory— *Agape* perfected. As we have learned, God's glory is His seven hidden attributes (Exodus 34:6-7). In order to allow the Seed to mature in us, we must allow "all things" (Romans 8:28) to conform us to the image of God's Son. To do so will infuse, nourish, and cultivate the seed which increases our capacity to love as Father loves.

The Wheat and the Tares

Jesus used the parable of the "Wheat and Tares" to show us an important lesson about the Eternal Seed of the Kingdom. This parable is illustrative of the *Eros/Agape* paradigm.

> [24]Jesus presented another parable to them, saying, "The kingdom of heaven may be compared to a man who sowed good seed in his field. [25]But while his men were sleeping, his enemy came and sowed tares among the wheat, and went away. [26]But when the wheat sprouted and bore grain, then the tares became evident also. [27]The slaves of the landowner came and said to him, 'Sir, did you not sow good seed in your field? How then does it have tares?' [28]And he said to them, 'An enemy has done this!' The slaves said to him, 'Do you want us, then, to

go and gather them up?' ²⁹But he said, 'No; for while you are gathering up the tares, you may uproot the wheat with them. ³⁰Allow both to grow together until the harvest; and in the time of the harvest I will say to the reapers, 'First gather up the tares and bind them in bundles to burn them up; but gather the wheat into my barn.'"

Matthew 13:24-30

Sometimes God is unwilling to pull the tares (*Eros*) until after the harvest because He does not want to risk injury to the wheat. This principle certainly applies in our own life. Pulling tares is a difficult and delicate procedure; it demands expertise that only the Master has. He is willing to pull the tares for us because of His love for us. Until the tares are pulled, we must learn to walk among the weeds in our own lives and in the lives of others. The weed-less field is an *Eros*-driven idea of human perfection that can only be accomplished by controlling and manipulating people in wrong and injurious ways. It is not a biblical model. The leader who seeks a weed-less field is missing the heart of the Savior.

Being cultivated and cultivatable, as well as assisting others in the care and nourishment of their Eternal Seed, requires that we understand the idea of *Agape* needing to be *perfected*—brought to its full and intended fruitfulness. When this occurs in our lives, the tares cannot and will not continue to be ignored. As the tares are exposed, they reveal themselves as the Seven Giants, creating a ruckus in order to be seen and remain in control. As the believer embraces the *Agape* Road and the process of being conformed to the image of God's Son, the tares are pulled. Uprooting *Eros* in the form of long-standing culture, tradition, family genes, religious presuppositions, personal prejudices, as well as personal preferences is not easy. The Lord provided the Wedding Garment for this very reason. Remember, the Father reserves the pruning and tare pulling process for Himself—He is the Vinedresser (John 15:1).

We need to be careful of eager tare-pullers who seek to keep the Kingdom clean from the very people the message of His love was offered. The blind, lame, poor, and marginalized are the objects of His affection, but He often cannot trust us with them. Jesus said, "It is not those who are healthy who need a physician, but those who are sick. But go and learn what this means: 'I desire compassion, and not sacrifice,' for I did not come to call the righteous, but sinners" (Matthew 9:12-13).

We do not want to be tare-pullers. We need to examine ourselves to see if *Eros*, like tares, is wrapped around the very roots of the life of God preventing us from knowing freedom and possibly making us a stumbling block to others. We cannot see, so we will not believe that *we* are the problem.

Three Dimensional Reality

Personal victory and true spirituality does not originate from us, but as a direct result of the presence of the Eternal Seed. That Seed is cultivated, nourished, and brought to maturity by three dimensions of Christ's Person. Seeing God in His three dimensions helps us understand His purposes in the earth.

> [4]John to the seven churches that are in Asia: Grace to you and peace, from *Him who is* and *who was* and *who is to come*; and from the seven Spirits who are before His throne. [8]"I am the Alpha and the Omega," says the Lord God, "*who is* and *who was* and *who is to come*, the Almighty."
>
> Revelation 1:4, 8

The Greek translates this verse something like this: "As I have been, so I remain, and I am coming." This is carefully restated in the book of Hebrews as, "Christ is the same yesterday and today and forever [tomorrow]" (Hebrews 13:8). Walking in three dimensional reality means that we follow Jesus who is the Light of the world so that we will not "walk in the darkness, but will have the Light of life" (John 8:12). The three dimensions of yesterday, today, and tomorrow look like this:

Hindsight—yesterday. He who *was* (Greek: as I have been). *Hindsight* is seeing what has happened, and what ought to have been done, after the event; it is perception gained by looking backward. It allows us to see that God was *Agape* from the beginning. As we know, *hindsight* is always 20/20. Because we know what the seed is like, pure and not a hybrid, we can reach into the past in order to build our foundation for the future. *Agape* was the Light of the world.

Insight—today. He who *is* (Greek: so I remain). *Insight* is internal sight, mental vision or perception, discernment, understanding, intelligence, wisdom. The fact of penetrating with the eyes of the understanding into the inner character or hidden nature of things; a glimpse or view beneath the surface; the faculty or power of thus seeing. *Insight* allows us to see that Christ as *Agape* Incarnate is with us now. We know what He is like because He sent us Jesus. The reality that *Agape* is present *now* keeps us from doing injury to our neighbor (Romans 13:8-10) and allows us to love others as He has loved us (John 13:34). Insight is walking in light because the incarnation is the revelation of the Father.

Foresight—tomorrow/forever. He who is *yet to come* (Greek: I am coming). *Foresight* is looking into the future. Perception gained by looking forward; prospect; hope; a sight or view into the future. When we really see Him, we shall become like Him. Our confidence is not in ourselves but in "the Spirit who lives in us is greater than the spirit who lives in the world" (1 John 4:4 NLT). We know what the Eternal Seed is like and know that only the Seed can continue to produce His likeness in us. *Foresight* is our confidence that the Seed will do what He promises. *Foresight* allows us to have the Light of Life.

We can be confident in the Eternal Seed of the past and the present so that we can also place our confidence in the future where Christ's high priestly prayer describes what the future will be like:

> [21]...that they may all be one; even as Thou, Father, are in Me, and I in Thee, that they also may be in Us; that the world may believe that Thou didst send Me. [22]And the glory which Thou hast given Me I have given to

them; that they may be one, just as We are one; [23]I am in them, and Thou in Me, that they may know that Thou didst send me, and didst love them, even as Thou didst love Me. [24]Father, I desire that they also, whom Thou hast given, be with Me where I am, in order that they may behold My glory, which Thou hast given Me; for Thou didst love Me before the foundation of the world. [25]O righteous Father, although the world has not known Thee, yet I have known Thee; and these have known that Thou didst send Me; [26]and I have made Thy name known to them, and will make it known; that the love wherewith Thou didst love Me, may be in them, and I in them.

John 17:21-26

Alpha and Omega

"I am the *Alpha* and the *Omega*, the first and the last, the beginning and the end" (Revelation 22:13). He is also everything in between. Understanding Christ as the Alpha and Omega implies that we understand hindsight, insight, and foresight—believing that He existed prior to creation, was the author of creation, and the One in Whom all things are to be consummated (see John 1:1-14). We begin our journey at *Alpha* on this *Agape* Road and move towards *Omega*—God, the Father. God is both the beginning and the end. He is revealed in Christ. This is also stated in Hebrews 12:2, "fixing our eyes on Jesus, the author and perfecter of faith, who for the joy set before Him endured the cross, despising the shame, and has sat down at the right hand of the throne of God."

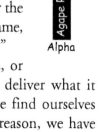

A false omega is a promise of life, circumstances, or ungoverned desire that does not have the ability to deliver what it promised. Rather than moving toward the Father, we find ourselves moving toward a false omega because, for whatever reason, we have become convinced that there is a pot of gold at the end of the rainbow.

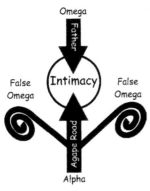

What is waiting is an *Eros* payoff that leads to an *Eros* prison. False omega's are both religious and worldly. Personally, I have experienced more than my share of false promises. Our twisted reasoning and ungoverned desires cause them to be desirous and appear to be real. False goals come in the form of business deals that seem too good to be true, or involvement in church groups, clubs, or friendships for the wrong motivations. One lady belonged to so many clubs that when she died they inscribed, "Clubbed to death" on her gravestone! People who are involved in numerous clubs at the same time are usually seeking security, identity, and belonging from the wrong source—nebulous false omegas. Remember, these false goals are legal and illegal, religious and worldly, valid and invalid. The one thing they have in common is that they always turn out to be disappointing!

Vivified or Unvivified

Father, in His providence and sovereignty, uses "all things" for the purpose of conforming us to the image of His Son. This is stated clearly in Romans 8:28-30:

> We know that in all things God works for good with those who love him, those whom he has called according to his purpose. Those whom God had already chosen he also set apart to become like his Son, so that the Son would be the first among many brothers. And so those whom God set apart, he called; and those he called, he put right with himself, and he shared his glory with them (UBS).

Paul states categorically in 1 Corinthians 3:1-4 that we can be an authentic believer in the Person of Jesus Christ, yet be immature, self-referential, and unspiritual. The footnote of 1 Corinthians 2:14 Weymouth Translation gives us the best description of what it means to be unspiritual:

Unspiritual. Or 'psychical;' or, if we had such a word, 'soulish.' In the psychical man "the spirit being *unvivified* and uninformed by the Spirit of God, is overborne by the animal soul with its desires—and is in abeyance, so that he may be said not to have it" (Alford).

The answer and response to this conflict is again in Weymouth's footnote called *The Message of the Cross* (1 Corinthians 1:18):

The Message of the Cross. Not merely the facts as to Christ's death and the doctrines involved therein, but also the truth expressed in Luke ix. 23: "If any man would come after me let him ignore self, and take up his cross daily, and follow me; for whoever would save his life shall lose it, but whoever shall lose his life for my sake, the same shall save it." We do not get the full benefit of Christ's atoning sacrifice unless we are willing, through faith, to die with Him to sin and the world (Gal. vi 14).—Ed.

The human spirit is *unvivified*, meaning the Eternal Seed is present, but for whatever reason, it has not sprung into life. The human spirit is *uninformed*—it is yet ignorant of the ways and processes of the Holy Spirit as to what will we look like and how will we act when the Eternal Seed has come to maturity within us (Galatians 4:19). Paul's answer is the message of the Cross. A casual reading of Paul's Epistles will show that he did not over emphasize the Cross, but carefully made the following four points to be the essence of what it means to follow Jesus:

❖ To follow Christ means to not be self-referential.
❖ To follow Christ means the Cross must be carried or embraced daily.
❖ To follow Christ means not complicating our journey with repeated attempts to 'save our life' in an *Eros* manner.
❖ To follow Christ means we are learning to die in the same manner that Christ gave us by His example (1 Peter 2:21).

De-centering and Re-centering

When we have, by choice or for any other reason, centered upon that which is less than or other than the Kingdom of God, Father employs "all things" to effectively de-center us from the wrong or inadequate *focus* or *object*. The de-centering process is always painful, but it always brings freedom. On occasion it has been so painful that I wasn't sure I wanted to be that free! Through this process Father seeks to "wash our eyes with tears" giving us new hindsight, insight, and

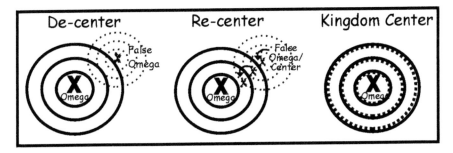

foresight. De-centering is applying the message of the Cross. Re-centering is the awakened, *vivified*, and instructed human spirit seeing the Kingdom and making the preferential choices necessary for the Eternal Seed not to be encroached upon nor hindered by the "worries of this world." We can see in Matthew 13:22 that external sin is not the only issue: "And the one on whom seed was sown among the thorns, this is the man who hears the word, and the *worry of the world* and the *deceitfulness of wealth* choke the word, and it becomes unfruitful." Both of these problems hinder the development and fruitfulness of the Eternal Seed. We can see in these diagrams how our priorities become restored when we seek the Kingdom Omega or center. Because of Father's jealousy toward us, He cannot continue to allow us to move toward a false omega. When we center on God and His Kingdom, then family, church, money, work, leisure, etc. all line up in proper order. This is what Paul was talking about in Romans 8:20-21:

> For the creation was subjected to *futility* (vanity, emptiness—false omega), not of its own will, but because

of Him who subjected it, in hope that the creation itself also will be set free from its slavery to *corruption* (unreality—false omega) into the freedom of the glory of the children of God.

Apart from Christ and an understanding of the Kingdom of God, every one of us is irrevocably committed to darkness, vanity, and futility (John 3:19). Our embracing the de-centering and re-centering process must not be based upon the disruption that de-centering causes, but the end result which is freedom. The process of de-centering and re-centering requires that we not run, hide, or shift blame, but embrace Father's care—this brings the freedom of the glory of the children of God.

There are three issues that face us in the de-centering and re-centering process:

1. *Despair of circumstances:* In the de-center and re-center process, events can become tumultuous and bizarre. It seems as if we have lost control of life itself. This is called chaos. God *is* in our chaos. He rules over all, including our circumstantially bizarre life.

2. *Unintended consequences:* This comes as a result of conscious decisions we have made. We are free to choose, but we are *not* free to control the consequences of that choice. Sometimes the consequences are far-reaching and extremely difficult. It is important that we allow every consequence to press us *into* God rather than cause us to run, hide, or shift blame.

3. *Personal failure:* This includes serious moral or sexual issues, ethical lapse, betrayal or denial of the Lord, spiritual failure in doctrine, leadership, or conduct that has inadvertently injured others. The recognition that we are the ones who have dirtied our own nest is exceedingly painful. It was not the devil, other people, or circumstances—we did it ourselves. Own it. Do not run, hide, or shift blame. In the re-centering process, God will use even our failures to conform us to the image of His Son.

Fireproof Wedding Garment

These three issues in the re-centering process should cause us to be exceedingly glad that the Seed of *Agape* is eternal and incorruptible. This is the primary reason for our unshakable confidence in the past, present, and future. It gives me great hope that the presence of *Eros* or even a mixture of *Eros* and *Agape* cannot corrupt the Eternal Seed. *Agape* cannot fail or disappear.

But, what happens if we seriously miss the *Agape* Road? Are we still a believer when we consciously journey up one of the alternate roads? If we died while we were on one of the alternate roads would we go to heaven? These questions have caused blood pressures to increase for 2000 years of Church history. Paul answers these questions about the consequences of human failure in the context of 1 Corinthians 3:15, "If any man's work is burned up, he will suffer loss; but he himself will be saved, yet so as through fire [fireproof wedding garment]." UBS makes this concept even clearer:

> But if the fire burns up anyone's work, then he will not receive an award. But he himself will escape destruction, like someone whom they pull out of the fire. He himself will be saved emphasizes the contrast between the person himself and the work he has done. He will be like someone who narrowly escapes death by running through flames. Literally, he will not be condemned and destroyed by God at the last judgment, although his work on earth has been destroyed *[fireproof wedding garment]*. In languages that do not normally use the passive one may say, for example, "he himself will not perish," or "he himself will not suffer (or, receive) destruction." UBS [Italics mine].

If the Seed is eternal and incorruptible, and Paul presents it as being fireproof, my biblical conviction would be yes, we would go to heaven irrespective of denominational and traditional positions. Mark 4:26-27 tells us that "the kingdom of God is like a man who casts seed upon the soil; and he goes to bed at night and gets up by day, the seed sprouts and grows — how, *he himself does not know.*" It is the unforeseen *possibilities* contained within the mysterious Seed that allows God to preserve His own freedom. Biblical faith in the Seed itself disallows the narrow, critical, and hardened attitude that is so prevalent among those of us who call ourselves evangelicals. It is faith in the Eternal Seed that will not permit us to become exclusive or demanding; neither will it allow us to be intolerant of those who struggle in their attempts to follow Jesus. It is our faith and confidence in the Seed that acts as preventive medicine, protecting us from becoming cynical with others and despairing toward ourselves.

Agape is inexorably and unfailingly committed to break the *Eros* prison in us and in those to whom we are sent to minister. Once *Eros* is broken, we gain security, identity, and belonging that rests in the providence of God because our ultimate confidence does not originate within ourselves, but in the power of the Seed (1 John 5:4).

Since *Agape* never fails, the pressures of time factors lose some of their demand. To hurry God is to find fault with Him. We *know* the chicken is in the egg. We *know* the flower or fruit is in the seed. We can *believe* in the Seed while observing the worst in human behavior. This confidence is not a false religious hope, but something I have personally experienced time and again in more than 50 years of ministering to hurting people. The humanist and the do-gooder do not understand this kind of *knowing* because it is only made possible by a bold, Kingdom confidence in the mysterious and Incorruptible Seed.

Faith in the Eternal Seed also allows us to give up our sheriff's badge; we are no longer driven to make sure everyone behaves with external conformity. Because of the Eternal Seed, we can become productive farmers or co-workers with God (1 Corinthians 3:9), cultivating, nourishing, and watering the Eternal Seed with our tears. Father will never be satisfied with anything less than the fruit of the Spirit being cultivated within those called by His Name. This is what it means to bring many sons to glory (Hebrews 2:10).

Each of us needs to understand why we are admonished to "keep ourselves in the *Agape* of God" (Jude 21). The wedding garment is God's gift to us through the Person of His Son, our Lord Jesus Christ. Our

Chapter 9 Glossary

Alpha/Omega: The first and last letters in the Greek alphabet, thus *alpha* and *omega*, the beginning and the end; used to describe God.

Decentered: The Eternal Seed remains unvivified and ignorant of the purpose of God and His Kingdom.

Eternal Seed: The sinless Son of God, *Agape* Incarnate, Whose nature is implanted in us when we believe in Him. The result is the new birth or being born from above. The Seed is incorruptible and imperishible (1 Peter 1:23); it abides forever.

False Omega: When anything other than God is at the center of our being. A false promise of life, circumstances, or ungoverned desires that do not have the ability to deliver what they promised. False omegas are legal and illegal, religious and worldly, valid and invalid, but they always turn out wrong.

Foresight: Tomorrow/Forever. He who is yet to come (Greek: I am coming). Perception gained by looking forward; prospect; hope; a sight or view into the future; opposite of hindsight. Foresight allows us to know what the Eternal Seed is like and know that only the Seed can produce God's likeness in us.

Hindsight: Yesterday. He who was (Greek: As I have been). Seeing what happened, and what ought to have happened after the event; perception gained by looking backward: opposite of *foresight*. Hindsight allows us to reach into *Agape* of the past in order to build our foundation for the future.

Insight: Today. He who is (Greek: So I remain). Internal sight, mental vision or perception, discernment, understanding, intelligence, wisdom. The fact of penetrating with the eyes of the understanding into the inner character or hidden nature of things; a glimpse or view beneath the surface; the faculty or power of thus seeing. Insight allows us to see that Christ as *Agape* Incarnate is with us now.

Omega/Alpha: The last and first letters of the Greek alphabet, thus from *alpha* to *omega*: from beginning to end; used to describe God.

Recentered: The awakened, *vivified,* and instructed human spirit seeing the Kingdom and making the preferential choices necessary for the Eternal Seed not to be encroached upon nor hindered by the worries of this world.

Three Dimensional Reality: Hindsight, foresight, and insight. Three dimensions of God which help us understand His purposes in the earth. Rev. 4:8, "the Lord God, the almighty, who was and who is and who is to come." Greek translation: "As I have been, so I remain, and I am coming" (also see Heb. 13:8).

Unvivified: Not sprung into life; unspiritual; ignorant of the ways and processes of the Holy Spirit as to waht we will look and act like when the Eternal Seed has come to maturity in us.

Chapter 10
Learning to Abide

The disciple who abides in Jesus *is* the will of God, and his apparently free choices are God's fore-ordained decrees. Mysterious? Yes, Logically contradictory and absurd? Yes, but a glorious truth to a saint.[1]

Oswald Chambers

Suppose, like the early Christians, we were required to defend our faith, perhaps even at the cost of our own lives. If everyday issues shake us, what will happen if some tyrant challenges our faith and our life is literally at stake? Much can be learned from the early Christians who learned how to stand in their love for God when they were forced into the arena with lions or assigned with others to be crucified or burned. They learned what it really means to abide in love and affection for the Father. Remember that love is as strong as death. Learning the skill of abiding is not superficial; it is preparatory for our continued journey on the *Agape* Road into God and His Kingdom. This is important stuff.

Isaiah 55:8-9 says, "'For My thoughts are not your thoughts, nor are your ways My ways,' declares the Lord. 'For as the heavens are higher than the earth, so are My ways higher than your ways and My thoughts than your thoughts.'" This ought not to be. His ways *should* be our ways; His plans *should* be our plans. This is the intimacy that we seek (John 10:30). For our thoughts to be transformed to God's thoughts

---

[1]Oswald Chambers, *My Utmost for His Highest* (Grand Rapids, MI: Discovery House Publishers, 1993, 1935), June 7.

(1 Corinthians 2:16) and for our ways to be transformed to God's ways (1 Corinthians 4:17), we have to learn to abide. It is a process, not an experience.

When the Kingdom of God comes, it demands repentance and promises intimacy with the Father. He cannot and will not leave us in an *Eros* prison. The skills we developed of running, hiding, and shifting blame do not give God the Father an opportunity to show Himself through our own personality. We must keep ourselves in the love of God and stop religious and worldly activity long enough to hear God's still small voice. This involves the skill of *abiding*—continuing to be present, to hold, and to be held in God's love in every situation, contradiction, and crisis that is presented to us on our journey. Abiding is the skill of being able to hunker down and effectively draw upon the "supply of the Spirit of Jesus Christ" (Philippians 1:19). It is the means to being conformed to the image of His Son. Like the simplicity of faith alone, the Kingdom comes to us in such a quiet and uncomplicated manner that we can easily walk right over it, missing the strength it provides us.

Abiding in the Gospel of John

The Apostle John gives us the application to *abiding*, the most basic of all spiritual skills. By using the word more than 80 times in his writings, he shows us the centrality of this issue. Abiding is a continued and uninterrupted relationship between Jesus and the believer. The discovery of mixture within ourselves is no surprise, nor shock to God as our Father. Jesus' disciples struggled with mixture, too, and had to be taught the urgent and necessary skill of abiding as Jesus prepared them for the chaos surrounding His death and departure to the Father.

Abide (Strongs #3306) is used 120 times in Scripture:
40 times in Gospel of John
12 times in John 15
31 times in I John 1, 2, 3

John 13-17 are the consummate chapters that promise intimacy for those of us who are seeking to know God and His revelation in the Person of Christ. The following verses from John 15 contain the essence of what it means to abide.

John 15:1, "I AM the true vine, and My Father is the vinedresser." Jesus is using the 'I AM WHO I AM' of Exodus 3:14. John uses the Greek construction of I AM eight times in his gospel. This statement is being made to the nation of Israel who was God's vine, but was in the process of being set aside because she failed to bring forth the fruit of the Kingdom (Isaiah 5:1-7; Matthew 21:33-46, note verse 43.) Remember that the Father, Himself, reserves the function of Vinedresser. He is the Gardener, the One who cultivates and brings forth the fruit for which He seeks.

John 15:2, "Every branch in Me that does not bear fruit, He takes away; and every branch that bears fruit, He prunes it so that it may bear more fruit." Fruit is the issue. God is never impressed or satisfied with the outward manifestation of leaves without the accompanying fruit. Father will cultivate and prune by means of de-centering and re-centering until we can produce Kingdom fruit. Our Vinedresser will never allow His vine to degenerate for lack of care and pruning.

John 15:3, "You are already clean because of the word which I have spoken to you." This is the Eternal Seed given to us as the wedding garment in the new birth. The result of the new birth is fruit that brings a revelation of God's glory as seen in the seven hidden attributes.

John 15:4, "Abide in Me, and I in you. As the branch cannot bear fruit of itself unless it abides in the vine, so neither can you unless you abide in Me." Abiding involves the skill of unbroken and uninterrupted communion allowing the sap of the Vine—God's *Agape*—to flow into our person (Ephesians 3:17). We must cultivate the Eternal Seed until that DNA which the Seed contains is brought to its full purpose, which is the Son of God *replicated* in the life of the ordinary believer. Abiding results in Christ formed in us (Galatians 4:19). Abiding sometimes appears inactive, because it is quiet and unpretentious, but waiting on God is His request (Isaiah 64:4).

John 15:5, "I AM the Vine, you are the branches; he who abides in Me and I in him, he bears much fruit, for apart from Me you can do nothing." Our union has made us one. We have been given authority to become a child of the Kingdom (John 1:12). It is the life of Christ flowing into us that produces the fruit of the Kingdom. "Apart from

Me" (meaning disjointed in union; injured or broken intimacy rather than a covenantal break) will produce nothing for which the Father waits. A son or daughter who has grasped the implications of *Agape* allows God's love to be *replicated* within them. Matthew 5:44-45 says, "love...*in order that you may be sons of your Father* who is in heaven...." The biblical evidence that the Kingdom has come and God's will is being done on the earth as it is in heaven is discovered when God's love is replicated.

John 15:6, "If anyone does not abide in Me, he is thrown away as a branch and dries up; and they gather them, and cast them into the fire and they are burned." If we do not learn the skill of abiding, we will dry up and fail to yield God's intended fruit. This is the professional Christian who does the right things without the promised results. The cultivation process, as administered by God the Father, is determined to bring forth the intended fruit of the Eternal Seed, which is Christ formed in us as believers (Ephesians 3:17; Galatians 4:19).

John 15:7, "If you abide in Me, and My words abide in you, ask whatever you wish, and it will be done for you." If we learn the skill of abiding, God's Word (Christ as *Agape* Incarnate) will abide in uninterrupted communion with us allowing the sap to flow from the vine into the branch in preparation for the fruit to appear.

John 15:8, "My Father is glorified by this, that you bear much fruit, and so prove to be My disciples." God's glory and the idea of governed desires are blending into one idea. Father's hidden attributes—compassion, gracious, slow to anger, mercy, truth, faithfulness, and forgiveness—given to us in His self-revelation are His glory. All seven of these attributes are *Agape* Incarnate and consist of Christ's very nature. The skill of abiding allows the Holy Spirit to form Christ in us. Father has effectively cultivated and pruned our vine of fruitless, religious activity until we have learned to abide in faith and in rest. Father is gaining a people who can love as He loves (Matthew 5:43-48). This is His glory. Only the solitary route of abiding in unbroken intimacy allows God's glory to fill the earth.

John 15:9, "Just as the Father has *Agaped* Me, I have also *Agaped* you; abide in My *Agape*." *Agape* is the ultimate issue. We are to love in the same manner and degree the Father loves us. Abiding in *Agape* is a skill we must develop. Jude 21 says, "Keep yourselves in the *Agape* of God." Abiding requires pure faith in the wedding garment and confidence that Father God is at work cultivating us towards His eternal purpose—to replicate His love to others. Remember that Father uses "all things" to conform us to the image of His Son "...that we may share His glory with them" (Romans 8:28-30 UBS). Uninterrupted abiding produces fruit that is slowly and carefully grown.

John 15:10, "If you keep My commandments, you will abide in My love; just as I have kept My Father's commandments and abide in His love." Notice that there are *two* sets of commandments here: Father's commandments and Jesus' commandments. Christ kept His Father's Ten Commandments on our behalf. He is asking that we keep His new command stated in John 13:34-35 (TLB), "And so I am giving a new commandment to you now-love each other just as much as I love you. Your strong love for each other will prove to the world that you are my disciples." If we keep Jesus' command to "love one another," we need not worry about keeping the commands God gave to Moses because Jesus kept all of them on our behalf (Galatians 5:14). The skill of abiding releases the sap of the vine—God's *Agape*—to flow through Christ, the Vine, into us, the branches, in uninterrupted union. Jesus told us He would teach us how to abide in Father's love.

It is impossible for us to abide by faith unless and until we have understood the wedding garment; security, identity, and belonging; and God's glory. The skill of abiding is the polar opposite of running, hiding, or shifting blame. Spiritual maturity means abiding in—continuing to be present, to hold, and to be held—in God's love in every situation, contradiction, or crisis we are presented with on our journey.

What Prevents Us From Abiding

There are two potentially undiscovered, *Eros*-motivated behaviors that tend to move us from our posture of abiding by faith. The first one we discussed in the chapter on the Seven Giants: *conforming truth to desire*. This is attempting to make the Scriptures say what we want them to say. We have learned that God's *Agape* is an absolute. We have also learned that *Eros* will use everything and everyone, including God and His Word to gain its own purpose (2 Timothy 4:3).

The second *Eros*-motivated behavior is *the Adam factor*. The very source of our problem is original sin. Oswald Chambers explains this concisely:

> Reconciling one's self to the fact of sin.
>
> This is your hour, and the power of darkness (Luke 22:53).
>
> It is not being reconciled to the fact of sin that produces all the disasters in life. You may talk about the nobility of human nature, but there is something in human nature which will laugh in the face of every ideal you have. If you refuse to agree with the fact that there is vice and self-seeking, something downright spiteful and wrong in human beings, instead of reconciling yourself to it when it strikes your life, you will compromise with it and say it is of no use to battle against it. Have you made allowance for this hour and the power of darkness, or do you take a recognition of yourself that misses out sin? In your bodily relationships and friendships do you reconcile yourself to the fact of sin? If not, you will be caught round the next corner and you will compromise with it. If you reconcile yourself to the fact of sin, you will realize the danger at once—'Yes, I see what that would mean.' The recognition of sin does not destroy the basis of friendship; it establishes a mutual regard for the fact that the basis of life is tragic. Always beware of an estimate of life which does not recognize the fact that there is sin.
>
> Jesus Christ never trusted human nature, yet He was never cynical, never suspicious, because He trusted absolutely in what He could do for human nature. The

pure man or woman, not the innocent, is the safeguarded man or woman. You are never safe with an innocent man or woman. Men and women have no business to be innocent; God demands that they be pure and virtuous. Innocence is the characteristic of a child; it is a blameworthy thing for a man or woman not to be reconciled to the fact of sin.[2]

What Chambers says about the undeniable existence of sin is accurate, despite the unpopularity of the word as it is used today. Society, and sometimes the Church itself, has a dangerous inclination to ignore sin, rationalize it, or go into actual denial that it exists.

These two undiscovered factors–conforming truth and the Adam factor–have a subtle, almost surreptitious way of moving us away from the skill of abiding by faith. When ungoverned desire becomes predominant, we have a frightening capacity to rationalize or explain away the plain meaning of truth. The Adam factor is our capacity to reconcile our spiritual understanding to the fact and the presence of sin (*Eros*), even after we have accepted Christ and have been baptized in water. There is a strange phenomenon called 'post-baptismal sin,' that is the presence of *Eros* within the heart and life of the believer. The skill of abiding transforms our desires and reconciles us to the fact that there does continue within us some "love for darkness" (John 3:19). Abiding is that skill which holds us into Christ until our thoughts are transformed into His thoughts (1 Corinthians 2:16) and our ways are transformed into His ways (1 Corinthians 4:17).

Keeping Ourselves in God's Love

Jude, for its small size, packs powerful insight into how to keep ourselves in God's *Agape*. He is seeking to keep the believers of his day in an effective abiding relationship in the presence of a strong *Eros* shift, the same sort of shift that preceded the fall of Jerusalem, the collapse of

---

[2]Oswald Chambers, *My Utmost for His Highest* (Grand Rapids, MI: Discovery House Publishers, 1993, 1935), June 24.

the entire Roman Empire, and the demise of every fallen civilization that has preceded us. Jude reminds his brethren that the Apostles of Jesus Christ had warned that in the last times scoffers will come who will follow *their own ungodly desires*. He then speaks to those of his own day, as well as to those of us as serious Christians, when he says:

> [18]. . . that they were saying to you, 'In the last time there shall be mockers, following after their own ungodly lusts.' [19]These are the ones who cause divisions, worldly-minded, devoid of the Spirit. [20]But you, beloved, building yourselves up on your most holy faith; praying in the Holy Spirit; [21]keep yourselves in the love (*Agape*) of God, waiting anxiously for the mercy of our Lord Jesus Christ to eternal life.
>
> Jude 1:18-21

Jude teaches about the unbroken abiding relationship by setting forth these four distinct points:

1. *Building ourselves up in the most holy faith*. This is consummate confidence in the righteousness we have described as the wedding garment. Without faith, it is impossible to please God (Hebrews 11:6). Jude reaffirms that abiding is a skill which comes out of faith alone. God will work if we can believe His intent to conform us to the image of His Son.

2. *Praying in the Holy Spirit*. To pray in the Spirit was "speaking to God and not to men" (1 Corinthians 14:1-3). The skill of abiding is enhanced and strengthened by cultivating the capacity to pray in the Spirit. God, as a Father, loves us so much that He personally gave us a language of the Spirit so we could speak to Him in mysteries. This is evidence that God seeks to know us and for us to know Him.

3. *Keep yourselves in the Agape of God*. *Agape* is God's absolute, so departure from *Agape* is departure from the seven hidden attributes of God given to us in the Person of Jesus Christ (Hebrews 1:3). To fail to keep ourselves in the *Agape* of God is the same thing as failing or refusing to abide. We have, for whatever reason, made a preferential choice to

do something other than or more than abide in God's finished work that was given to us in the Person of His Son, our Lord Jesus Christ. We are trying to improve on God's plan!

4. *Wait for the mercy.* Mercy is what triumphs over that which is critical and judgmental. Jesus said, "I desire mercy, not sacrifice" (Matthew 9:13). Mercy is *Agape* applied. It is God's glory revealed because mercy is one of the hidden attributes of God's own Person. Mercy comes in a manner similar to the Kingdom, it comes quietly, almost imperceptibly. When mercy appears, it is symptomatic that the storm is over and victory has been assured.

Saved by His Life

One of the more important, yet hidden phrases found in the New Testament is the unobtrusive text of Romans 5:10, "we are saved by His life." The significance of being saved by His life is that the Eternal Seed has taken up residence in our life (Ephesians 3:17). We have already learned the importance of cultivation and nourishment of that seed which is *Agape* perfected or "Christ being formed in us" (Galatians 4:19). Abiding allows His life to be passed into ours by the functioning of the Vine imparting His life to the branches. This is being saved by His life.

John 1:4 states that "In Him was life…." Christ came that we might know life. When, in the new birth, God implanted the Eternal and Incorruptible Seed, He gave us value and claimed us as His very own (1 Peter 1:20-23). The Life in that Eternal Seed is what does the saving. His *Agape* comes and effectively displaces all that would compete or resist the giving of our entire affection–heart, soul, mind, and strength– to God.

Agape will release God's glory. Keep yourselves in the *Agape* of God for the end result is Kingdom fruitfulness (John 15:7-8). Jude, whom many scholars believed to be the Lord's biological brother describes the results of discovering and abiding on the *Agape* Road:

> But to Him who is able to keep you safe from stumbling,
> and cause you to stand in the presence of His glory *free*
> *from blemish and full of exultant joy*—to the only God

our Savior—through Jesus Christ our Lord, be ascribed
glory, majesty, might, and authority, as it was before all
time, is now, and shall be to all the Ages! Amen

Jude 24, Weymouth

If, for whatever reason, we may feel God is still angry at us, we are
totally missing the freedom of His gift. All of God's anger was exhausted
and expended upon Christ, so that we might know the peace of God
(Romans 5:1). God's favor is His gift to us, purchased by Christ's death
and resurrection. *Believe* that we are valuable to Him. *Believe* what Christ
has accomplished in our behalf. *Believe* His redemptive act has released
us from all guilt and condemnatory accusations, those that come from
others and those that are self-generated. *Believe* that all His anger is
past, and that we are looked upon as His Bride, His Inheritance, whom
He seeks to release into a hurting world to love as He loves. We are,
indeed, forgiven by His death and saved by His Life. We live because
He lives.

Paradox of Grace

If grace is unmerited favor, why would Scripture say, "God is opposed
to the proud, but gives grace to the humble" (Proverbs 3:34; James 4:6;
1 Peter 5:5)? This appears to be contradictory, but when understood, it
proves to be well-founded. We should learn never to trust in anything
or anyone other than the grace of God in ourselves and in others. We
understand grace as God's way of coming to us, dismantling our own
works, and self-conscious efforts (Ephesians 2:8-9). Scripture says that
"God is able to make all grace abound toward you." He provides these
means of grace as tools for the care, nourishment, and protection of the
Eternal Seed. Some of the means of grace are:

1. *Scriptures* .... God's love letter to His own Bride
2. *Prayer* .... Returning God's affection to Him in a pure form
3. *Church* .... Mutual encouragement; breaking individuality
4. *Lord's Table* .... Receiving the Bread of God and forgiveness
5. *Deliverance* .... Release from cyclical behavior; ungoverned desires

6. *Worship* .... Declaring our love privately and corporately
7. *Forgiveness* ..... Freely receiving and giving forgiveness
8. *Fasting* .... Humbling our soul by governing food, talk, activity
9. *Abiding* .... Resting in faith; keeping ourselves in the *Agape* of God

If we put the means of grace into the context of the Eternal Seed, we will see that the means of grace are not religious merit, but activity upon which the cultivation, nourishment, watering, and protection of the Eternal Seed is accomplished. None of the means of grace carry any sense of religious reward or human merit. None of these are recommended as *proving* our love for God. Rather, we were created to respond in this manner, for we seek to cultivate and release that Eternal Seed into all of God's created intent. "Greater is He that is in you, than he that is in the world," allows us to see clearly that the Seed is what overcomes, not the person.

Our human tendency is to over-emphasis one or more of the means of grace compared with a more mature and biblical balance of all that Christ has provided for us. The cessation of extremes can be seen in the caution given in Proverbs 25:16, "Have you found honey? Eat only what you need, that you not have it in excess and vomit it." We can apply such wisdom to all of the means of grace. Over-indulgence, even in that which is sweet and desirable, can be detrimental and become one more form of ungoverned desire. We must cease striving because striving and abiding are polar opposites.

The Skill of Abiding

Learning to remain in Christ's completed work is an absolute necessity to our Kingdom fruitfulness. It is the only thing that will hold us in times of conflict. Abiding is a skill we must learn, like skiing or riding a bicycle. Remember that abiding is rest in God's ability to work all things together for good. It signifies spiritual consistency that has come from our learning to trust God in all circumstances, even when we may feel like pressing the alarm. God's pleasure and design is that we rest in the finished work of Christ (Hebrews 4:11) knowing that we are acceptable to God and that we do so without guilt or anxiety knowing that God is not angry with us. Abiding yields freedom, fruit, and releases Father's glory. It is the clear and biblical example given to us by the Person of our Lord Jesus Christ. Peter, who witnessed Jesus' uncomplaining endurance (abiding) said,

> [19]For this finds *favor*, if for the sake of conscience toward God a man bears up under sorrows when *suffering unjustly*. [20]For what credit is there if, when you sin and are harshly treated, you endure it with patience? But if when you do what is right and suffer for it you patiently endure it, this finds *favor* with God. [21]For you have been *called for this purpose*, since Christ also suffered for you, leaving you an *example* for you to follow in His steps, [22]who committed no sin, nor was any deceit found in His mouth; [23]and while being reviled, *He did not revile in return*; while suffering, He uttered no threats, but *kept entrusting Himself* (abiding) to Him who judges righteously.
>
> 1 Peter 2:19-23

Abiding is the only skill known that allows us to put biblical demands upon the Eternal Seed, causing *Agape* to manifest as the fruit of the Holy Spirit (Galatians 5:22-23). Running, hiding, and shifting blame are not an option. Only when we draw upon the life of the Eternal Seed can God's supernatural *Agape* rising *within* us can meet the demands of our present circumstances. This is how the fruit of the Spirit appears even though our circumstances have not changed. We are the ones being transformed by the *Agape* of God in the midst of difficulties.

The skill of abiding is needed to fulfill what God asks from each of us in the following four areas (Matthew 5:43-48):

Loving God. As we know, God loved us first. He is the very source of *Agape* and without Him we can do nothing (John 15:5). He is our Enabler who works His will within us (1 Corinthians 12:6). Our choice in compelling and unchanging sets of circumstances is to abide in His love. To do so reveals His glory. Only our love for God can enable us to stand.

Loving ourselves. We know that we are complete in Christ, lacking nothing. His wedding garment was sufficient and it is fireproof; it will hold. Love for God and for myself results in security, identity, and belonging which cannot be self-generated; they are given by God the Father as the direct result of the *authority* imparted when we believe on the Person of Christ (John 1:12).

Loving others. Only abiding in the security, identity, and belonging provided by Christ will allow us to be slappable and spitable in the midst of conflict.

Love our neighbor. *Agape* always reaches out to others. Because of *Agape*, we are committed to do all we can to help others who are in difficulty. Rather than murmur, we are asked to assist, nurture, and strengthen others in our sphere or those who come across our path. Jesus consciously demonstrated concern and forgiveness to the two Roman soldiers who were assigned to crucify Him. Likewise, we must exert conscious effort to express forgiveness and help to others. It is a supernatural demonstration of the Kingdom of God. As we abide, the walls of our *Eros* prison weaken and are destroyed. Our confidence is that though the circumstances may not change, we are being transformed and experiencing the freedom that Jesus promised.

Love our enemy. This is a stretch for most of us. We live in a fallen world and while we should certainly seek relief from personal pain and pressure, we cannot do so by wishing death or injury on those who may be the cause of our suffering. We must keep in mind that an abusive person is controlled and driven by forces that are way beyond their control. They do not understand it any more than the Roman soldiers understood what was happening. Security, identity, and belonging give us the resources needed to forgive and release those who have hurt us. Only by abiding in what Christ has provided can we come to the place where we love our enemies. Abiding allows us to entrust ourselves to Him who judges righteously. Abiding provides us that needed ability for us to say: *Abba, Father. God is my refuge, a very present help in the time of trouble!* If the detours are not open to us, we must learn how to abide.

Results of Abiding

Only in abiding can we effectively learn to reveal God's glory (John 15:8). Abiding is a means of grace that acts as a preventative measure toward the human propensity to establish our own righteousness (Romans 10:3). Paul explains it to the Galatians in a similar manner, "Are you so foolish? Having begun by the Spirit, are you now being perfected by the flesh?" Abiding is the only way we can embrace self-government which leads us to the freedom the Father has promised. As we have learned, *no one can set us free from that which we still love.* Through

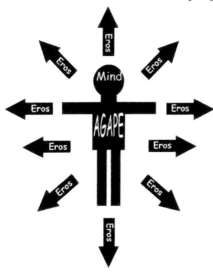

the skill of abiding, we can see ungoverned desires *transformed* into desires that are controlled by *Agape* (2 Corinthians 5:14). As a direct result of abiding, *Eros* is displaced and *Agape* is released at the center of our person.

Jesus, teaching on the skill of abiding said, "the Son can do nothing of Himself, unless it is something He sees the Father doing; for whatever the Father does, these things the Son also does in like manner" (John 5:19). He also said, "apart from Me you can do nothing" (John 15:5). Joining these two statements develops the skill of abiding. The solitary route to bringing glory to the Father (John 15:8) is by learning to abide in an uninterrupted dependence on the Person of Jesus Christ whereby the life-source and the internal sap of the True Vine flows into our mind, emotions, and will. In this quiet state of depending on faith comes the transformation of our personality that results in our being able to bring glory to God as our Father.

Summary

When I was learning to snow ski, the first lesson was to stay upright. The second was how to fall and get back up. Paul in his serious teaching on spiritual warfare in Ephesians 6:10-16 uses the word "stand" three times (vs. 11, 13, 14). My impression is that he knows something about what it means to run, hide, and shift blame. The simple skill of standing in faith brings release into all that God has for us.

The pressures of life are attempts to force us up one of the alternate roads and into an *Eros* prison. God uses all things—good and bad—to conform us to the image of His Son (Romans 8:28-29). This means that nothing can touch us without the Father's permission. This is the biblical concept of providence. The Christian faith will always remain a mystery. We cannot always know for certain the cause of events. What we do know is that God has the ability to use them for His purpose in our lives. We can say, "Lord, I don't know what You are doing, but I know Who You are." In this we can abide being consciously aware of His compassion, grace, mercy, and truth. Abiding is the means to being conformed to the image of His Son.

Glossary Chapter 10

Abiding: Rest in God's ability to work all things together for good. Continuing to be present, to hold, and to be held in God's love in every situation, contradiction, or crisis that is presented to us on our journey. To continue on in uncompromising devotion to the Lord; lasting or enduring. Remaining in Christ's completed work. Abiding means not running, hiding, or shifting blame and is the means to being conformed to the image of His Son. Abiding is the skill of being able to hunker down and effectively draw upon the "supply of the Spirit of Jesus Christ" (Phil. 1:19). (See John 15).

Adam Factor: Our capacity to reconcile our spiritual understanding to the fact and the presence of sin (*Eros*), even after we have accepted Christ and have been baptized in water. There is a strange phenomenon called 'post-baptismal sin,' that is the presence of *Eros* within the heart and life of the believer even after we have been saved. It is original sin.

Conforming Truth to Desires: Attempting to make Scriptures say what we want them to say. "There are ultimately only two alternatives in the intellectual life: either one conforms desire to the truth or one conforms truth to desires" (E. Michael Jones).

Paradox of Grace: Something that appears to be contradictory, but when understood, proves to be well-founded. We should never trust in anything or anyone other than the grace of God in ourselves and in others. (See Prov. 3:34; Jam. 4:6; 1 Pet. 5:5).

Chapter 11
Avoiding Detours

You have to learn to go out of convictions, out of creeds, out of experiences, until so far as your faith is concerned, there is nothing between yourself and God.[1]
Oswald Chambers

This chapter is intended to provide practical suggestions and personal instruction so we can avoid as many detours as possible on our journey to intimacy with the Father. In the 12 years that I was backslidden, I made many detours and learned some desperate lessons that caused me to earnestly seek an authentic love and affection for God. Detours take us to dead-ends that can easily turn into *Eros* prisons if we are not careful. Responding to God's *Agape* is what enables us to recognize and avoid the detours and to stand firmly when facing the temptation of ungoverned desire.

As we know, alternate roads to the *Agape* Road do not yield answers; they simply complicate the issues further. We cannot and must not continue to run, hide, or shift blame. Abiding is the only antidote to taking detours. When we, at any time or for any reason, take a detour, the result is the disruption of the abiding relationship disturbing the flow of the sap from the Vine, which is our vital life source. When we cease or fail to remain in an abiding posture, we interrupt that mystical growth and fruit-bearing process. This is the primary cause of the eternal

---

[1]Oswald Chambers, *My Utmost for His Highest* (Grand Rapids, MI: Discovery House Publishers, 1993, 1935), January 2.

childhood of the believer. We remain like children, playing with our religious toys, failing to understand Father God's larger purpose in our own life and in the earth.

Focus and Object

A primary problem with choosing detours off the *Agape* Road has to do with where we place our focus. A young man had some sexual problems so he went to a Christian psychiatrist. The counselor did an exercise of picture associations with him. He showed the young man a picture of a square and asked him, "What do you see?" The young man looked at it carefully and said, "Well anybody knows what that is. That's a couple making out under a beach blanket." The psychiatrist thought, "My, my, my." Then he pulled out a picture of a circle and asked the young man what he saw. He said, "Oh, that's a couple making out under a beach umbrella." The psychiatrist rolled his eyes for a moment, and tried one more time with a picture of a triangle asking, "What do you see in this picture?" He looked at it and said, "Oh, that's easy to interpret. That's a couple making out in a tent." The psychiatrist said, "Young man, you really have some problems." He says, "Me? You're the one who showed those lewd pictures!"

If we can change the focus and object of our life from the things that have held us in bondage and put our focus on God the Father, we begin to abide. The moment we start saying, "Father, I love You with all my heart, soul, mind, and strength, You are the object of my life," our focus on God begins to expand in our life and because He has free access to us, a reciprocal relationship begins to grow.

The law of sin works exactly the same way. If we focus on the problem, it expands. If we focus on failure, anger, sex, clothes, finances, or even on the necessity for change, then feelings of insecurity, illegitimacy, and abandonment start to encroach upon our faith. The temptation to take one of those alternate roads looking for fulfillment increases in strength. We only go up one of those roads because we think we need something or hope to get something. If we can hold ourselves in the *Agape* of God and abide in Christ, our needs, both spiritual and natural, will be supplied by virtue of Who Christ is. "And my God shall supply all of your needs according to Christ Jesus..." (Philippians 4:19).

Remember that abiding means choosing to stay on the *Agape* Road rather than going up one road or the other at the point of conflict. Opportunities for us to take journeys off the *Agape* Road by running, hiding, and shifting blame present themselves by the dozens. There can be hundreds of points of conflict in our journey because those religious and worldly roads beckon to us continually. We defined temptation as something we want more than our freedom. Remember, freedom involves our ability to start or stop. God has given us freedom in

Christ Jesus that allows us the ability to be free from both anger and anxiety, but no one can set us free from what we still love.

Detour Strategies

Keeping ourselves in the *Agape* of God may well depend on our understanding the six strategies that seek to take us from that place of abiding in the Lord. Each of these can appear to be a perfectly normal solution to the problem at hand. We may even experience a combination of one or more of these at the same time. Each of these is an effective detour that causes injury to the young shoot transforming into fruit. The detours are like taking the wrong exit off the freeway; it may be miles before the next exit. Taking a detour can be a serious problem.

1. *Pride.* Proverbs 16:18, "Pride goes before destruction, and a haughty spirit before stumbling." Pride is inordinate and unreasonable self-esteem, attended with insolent and rude treatment of others. It seeks distance from other humans considered less worthy or different from us. Once we respond in pride, we leave the *Agape* Road. Responding in pride prevents us from dealing with the problem.

2. *Rage.* Luke 6:11, "But they themselves were filled with rage, and discussed together what they might do to Jesus." Rage is violent anger or furious passion usually

manifested in looks, words, or actions. It is the result of pride being revealed or frustrated. Both pride and rage cause us to react in such a way that we depart from dealing with the real issues.

This happened to Naaman in the Old Testament. He was the captain of an army and a valiant warrior, but he was a leper. Naaman came to Elisha for healing, but when Elisha did not heal him in the manner he thought appropriate, he went away enraged. His pride nearly caused him to lose his healing (2 Kings 5:1-14).

When the events of life are successful in turning us in upon ourselves, we quickly spin downward into self-pity. We find ourselves in despair, convinced that no one cares, including God. At this point, all of the detours look promising. Self-pity promptly moves from despair to outright rage. If we are particularly religious, this rage will be sublimated and eat like a cancer at the root of our soul, but we are too proper to tell God what we really think. At first our rage is directed at the perpetrator or the cause of our downward spiral, then at ourselves because of the paralysis or sense of helplessness that we feel. Ultimately, our rage is directed toward God because He could have prevented all of this if He really wanted to.

3. *Deny.* Luke 20:27, "Then some of the Sadducees, who *deny* that there is a resurrection, came to Him" (NKJV). Denial is not a river in Egypt! It is the first-fruit of running, hiding, and shifting blame; it is alive

and well in the larger body of Christ. We come right up to a problem, but deny its existence. All of us have experienced going into denial at one time or another. Denial can be illustrated by Sarah's famous laugh at the angel's word that she would have a child (Genesis 18:13-15). It was a pure form of denial.

4. *Avoid.* James 3:14, "But if you have bitter jealousy and selfish ambition in your heart, do not be arrogant and so *lie against the truth.*" We very carefully work our way around the problem and continue on our own way because we do not want to

deal with the issue. Our determination to avoid the problem can go so far as to cause us to lie against the very truth we know will set us free. Ananias and Sapphira (Acts 5) used both avoidance and lying against the truth. Avoidance is another form of denial, but is much more subtle. It is playing intellectual or emotional games for the purpose of getting our own way. We seek to avoid certain people, issues, problems, and conversations. Circumvention, or knowing how to get around something, becomes an acquired skill as contrasted to developing the skill of abiding and missing the detour.

5. *Endure.* Jeremiah 12:5, "If you have run with footmen and *they have tired you out,* then how can you compete with horses? If you *fall down* in a land of peace, how will you do in the thicket of the Jordan?" We enter the circumstance, but do so with deep, internal resistance. This is how we survive the time factor, yet remain unaffected or

unchanged. A person can survive four years in the military or ten years in prison without benefit or personal change. He or she simply endures. All they are concerned about is doing the time. Many people endure marriage in a similar manner. Christians even approach their spiritual journey, including church services and Bible reading, from an attitude of enduring.

6. *Turn back.* In Galatians 4:9, Paul asks the Galatian believers, "But now that you have come to know God, or rather to be known by God, how is it that you *turn back again* to the weak and worthless elemental things, to which you desire to be enslaved all over again?" This is what Israel tried to do coming out of Egypt because they missed the leeks

and the onions. Turning back is more drastic than the other detour strategies. I turned back as a new believer because the unexplored world of the Kingdom of God was too threatening and cost too much. Few things give us a clearer insight into the twisted nature of fallen man than seeing how easily we can turn back even after understanding the demonstration of God's love in the Person of Christ.

All of these detours present themselves as sophisticated occasions to run, hide, and shift blame. The only way through is to embrace and abide. This is God's prescription in John 15:7-10:

> If you abide in Me, and My words abide in you, ask whatever you wish, and it shall be done for you. By this is My Father glorified, that you bear much fruit, and so prove to be My disciples. Just as the Father has loved (*Agape*) Me, I have also loved (*Agape*) you; abide in My love (*Agape*).

Embrace. Hebrews 10:7, "Then I said, 'Behold, I have come...to do Your will, O God.'" When we are in the middle of a problem or circumstances that we would prefer to *avoid,* or when everything within us wants to *deny* what is happening, we must see that abiding is the only manner in which we can *embrace* the situation. When the pressures of life

are multiplying and telling us we had better *turn back* or we will perish in the wilderness, and we are gritting our teeth *enduring,* it is then we need to say: "*Father, I am Yours. You know I believe You are able to work all things together for good because I love You. My focus is on You. You are the object of my affection.*" Only our response to God's love for us can make the circumstances unfold to serve the purposes of God in our life.

John 15:7 says, "Ask what you will." It is possible to ask our way out of a set of circumstances in which the Father would prefer us to abide. He does use all things, even our insistence for Him to do what He would prefer not to do at the time. Father knows the end from the beginning and due to His knowledge of the long-term results, He would have preferred us to abide, but may choose to honor our insistent and determined prayer for release. The only problem is that we will have to repeat the lesson at some point in our journey and we already know the futility of cyclical behavior.

A friend of mine wrote a song lyric that said, "I'd rather lose me than You, Lord." One of the ways I have learned to abide on the *Agape Road* is the increased comprehension that my personal preference to go up either of the alternative roads costs me an injured relationship with the Lord. The same thing happens in a natural relationship. We are not talking about the loss of our salvation or some gross failure, but broken intimacy and injured friendship. We are the losers when we insist upon our own way (Isaiah 53:6). Once we understand what detours cost us, we find ourselves wanting to reject even the smallest one simply out of a desire to protect that tender, familiar closeness with the Lord. The secret to dealing with temptation is not will-power, but learning to be a Father-pleaser. When our whole life is centered on the Father, the power of the things that formerly wanted to capture and lead us off as prisoners begin to break. It may not happen immediately, but the tentacles of *Eros* begin to loosen their hold until we find ourselves free to love and follow God. Avoiding detours results in the rest of God presented in Hebrews 4:11, "There remains a rest for the people of God" (AMP). The skill of abiding will produce in us *uncomplaining endurance.* This will act as the spiritual antidote, restraining us from turning in upon ourselves.

Abiding

As reality forces itself upon us, we realize we cannot go on, we cannot go back, and God knows we cannot stay where we are. We find ourselves at the Red Sea: mountains on either side, the sea before us, and the enemy crowding the rear. Our only real choice is to abide and watch the Lord adjust the circumstances *or* transform our own nature into His Image. Like Moses, we can watch the Lord open a way through rather than take the detours so freely and willingly being offered. The Lord Jesus *causes* us to stand and hold our ground of faith and relationship with God our Father while we are still *in the difficult circumstances.* This requires the skill of abiding and is the only known antidote to taking the detours. It is not magic, nor is it instantaneous; it is God's nature being formed in us (Galatians 4:19).

Once we have taken a biblical position of abiding, God has the freedom to change us or change the circumstances. Those who are instrumental in creating the difficult circumstances may need us to be there for them at the right time, therefore, we are not *permitted* to run, hide, or shift blame. We may not be allowed to change jobs, churches, or alter our geography. Others may be able to divorce, but we are not allowed to use divorce in order to run, hide, or shift blame, for we know the implications of the detours. Others may be able to disinherit their disobedient and embarrassing child, but not us. We must abide in the circumstance with them. Father may not allow us to change difficult mates. God may deny us the freedom from using these detours as a means to find relief and think it is the peace of God. Detours are essentially *cyclical* behavior. We must choose to abide in such a manner that the glory of God can be released. This can only happen *through* us.

Refusing the detours is not striving or self-conscious religious effort; it is faith and personal confidence in the Eternal Seed. We are beginning to see ourselves in God's gymnasium (Hebrews 12:11). Father wants to reveal Himself *to* us in the pressure and *through* us in the circumstances. *Agape* emerges gradually from the wreckage and chaos of the *Eros* environment. *Agape* comes as the Kingdom does: "first the blade, then the head of the grain, then the mature grain in the head" (Mark 4:28). It is the mysterious process of growth toward fruitfulness.

When Moses was standing at the Red Sea, God was not angry with Him, but He was asking Him to abide. Likewise, when we are in a difficult circumstance and one or more of the detours looks promising, remember that God is not punishing us, nor is He judging us. As Isaiah 54:15-17 plainly tells us, Father is not angry with us either:

> If anyone fiercely assails you it will not be from Me.
> Whoever assails you will fall because of you.
> Behold, I Myself have created the smith who blows the
> fire of coals,

And brings out a weapon for its work;
And I have created the destroyer to ruin.
No weapon that is formed against you shall prosper;
And every tongue that accuses you in judgment you
will condemn.
This is the heritage of the servants of the Lord,
And their vindication is from Me," declares the Lord.

That

One of the most important tools to avoiding detours is
understanding what Father had in His mind when He created us. A
small boy about 3 ½ years old was drawing with his crayons on a huge
piece of butcher-block paper, sitting at the dining room table. His mother
asked him what he was drawing.

He said, "I'm drawing God."

His mother replied, "Well, nobody knows what God looks like."

With great confidence, the three year old said, "Well, they will when
I'm finished!" In order to avoid detours, it is important that we
understand what God had in mind when He created us. Hopefully this
primitive diagram will help.

Philippians 3:12 says, "I press on in order that I may lay hold of
that for which I also was laid hold of by Christ Jesus." In God's *mind*
was something for you called *that*. When I personally
saw *that*, my whole life and ministry changed. We must
see the difference between running, hiding, and
shifting blame and the serious prayer: "I want *that*
which God had in His mind when He saved me." Like
Paul, I actually became disinterested in *success*, but
found myself pressing toward *that*. The over-all *that*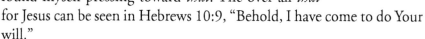
for Jesus can be seen in Hebrews 10:9, "Behold, I have come to do Your
will."

That is different for every person. God, as a Father, has something
personal and specific in His mind for each of us; it was in His mind
before the foundation of the world. *That* is specific and personal for
every one of us; it is designed by the Father to be a central focus of our

life. We cannot design or create for ourselves or for others what *that* is because it originates in the mind of God the Father. Only faith and security, identity, and belonging can give us the needed courage to stop trying to make our life what *we* think it ought to be and say to God, "I want *that* which You had in Your mind when You saved me." This is one of the most revolutionary, life-changing prayers anyone could verbalize, but it does take courage. When we pray this prayer with understanding and faith, it will be the beginning of a real adventure. It takes us out of ourselves, our own definitions, and our own understanding and guides us to a place where we can find *that*.

In my early Christian walk, I thought *that* for me was to be a missionary. I love missions and the nations of the world, so I nearly put myself on the mission field by human strength. My self-willed determination to be a missionary caused me to press for a missionary appointment from a major denomination. I was ready to go. Within several months of leaving, one team member got sick, another's plans were unalterably changed, and then the rest of our man-made plans fell apart.

So, if I was not supposed to be a missionary, I quickly decided *that* for me was to be an evangelist. I eagerly pursued opportunities to win souls to Christ. After preaching one time there were about six or eight people who had come forward to accept the Lord and I was ready to pray for the first one when I heard the Lord say, "I didn't call you to be an evangelist."

I thought, great, now is a fine time to tell me! Afterwards I went home and said, "So, what do You want from me?" I was essentially asking, "What is *that* for me, personal and specific?"

The Lord said, "I called you to teach."

All I can say is when I discovered *that*, it contained all of the deeply satisfying things my heart ever longed for because I was *created* for *that*, and *that* was created for me. When these two things came together, it was like a wedding made in Heaven.

That for me is teaching—I found it! One of the ways I know I found *that* is God gives me stuff to teach. If you have not found *that* yet, hopefully my testimony will give you the same hunger and eagerness to discover what God had in His mind for you when He created you.

There is a very clear difference between destiny and success. Many people have been an outward success in this life, but completely missed their destiny. Someone said if God called you to be a missionary, don't shrivel up to be a millionaire! If you have the courage and the faith to believe God for *that*, then it takes it out of your hands and puts it into the hands of the Father and we rest in His unfolding purposes. God, as a Father, begins to set into motion the people, events, finances, and education to take you to *that*. God will move heaven and earth to get you to what *that* is for your life.

One of the best things we can do to serve our generation is to function in *that* which God had in his mind for each of us. *That* allows us security, identity, and belonging, making each of us equally valuable in our own sphere.

Embracing *that* is probably one of the most clear and strengthening biblical truths to keep us on the *Agape* Road. When we discover and embrace *that* which God saved us for, we are less enchanted by and less desirous of anything these detours are offering. From the point of embracing *that* and abiding in the completed work of Christ, we will find ourselves free to become Father-pleasers.

Glossary Chapter 11

Focus and Object: The objects we focus on expand. When God is the object of our life, our focus on Him begins to expand and a reciprocal relationship begins to grow. Diverting our focus from the Father is a primary reason we choose detours off the *Agape* Road. As we change the focus and object of our life from things that hold us in bondage and put our focus on God the Father, we begin to abide.

Detour Strategies: Pride, rage, deny, avoid, endure, and/or turn back.

Freedom: The end result of the journey that has taken us through the Cross. All freedom has its source in God the Father. Freedom can be lost or preserved; it involves choices and the ability to start and stop. No one can set us free from that which we still love. It is the liberty for which Christ died (Gal. 5:1). Freedom is release from un-freedom.

That: The purpose God had in mind when He created me (Phil. 3:12).

Chapter 12
Becoming a Father-Pleaser

I wish that when I speak, many may believe, not on me, but with me on him.
Saint Austin[1]

Some years ago, while teaching the Scriptures to San Quentin prison inmates, an older, Latin prisoner was waiting for me as I entered the chapel. We had developed a trust and friendship that was real. He grabbed me, we embraced, laughed and hugged, saying, 'Un gran abrazo', meaning one, big hug. As we exchanged this mutual expression of affection, I noticed a young, white male watching us. His lip was quivering, and he was almost on the edge of tears. I asked him, "What is happening? Do you need to say something?" He responded very quietly, "Could I have one of those hugs?" I reached out and grabbed him, loved on him, ruffled his hair, and waltzed him around lifting him off the floor. He began to laugh. The prison chaplain who was with me later told me that in prison no one ever physically touches another person in a positive manner. Boundaries of personal space are part of survival. When that young man gained enough courage to ask me for a manly, Christian hug, he was expressing what can only be defined as touch deprivation. He urgently needed to be touched, held, and reaffirmed in a nonsexual manner. The importance of that hug cannot

---

[1]*Matthew Henry's Commentary on the Whole Bible*: New Modern Edition, Electronic Database. Copyright (c) 1991 by Hendrickson Publishers, Inc.) John 8:31.

be underestimated. Since my own family touches, hangs on one another, and interacts physically, this was a totally new concept to me. It never dawned on me how valuable and necessary touch was.

Touch deprivation is addressed by the biblical admonition to greet one another with a holy kiss. This is the *Agape* touch, not Judas' touch of betrayal. Only *Agape* meeting *Agape* can fulfill our own personal touch deprivation. Finding the Father is not a deeper life issue for extraordinary believers; it is most basic and increasingly urgent.

The larger institutional Church suffers from spiritual touch deprivation. We do not understand our deep need to have the Father touch, affirm, and confirm us as His own child. In John 14:21, Jesus says, "he who loves Me will be loved by My Father, and I will love him and will *disclose* Myself to him." The word 'disclose' comes from a Greek word (Strong's #1781) meaning to show myself plainly; to be seen, heard, felt, or tasted. Jesus knows that we must have Father's touch. Father has taken us 'out of Himself' and made us for the purpose of bringing us 'into Himself.' He said, "I *will* welcome you, I *will* be a Father to you, and you shall be My sons and daughters" (2 Corinthians 6:17-18 NKJV). This relationship is not in the Millennium. We are not talking about heaven after we die; this is Father's house now. We know that the church is not always a safe place, but the biblical hope is that when Father is home each of the children will feel secure. He has been waiting for us as we have been waiting for Him. We all live for the day when we will meet the Father before we meet the religious elder brother on our journey home. His house is a safe place.

God does not *make* us sons and daughters; He gives us the right or authority to *become who we already are*—His sons and daughters (John 1:12). Just like the acorn has everything it needs to become an oak tree, we have everything we need to become God's son or daughter. Everything God had in His mind when He created us in His Own Image has already been written into the DNA of the Eternal Seed. Father waits for us to *become* who we are!

It was not long after I came back to the Lord from one extended detour of being backslidden that I discovered this life-changing verse, "He who sent Me is with Me, He has not left Me alone. I always do the things that are pleasing to Him" (John 8:29). The reciprocal implications of Jesus' statement was highly motivating to me. Jesus sought to please the Father and was deeply confident that Father would never leave Him alone. This simple, but profound, lesson has been my life's verse.

A Father-pleaser follows the Person of Jesus rather than a doctrine, an institution, or even the Church. When Jesus says "follow Me," He always speaks as the Son Who seeks to lead us on the *Agape* Road to His Father. While doctrines or institutions may serve the purpose of God and His Kingdom, they must never be given final authority. We can and should remain faithful to the local church without yielding ownership of our soul. It is possible to make great progress on the wrong road trying to get home. It is like an airplane pilot who says to his passengers, "We're lost, but we're making great time."

What Does a Father-Pleaser Look Like?

A Father-pleaser is a man or woman who has matured in *Agape* and is walking in the Kingdom of God. Being a Father-pleaser does not mean we will never do anything wrong or that we are the teacher's pet. A Father-pleaser is someone who can not and will not be satisfied with anything less than Father's approbation. The following statements are what it means to *become* experientially what God has made us to be conceptually when He said, "It is finished" (John 19:30) and "I make all things new" (Revelation 21:5). Note that Jesus did not say He would make all new things.

❖ We *think* like Father thinks. We have been given the mind of Christ (1 Corinthians 2:16); therefore His ways are becoming our ways, our thoughts are becoming His thoughts.

❖ We *feel* what Father feels. We have been given the compassion of Christ (Philippians 2:1). It may be limited, but it is real.

❖ We *judge*, measure, and understand the way Father does because we have been given the biblical standard of judgment (John 5:30).

❖ We *approach* Father with confidence. We have been given Christ's assurance of acceptance (Hebrews 9:24); therefore we can go within the veil of the Holy of Holies without fear.

❖ We *love* as Father loves. We have taken up Christ's burden (Matthew 28:19-20); therefore we see Father's love for the lost and hurting being replicated in our own person. We, too, must be about our Father's business.

If we interpreted the Sermon on the Mount (Matthew 5, 6, 7) in light of *Agape*, we could imagine Jesus saying something like this:

> *So you have decided to follow Me up this Agape Road. You have chosen My cup and want to be a Father-pleaser like Me. Since I always put everything up front, let Me explain to you how you will look and act as the direct result of your following Me. I do not want you to be surprised or stumbled by the unexpected. My Father has already decided where He wants to take you and what the end result will be. There is little you can do to make any of these things I am describing come to pass, but you can delay or thwart the process by running, hiding, or shifting blame. If you learn to abide and consciously move towards Me in preferential choice, I will take you to the Father (John 14:6). During the journey, a transformation will be taking place in your life called the coming of the Kingdom. I am explaining all of this to you so you will be able to recognize the road signs and understand more accurately what is happening.*

Out of this mysterious journey and the inexplicable haze that seems to lie ahead, we can discern Christ as the I AM, taking our hand and leading us out of ourselves into the *Agape* understanding of Himself and His Father. He, Who was totally selfless, seeks to be born in our heart. We are increasingly able to recognize Father's Person eagerly waiting for us like the prodigal's father; for we have seen the glory of God in the face of Jesus Christ. We are not stopping short on this journey. We will never be satisfied with anything less than intimacy with God as our Father. We are not looking for some spiritual experience or *Eros* payoff, even a good one; we are looking for *Him*. It should be more than acceptable to us if He decides that some particular experience is necessary for us to know Him. Our intention is to know Him for Himself, not because of what He has done on our behalf.

Abba, Father!

God gives us the privilege of spiritual touch by giving us use of the endearing words "Abba, Father." Abba, in the original language, is a child's word. When we have learned to pray "Abba, Father" with spiritual understanding, the Father, Himself, *"bears witness with our spirit that we are the children of God"* (Romans 8:16 NKJV). Paul is seeking to give us access to Father's touch in this life and in a way that will satisfy something that can hardly be expressed. Father is seeking to know me, and, like a small child, I am seeking to know my Father. God is known slowly, intimately, and progressively (John 17:3). Only following Jesus on the *Agape* Road will take us to the Father. If we allow Him to lead us, His Spirit will bear witness with our spirit and intimacy results. We must not live in the past or the future without fully recognizing that we *do* have touch deprivation. We are in desperate need of Father's approbation: *This is my beloved, in him/her, I am well pleased.* It is Father's approbation that increases or intensifies our desire to be a Father-pleaser.

The whole redemptive plan is called the promise of the Father. This should give us courage to pray "Abba, Father" with intention and confidence. It was the Father who drew us to Jesus Christ in the first place (John 6:44). Father chose us and set us free so we would be able to choose Him. Father gave us the Holy Spirit so we could speak directly to Him in a spiritual language that is a godly mystery. His love was so intense that He made special provision for a language He knew we would need (1 Corinthians 14:2). It is a Father, like the prodigal's own father, who is waiting for us. Let us cease our excuses, put confidence in our wedding garment, and begin to search out the implications of the *Agape* Road. We do not have to be mature, spiritually skilled, or memorize more Scripture for God to love us. He has already set His love upon us and there is nothing more that we can do to make God love us more.

Jesus, in saying that He would take us to His Father, acknowledges that our ultimate need is to know the touch of Father God. The Trinity is not competing for our affection nor is the Holy Spirit a substitute for the Father. The Church, as God's instrument of maternal nurturing and care, must never attempt to displace our need for the Father's touch. Likewise, the Scriptures, however important, must never become a substitute for having a personal, intimate relationship with the Father (John 5:39).

Father Waits for the Eternal Seed

Father does not possess, acquire, or control. He is the Farmer and He *waits*. James 5:7, "The farmer waits for the precious produce of the soil, being patient about it, until it gets the early and late rains." We are the soil into which the Eternal Seed has been implanted. We need to cultivate, protect, water, and nourish the Seed within ourselves and give others a hand in their cultivation so God's glory can be seen in the earth. How urgently we need to see beyond ourselves and recognize that all of creation waits and depends on our discovering the freedom and the transformation God has promised. The prayer "Abba, Father" nourishes the Eternal Seed within us. At some point on our journey on the *Agape* Road our focus is no longer on ourselves; we begin to understand that 'Abba, Father' is the freedom for which creation waits and longs (Romans 8:16-21).

Personal Victory

I began this book by sharing about my own father's rejection, resulting in my anger, critical mouth, and free-floating anxiety. Those three things, oblivious to me, were deep in my person and were very obvious to others. They came out of an absence of security, identity, and belonging. Yet, God continued to love me and use me in the work of the Kingdom and "I was shown mercy because I acted ignorantly in unbelief" (1 Timothy 1:13). As I increasingly put my confidence in the wedding garment, refusing to rest in personal merit and religious works, Father God became the focus and object of my being. Almost immediately, I found myself crying out to know what it meant to be a

Agape Road

Father-pleaser. I began to realize that the Lord knew what He was doing when He said, "I want you to love Me with all your heart, all your soul, all your mind, and all your strength" (Deuteronomy 6:5; Mark 12:30). He knew that if He could teach me how to put my love on Him, I would find freedom that I didn't know existed.

When I was in the midst of deep struggles with seemingly unsolvable problems, I was forced to work out what *Agape* really meant to me so that I could personally survive. I held on to the following seven points like a knot tied to the end of a rope. They enabled me to abide during the crazies that were going on in my own life. Perhaps they can serve you in a similar manner.

> *Agape is* God's Person; God *is Agape.*
> *Agape is* the whole redemptive act.
> *Agape is* an active force, not a passive attitude.
> *Agape is* God's action upon humanity. God loved, God gave....
> *Agape is* the Summum Bonum—the highest good; beyond *Agape*
>   there is nothing.
> *Agape is* governed desire as contrasted to ungoverned desire.
> *Agape is* the Kingdom absolute. Submission or resistance to God
>   as Father can only be measured or determined by *Agape.*

This journey on the *Agape* Road has personally transformed me into a Father-pleaser and is now transforming my own personal difficulties. Finally, after almost 20 years of struggling with some of these issues, I can see a significant degree of change. My seemingly unsolvable problems are being resolved. I can truthfully say to my Father, "You do all things well" (Mark 7:37).

My critical mouth is being conquered as a result of learning the skill of abiding. *Agape* has imparted to me a confidence in the form of security, identity, and belonging that has had an anti-anxiety effect for which I have searched most of my life, however it did not come prepackaged, I had to walk it out. I am learning that *different* may not be wrong and that I no longer have to be *right*. I am learning that acting like the Son of Thunder does not always bring glory to God. I am learning that religion can be an *addiction*, difficult to expose and almost impossible to correct. I am learning that the swamp of criticism, condescension, and superiority that religion produces can be drained and turned into a cultivatable farm that will yield the fruit of the Holy Spirit for which this hurting world hungers. This can be accomplished by anyone who will choose to be a Father-pleaser and abide on the *Agape* Road.

Conclusion

God is a rewarder to all who come in faith. He does not tease. My personal prayer is that you will have discovered for yourself and through the content of this book, the benefits and rewards of walking the *Agape* Road. These concepts have been sought out and written without regard to our personal comfort or denominational distinctives. They have been stated out of the deep conviction that they are biblically true. Spiritual experience and personal testimony bear witness that each progressive step has contributed to the larger concept of the *Agape* Road journey.

Personally, I have lived and experienced every concept in this book and have sought to embrace each one with all of my heart, soul, mind, and strength. It has transformed me. Those who have walked with me on this journey and embraced the lessons in their own lives have also been transformed. There are many who are seeking the Father and He is eagerly waiting for them. Perhaps sharing with them the manner in which the Lord meets you on the *Agape* Road will help cultivate and nourish that Eternal Seed which is "Christ in you, the hope of glory."

Necessity for Creating the New Word *Agape*
by Alan Richardson

Agape = (ä-gä'pā) quality of life

It is sometimes said that the NT writers had to invent a new word, agape, for a new quality of life which came into the world of Christ. It is true that the noun hardly occurs in pre-biblical Greek literature, but this does not mean much. The important point is that LXX translators had adopted the colourless verb άΥάπάυ to translate the Hebrew for 'love" (root *ahebh*), a very frequent OT conception found in many forms. There were obvious objectsion to the use of έράυ and even to Φιλέιυ since these words had been spoilt by Greek mythology and pagan "erotic" religion. The verb άΥάπάΥ is frequent in OT; God loves Israel (Deut. 10:15; Hos. 11:11, etc.) and it is the Israelite's duty to love God (Deut. 6:4f, the Shema; 11:1, etc.) and his neighbor (Lev. 19:18), including even "the stranger" (Deut. 10:19). The noun άΥάπη (or άΥάπηοιl, a form not found in the NT) occurs some 30 times in LXX. The difference between the OT and the NT teaching about άΥάπη is that whereas the former develops an attempt to organize άΥάπη into codes of law, and so loses spontaneity, the latter regards άΥάπη as an eschatological reality, a quality of life in the Age to Come, but one which is nevertheless even now "shed abroad in our hearts through the Holy Spirit" (Rom. 5:5). But in OT and NT alike άΥάπη differs from έρως in that the latter is brought into action by the attractiveness of the object loved, whereas άΥάπη loves even the unlovable, the repellent and those who have nothing to offer in return. It is thus a word which exactly describes God's attitude of free and utter grace in his dealings with Israel, old and new. The words έράυ and έρως do not occur in NT.

---

[1]Alan Richardson, *Introduction to New Testament Theology* (London: SCM Press Ltd.), 269.

Agape Road Glossary

Abiding: Rest in God's ability to work all things together for good. Continuing to be present, to hold, and to be held in God's love in every situation, contradiction, or crisis that is presented to us on our journey. To continue on in uncompromising devotion to the Lord; lasting or enduring. Remaining in Christ's completed work. Abiding means not running, hiding, or shifting blame and is the means to being conformed to the image of His Son. Abiding is the skill of being able to hunker down and effectively draw upon the "supply of the Spirit of Jesus Christ" (Phil. 1:19). (See John 15).

Adam Factor: Our capacity to reconcile our spiritual understanding to the fact and the presence of sin (*Eros*), even after we have accepted Christ and have been baptized in water. There is a strange phenomenon called 'post-baptismal sin,' that is the presence of *Eros* within the heart and life of the believer even after we have been saved. It is original sin.

Agape: (ä-gä′pä) (Strong's #25) is an exercise of the divine will in deliberate choice, made without assignable cause save that which lies in the nature of God Himself (Deut. 7:7-8). It is a quality of life and is used both as a noun and a verb. *Agape* unfolds in three progressive steps, none of which can be omitted: *1. Love God* with all of our heart, soul, mind, and strength (Mark 12:30); *2. Love myself* because God has given me value and worth by pouring His Own love into me while I was yet a sinner (Rom. 5:8). *3. Love others*, even our enemies, in the same manner and degree that He has loved me and gave Himself for me (Matt. 5:43-48). God Himself is *Agape* (1 John 4:8). His love—covenantally faithful, unconditional, and self-giving—is depicted as a straight arrow. *Agape* is God's absolute by which He judges all things and is His Nature imparted to His own. *Agape* is ultimate reality.

Agape **Conversion:** Release from the power of *Eros* and our self-referential human nature. It is the decisive adoption of *Agape* as a life-style.

Agape **Road:** *Agape* is the Greek word for love. The *Agape* Road is a road of love that God created to bring us to intimacy Himself. Jesus is the road–the Way, the Truth, and the Life–to the Father (John 14:6).

Alpha/Omega: The first and last letters in the Greek alphabet, thus *alpha* and *omega*, the beginning and the end; used to describe God.

Area of Conflict: The area where the human will and life's choices come together and force us to make a decision. We are presented with three choices: We can seek fulfillment on the religious road, the worldly road, or abide on the *Agape* Road.

Audience of One: The consciousness of becoming a Father-pleaser. Learning to be totally satisfied that the Father alone knows what we are doing and why we are doing it. Never doing or saying anything for the purpose of being seen nor refusing to do anything because we are being seen.

Barriers to Intimacy: Three main categories hinder us from having an intimate relationship with the Lord: the satanic or demonic, the original fall, and as a result of the first two, human failure—the mistakes and injuries whose origin and source, for the most part, come from us.

Belonging: One of the three qualities that grow out of intimacy with the Father; replaces the feeling of abandonment, rejection, and worthlessness.

Be Right: One of the Seven Giants. The inability to admit that we are wrong. A "know-it-all" paralyzed by the domino theory—if wrong once, how can we be sure we have ever been right? Because the mind rules the emotions, *Be Right* is focused, controlled, and overly committed to his or her own evaluations, ideas, and concepts. The fear of being wrong or challenged makes them increasingly rigid—a form of stubbornness and rebellion. *Be Right* often uses anger and rage as protective mechanism to prevent being discovered. (Job 40:8).

Bread of God: "In order to really live, man needs every word from God. Food alone is not enough to sustain him" (Matt. 4:4 UBS). The Bread of God is sustenance that originates from God Who is spiritual, eternal, and uncreated. Every word that proceeds from the mouth of God is *Agape* because God is *Agape*. Father spoke into the human predicament with His Word–Christ as *Agape* Incarnate.

Bread of Man: Bread of man is sustenance that originates from us. It is doing our own thing (*Eros*) rather than keeping ourselves in the *Agape* of God. The bread of man brings death (1 Tim. 5:6).

Changing the Rules: God's favor no longer depends on external behavior; He wants us to focus on the internal reality of the Kingdom of God. Jesus changed the rules stating that it is not what goes into us that is important, but what comes out of us that matters. (Matt. 15:11-20).

Childhood Tapes: Memories of events from childhood that continue to play in our minds and control our behavior long after we have reached adulthood. They are strongholds, untruths, or forms of deception that we hold in a fortified place of defense within our mind.

Choose the Cup: Symbolism for preferentially chosing the Father's will above our own. By choosing the cup, we follow Jesus' example even at great personal expense. (See Preferential Choice).

Compassion: (Strong's #7349 / #3628) Greek word *splagchnon*—splangkh'-non; meaning bowels of compassion or mercy (Phil. 2:1). The word means suffering with another; painful empathy; a sensation of sorrow excited by the distress or misfortunes of another; pity; commiseration. Compassion is a mixed passion, compounded of love and sorrow; at least some portion of love generally attends the pain or regret, or is excited by it. Extreme distress of an enemy even changes enmity into at least temporary affection. Compassion means my very insides are moved in concern and care toward you in a supernatural way.

Confidence in the Wedding Garment: Trust, reliance, bold assurance that Christ alone is our righteousness demonstrated by our acceptance of the wedding garment (Heb. 3:6).

Conforming Truth to Desires: Attempting to make Scriptures say what we want them to say. "There are ultimately only two alternatives in the intellectual life: either one conforms desire to the truth or one conforms truth to desires" (E. Michael Jones).

Cross-less Christianity: Being an enemy of the cross of Christ due to ungoverned desires (Phil. 3:18-19). Note that we are not enemies of Jesus, because ungoverned desires still need the good things He can do for us, i.e., salvation and healing. Embracing the cross of Christ is the only way our human behavior can be changed. The daily need for the Cross will appear and reappear as we discover the Seven Giants operating in our own life and in the lives of others whom we know and love.

Cyclical Patterns: Traveling in circles and ending up at the same place (Rom. 8:20). If we miss God and head in the wrong direction, God, in His love and mercy, sends us in a circle, bringing us back around to the issue again and again, giving us as many opportunities as possible to get it right.

Death Line: When Adam and Eve transgressed, it created a separation between God and His creation causing *death* to come upon all men (Romans 5:12). The death line represents the broken relationship between God and His creation and as a result, sin, shame, and guilt came upon all humanity. God, however, transcended the death line by sending us Jesus. Our path to God is the Holy Spirit, the Scriptures, and Jesus as the Word of God made flesh. These three things are the source of life for those who have been brought over the death line.

Decentered: The Eternal Seed remains unvivified and ignorant of the purpose of God and His Kingdom.

Detour Strategies: Pride, rage, deny, avoid, endure, and/or turn back.

Eros: (er′os′) The original unreality and vanity that entered at the fall of man and it holds all creation in bondage (Rom. 8:19-21). *Eros* is a Greek word, but it is not used in the New Testament because of its sexual corruption. *Eros* does not seek to be accepted by its object, but to gain possession of it. *Eros* has an appetite or yearning desire that is aroused by the attractive qualities of its object. It is man-centered, self-centered love recognized by three manifestations–possess, acquire, and control, and is depicted by the hooked arrow.

Eros **Payoff:** The reward we receive for seeking to influence or be seen doing things to impress people. Jesus spoke of that as having our reward (Matt. 6:1-6). That reward is an *Eros* payoff. The opposite is acting and responding for the Audience of One–God, as a Father. (See 1 Kings 21:25).

Eros **Prison:** The end result of detouring off the *Agape* Road because *Eros* is at the center of our life. Cyclical behavior causes us to spiral downward until the walls become thicker and the bars become stronger than iron.

Eros **Shift:** A move toward man-centered, ungoverned desires, individualism, anarchy, and entitlement. The *Eros* shift involves all levels and units of society–individual, family, church, and government. The five steps of an *Eros* shift are: 1. Religious Passion; 2. Religion nourished in self-righteousness; 3. Religious violence; 4. Training in skills of intrigue and suspicion; 5. Buried in disgrace.

Eros **Symbol:** The snake eating his tail. Being convoluted and turned in on ourselves.

Eros **Toxicity:** Like radium, *Eros* creates spiritual toxicity when we are taught by our culture, including the Church, to be self-referential and how to get things from God. *Eros* toxicity is not easily detected, and it is deadly. The Church, seriously infected with *Eros*, passes on a double-dose of the infection that was our problem before we came to Christ.

Agape Road

Eros Virus: When we are taught by the Church to be self-referential and to get things from God, *Eros*, like a virus, emerges. Attempts to eradicate it make it increasingly lethal and resistant to counter measures, even giving it the ability to mutate. Like a viral strain, one dose of repentance or spiritual breaking is seldom sufficient to kill *Eros*; it goes through a metamorphosis, continues to develop immunity in a different form, and rapidly re-emerges in religious clothes quoting Bible verses.

Eternal Seed: The sinless Son of God, *Agape* Incarnate, Whose nature is implanted in us when we believe in Him. The result is the new birth or being born from above. The Seed is incorruptible and imperishible (1 Peter 1:23); it abides forever.

Faithfulness: (Strong's #5375 / #5746). The Greek word is *hesed* meaning fixed, determined love. God, Himself, causes His love to be kept, guarded, watched over, and preserved. Once God gives Himself covenantally, it is impossible for Him to desert or abandon the person or the covenant (Heb. 13:8). It is firm adherence to truth and duty, true to allegiance, careful to observe all compacts, treaties, contracts, or vows. In other words, true to one's word. (Deut. 7:9; Heb. 13:5).

False Omega: When anything other than God is at the center of our being. A false promise of life, circumstances, or ungoverned desires that do not have the ability to deliver what they promised. False omegas are legal and illegal, religious and worldly, valid and invalid, but they always turn out wrong.

Father-Pleaser: A person whose center is outside self and focused on Father God; obedience of faith grows out of affection for the Father. Father's approbation increases or intensified our desire to be a Father-pleaser.

Feel Good: One of the Seven Giants. The pure pleasure principle. *Feel Good* avoids pain and discomfort at any cost, is committed to personal pleasure or gain, and is given to the senses or is sensual. *It* controls the emotions, mind, and heart and is the source or first cause of all compulsive and addictive behavior. (Jam. 4:3).

Focus and Object: The objects we focus on expand. When God is the object of our life, our focus on Him begins to expand and a reciprocal relationship begins to grow. Diverting our focus from the Father is a primary reason we choose detours off the *Agape* Road. As we change the focus and object of our life from things that hold us in bondage and put our focus on God the Father, we begin to abide.

Foresight: Tomorrow/Forever. He who is yet to come (Greek: I am coming). Perception gained by looking forward; prospect; hope; a sight or view into the future; opposite of hindsight. Foresight allows us to know what the Eternal Seed is like and know that only the Seed can produce God's likeness in us.

Forgiving: (Strong's #5375 / #5746). Forgive means pardoning, remitting, inclined to overlook offense, mild, merciful, and compassionate as a forgiving temper (Matt. 6:12). It is one of God's hidden attributes. Forgiveness is part of His Nature.

Freedom: The end result of the journey that has taken us through the Cross. All freedom has its source in God the Father. Freedom can be lost or preserved; it involves choices and the ability to start and stop. No one can set us free from that which we still love. It is the liberty for which Christ died (Gal. 5:1). Freedom is release from un-freedom.

God's DNA/Nature: God's DNA is His communicable attributes, His nature which are able to be imparted to humans (Gal. 5:23). He is compassionate, gracious, slow to anger, merciful, truthful, faithful, and forgiving (Ex. 34:6-7). God also has incommunicable attributes: He is eternal, omnipresent, omniscient, immutable, and self-revealed. When Jesus was on earth, He laid aside the incommunicable attributes, picking them up again after His death and resurrection (John 17:5).

God's Name: God's reputation (Ex. 33:18-19). His Name is His identity, authority, and revealed character; it is all that He wants us to know about Him. To call upon His Name is to worship Him. When we pray for someone in God's Name, we are revealing at least one of His seven character traits.

Governed Desires: Christ's love controls us; therefore we are able to govern our desires under the Lordship of Christ (2 Cor. 5:14).

Gracious: (Strong's #2587 / #5485). It means to find favor, be kind, friendly, benevolent, courteous, disposed to show or dispense grace and forgive offenses, and to impart unmerited blessings. Gracious is a substitute for the name of God.

Hidden Agenda: One of the Seven Giants. He is covert with words of peace and a heart of criticism. *Hidden Agenda* is like a snowball with a rock in it. With this Giant in operation, we lie in ambush with undisclosed motives, watching for weakness and vulnerability, ready to spring the trap, which has been disguised and then set with lies or half truths. We hide one thing in our hearts while proclaiming another. This Giant is a user; it seeks to use life, people, and every situation to advance his own interests (Matt. 10:26-27).

Hidden Shame: Feelings of failure that others cannot see. An *Eros* phenomena of being turned in upon ourselves with such a force as to precipitate paralyzing fear, disgust with our own weakness, self-hate, and often, thoughts of suicide. We experience strong urges to run and hide as well as the desperate need to find someone else to blame for our failures. The manifestations of hidden shame are insecurity, illegitimacy, and abandonment.

Hindsight: Yesterday. He who was (Greek: As I have been). Seeing what happened, and what ought to have happened after the event; perception gained by looking backward: opposite of *foresight*. Hindsight allows us to reach into *Agape* of the past in order to build our foundation for the future.

Identity: One of the three qualities that grow out of intimacy with the Father; realizing my significance or value as God's child; replaces the feeling of illegitimacy.

Imparted Righteousness: Allowing Christ's righteousness to be worked in us; becoming conformed to the image of Christ (Rom. 8:29). Illustrated by the white handkerchief.

Imputed Righteousness: The righteousness of Christ given to us as God's gift which completely covers us. We did nothing to deserve or earn it. It is God's righteousness imputed or implanted within us as the Eternal Seed giving us the authority to *become* sons and daughters of God by faith (John 1:12). Illustrated by the white handkerchief.

Iniquity: (Strong's #5771 / #458). A biblical term meaning lawlessness, crooked, that which is not straight, to bend, go astray, deviation from the right path. It is the result of the fall of man when ungoverned desire caused Adam and Eve to go their own way (Gen. 3:6). Iniquity defines the innate and ubiquitous desire that has broken loose from God's restraint, motivating us to go our own way and do our own thing (Is. 53:6). (See Transgression, Sin).

Injured Expectations: The result of broken promises, misconceptions, illusions, unfulfilled prophecy, or failed words of "encouragement" from well-meaning people, false brothers, or selfish desire (Prov. 18:14). Injured expectancy can turn into resignation, subtle forms of fatalism, or suppressed anger, especially if we are too religious to admit we are angry.

Insight: Today. He who is (Greek: So I remain). Internal sight, mental vision or perception, discernment, understanding, intelligence, wisdom. The fact of penetrating with the eyes of the understanding into the inner character or hidden nature of things; a glimpse or view beneath the surface; the faculty or power of thus seeing. Insight allows us to see that Christ as *Agape* Incarnate is with us now.

Intimacy: Into-me-He-sees. God wants us to know Him (Heb. 8:11) and He wants to know us (1 Cor. 8:3). This is the normal Christian life made possible through Jesus.

Land of Promises: The New Testament fulfillment of the Promised Land. In the New Testament, all that was type and shadow (Col. 2:17) is brought to spiritual reality in the Person of Christ. Rom. 8:1-39 is the most succinct description of the Land of Promises which speak of intimacy and usefulness.

Lawlessness: Failure or refusal to bring my entire personality, including my love and affection, into conformity to the likeness of Jesus Christ. Lawlessness in the Old and New Testament is often translated 'iniquity'. It includes giving other people truthful advice, but not applying it to our own life. It is desire and intent determined to go its own way; quiet rebellion; and sweet refusal to do the will of God. (1 John 3:4).

Law of Reduced Return: The more we expect or demand from the bread of man or living in our own strenght, the less benefit we receive.

Linear Progress: Linear movement is life as God intended it—always moving forward in measurable growth or progression. Everything that God does has a beginning and an end. We are designed to be moving incrementally in a linear direction towards the planned unfolding of His purpose in our lives (Rom. 8:21).

Look Good: One of the Seven Giants. Over-concern for appearance or image rather than character. *Look Good* is not just concerned with outward appearance, but with creating a reputation that is not established in truth. It involves an improper or illegal search for originality, uniqueness in dress, language, automobile, skills, etc. It will pay any price and exerts a tremendous amount of effort to preserve its image. (Matt. 6:1).

Love: Our English word "love" is translated from four very different Greek words: *Storgos, Phileo, Agape,* and *Eros.* "I love God" and "I love my dog" have different meanings. See individual definitions of these words.

Mercy: (Strong's #2617 / #1656). Mercy is mildness, tenderness of heart, which disposes a person to overlook injuries or to treat an offender better than he deserves. There is no word in the English language precisely synonymous with mercy.

Mother's Milk: "Mother's milk" of the Church (1 Pet. 2:2) has become seriously infected with *Eros.* As we feed from an *Eros*-centered church, we will likely get a double dose of the *Eros*-infection that was our problem before we came to Christ. The nourishment which should heal and deliver us from our selfishness has the capacity to inadvertently injure us by reinforcing all that is self-referential.

Mountains and Valleys: This is the path that Yo-Yo Christians tend to follow. Alternating between being puffed up in pride on the mountain top of spiritual experience and cast down in rage in the valley of despair. Pride (the mountain top) and rage (the valley of despair) are Satan's twin arsenals used to beat up and wear down the unsuspecting believer.

Omega/Alpha: The last and first letters of the Greek alphabet, thus from *alpha* to *omega*: from beginning to end; used to describe God.

Paradigm Shift: A complete and expanded change in the model or the pattern of the way something is perceived. The human mind sees different things when looking at the same object, seeing more of what was there all the time, often in a different manner. This is especially true of spiritual concepts. It requires a paradigm shift to accept the New Birth and to see the Kingdom of God.

Paradox of Grace: Something that appears to be contradictory, but when understood, proves to be well-founded. We should never trust in anything or anyone other than the grace of God in ourselves and in others. (See Prov. 3:34; Jam. 4:6; 1 Pet. 5:5).

Parasite: One who habitually takes advantage of the generosity of others without making any useful contribution in return; it is the result of entitlement. Early description of a person who continually seeks invitations to meals, rewarding his host with flattery (Jude 12-13).

Personal Advantage: One of the Seven Giants. This Giant uses other to accomplish its own agenda. It is constantly maneuvering for title, position, or recognition. When not the center of attention, it suffers envy and pain. We ask, "What's in it for me?" and will help others only if it directly benefits us. Selfish ambition. (See Jude 1:16).

Phileo: A *reciprocal* friendship; a relationship characterized by affection aroused by certain qualities seen in another.

Poisoned Love: Being so in love with oneself that we are determined not to let anything interfere with our satisfaction. This determination will go to the point of eliminating another if that becomes necessary. Poisoned love is an *Eros* payoff.

Predator: (Jude 12-13 AMP) One who victimizes, plunders, or destroys, particularly for one's own gain or personal agenda. There are predators in business, law, medicine, ministry, etc.

Preferential Choice: Choosing to accept God's *Agape* rather than resist it. It is a matter of how we set our love. God restored our freedom of choice through the redemptive act of Christ. He first chose us so that we could have the capacity to choose Him. God gave us preferential choice because He wanted to be wanted. Love that is not based on our preferential choice is not love at all—it is bought and sold.

Projection: Seeking to create the impression that we are more spiritual, advanced, and mature than we really are. Once we have created an image based in unreality, we are forced to create another one to maintain that impression.

Recentered: The awakened, *vivified*, and instructed human spirit seeing the Kingdom and making the preferential choices necessary for the Eternal Seed not to be encroached upon nor hindered by the "worries of this world."

Reciprocal Lawlessness: I give you permission to annul or change what the Bible says, if you, in turn, will do the same for me (Matt. 5:19-20). Reciprocal lawlessness has hidden agendas and is one source of the increase in velocity and strength of the *Eros* shift.

Regressive Paradigm: Not wanting to grow up; acting childish (1 Cor. 13:11). Child-like must be carefully distinguished from childish. Growing up involves response-ability, cultivating our ability to properly respond to the demands and expectations of life.

Religion: Religion, in the negative sense of the word, is man's effort to replicate what only God can do.

Religious Road: A detour off the *Agape* Road due to a rule-keeping, legalistic focus that captures and controls. The end of the road is a prison is constructed from a self-referential perspective that is the result of refusing God's righteousness and seeking to create a righteousness of our own (Rom. 10:3).

Remain Undisturbed: One of the Seven Giants. Unwilling to be inconvenienced. *Undisturbed* is not as blatant as the other six—he is insidious, secretive, subtle, and sophisticated. This Giant disguises himself as the need for stability, perhaps as the need to preserve his reputation or the honor of respectability when more is asked of him than he wants to give. *Undisturbed* says "I will follow you, but I cannot follow you *that* far!" It is that subtle difference between admiration for Christ and identification with Him. (Jer. 48:11).

Revival vs. Reformation: Revival is the act of reviving after a decline or discontinuance. Reformation is a visitation of the Holy Spirit accompanied by radical and permanent change in political, religious, and social affairs.

Right and Left Swings: Repeated, never ending swings from left to right and right to left–always swerving across the *Agape* Road but never stopping on it. (Is. 30:21).

Agape Road

Security: One of the qualities that grow out of intimacy with the Father; replaces insecurity. Knowing and accepting that God has chosen me.

Seven Giants: Manifestations of *Eros*; behavioral patterns which hinder us from coming into intimacy with God: Look Good / Feel Good / Be Right / Stay in Control / Hidden Agenda / Personal Advantage / Remain Undisturbed. Slaying these Giants is essential to maturity.

Sin: The Hebrew root of sin means 'to miss the mark' or failing, omitting, or refusing to do what we ought to do. All of these result in our inability to reveal God's glory. Sin involves some degree of choice, intentions, and culpability. (Rom. 3:23). (See Iniquity, Transgression).

Slow to Anger: (Strong's #639/ #750 / #3115). Longsuffering is God's forbearance or patience and involves not being easily provoked but able to patiently bear injuries or provocation for a long time. (Num. 14:18; Rom. 2:4; Jam. 1:19).

Spiral Downward: Once we are trapped in the *Eros* prison, we begin a downward, ever-tightening spiral. There are three stages in this *Eros* prison: alone, mean, rage.

Stay in Control: *Stay in Control* demands to have his hands on the steering wheel—he always wants to be in control because then everyone is safe and the results are guaranteed. Because he thinks he is god, *Stay in Control* must determine the outcome of everything for everyone. He experiences anxiety regarding the future because it may be just beyond his control. *Stay in Control* refuses to take *no* for an answer. He is a control freak determined to have everything and everyone that touches his sphere of life within his power and subject to his influence. (Esther 1:12).

Storgos/Astorgos: Without love, heartless, or without family or natural affection. Used to describe a degenerating society. (Rom. 1:31; 2 Tim. 3:3).

Temptation: Opportunities, suggestions, or pressures to yield to desires which are self-serving. Temptation is something we want more than our freedom. Tempted to do good is activity that is good, but outside of Father's purpose for us at the time.

That: The purpose God had in mind for each of us when He created us (Phil. 3:12).

Three Dimensional Reality: Hindsight, foresight, and insight. Three dimensions of God which help us understand His purposes in the earth. Rev. 4:8, "the Lord God, the almighty, who was and who is and who is to come." Greek translation: "As I have been, so I remain, and I am coming" (also see Heb. 13:8).

Transgression: Intentionally going beyond known limits, breaking or violating a law, principle, or relationship. The word 'transgression' occurs 80 times and it's meaning is essentially a rebellious *attitude*. (See Iniquity, Sin).

Truth: (Strong's #571 / #225). Truth is conformity with fact or reality; exact accordance with that which is, has been, or shall be. Truth is a Person, the Lord Jesus Christ, who is the Word of God. (Prov. 8:7; John 17:17).

Ungoverned Desires: Ungoverned desire, awakened in the fall (Gen. 3:6), caused us to raise the fist (stubbornness/rebellion), run away from home (run, hide, shift blame), prefer to live as orphans (denying God's Fatherhood), masters of our own destinies (little gods), planners of our own tomorrows (all we like sheep have gone astray each to our own way), and rulers of our own worlds (be right, stay in control). The Seven Giants utilize the power of ungoverned desire to implement their *Eros* agenda.

Unvivified: Not sprung into life; unspiritual; ignorant of the ways and processes of the Holy Spirit as to what we will look and act like when the Eternal Seed has come to maturity in us.

Wedding Garment: The white robe of righteousness bought for us by Christ's death for our sins. Illustrated by the white handkerchief. God provided the wedding garment so we would be comfortable in His presence (See Is. 61:10; Rev. 6:11).

Worldly Road: A detour off the *Agape* Road in an attempt to *get something* we believe God has been withholding from us. It is rooted in a desire to use God for one's own personal success or advantage.

Recommended Reading

Agape and Eros by Anders Nygren (Philadelphia, The Westminster Press)

Works of Love by Soren Kierkegaard (Harper, 1962)

Agape, An Ethical Analysis by Gene Outka (Yale Press, 1972)

The Idea of Love by Robert Hazo (Praeger Press, 1967)

The Nature of Love: Plato to Luther by Irving Singer (Random House, 1966)

The Four Loves by C.S. Lewis (Harcourt Brace & Co., 1960)

The Agape Road Video Series

The *Agape Road* video series by Bob Mumford
was filmed with LifeWay. This series is a
culmination of Bob's life message.
Recording artist, *Geoff Moore*, introduces
each session and his music video of
"God Bless the Broken Road" is on
the end of Session One.

What you will learn:

❖ Believers are on a journey called the *Agape Road*. Jesus takes us on this journey.

❖ Believers get off the *Agape Road* when they take an excursion into worldliness or
man-made religion. We can get off the road in both directions at the same time or go
back and forth.

❖ Seven Giants are identified that entice us to take a detour. These Giants are
manifestations of *Eros*, the opposite of *Agape*, or God's love.

❖ God sets His love on us and if we get off the *Agape Road*, He draws us back to Himself.

❖ We learn to stay on the Agape Road through abiding—holding steady—in the
crises of life that tempt us to take a detour.

❖ We make progress on the *Agape Road* when we become Father-pleasers.

Session Titles:

God the Father	The Healing Power of Agape
The Human Dilemma	The Point of Conflict
The Eros Prison	Intimacy with the Father
A Word From God	Avoiding Detours

Agape Road consists of:

❖ 4 Video tapes with 8 teaching sessions

❖ 4 Audio tapes with 8 teaching sessions

❖ Extensive Viewer's Study Guide & Leader's Guide

Agape Road Video Series: Catalog #V325

Additional Viewer Guides available: Catalog #V325OL

LIFECHANGERS®

P. O. Box 3709, Cookeville, TN 38502 U.S.A.
800.521.5676 ❖ 931.520.3730
lc@lifechangers.org ❖ www.lifechangers.org

About Bob Mumford

BOB MUMFORD is a dynamic Bible teacher with a unique and powerful gift for imparting the Word of God. His anointed messages are remembered years afterwards, because he captivates his audiences by humor in the form of word pictures, which penetrate deep into hearts with incredible authority, clarity and personal application. Since 1954, thousands of Christians worldwide have attributed their spiritual growth and determination to follow Jesus Christ to his prophetic teaching, helping them understand Father God and His Kingdom.

Bob has written for major Christian periodicals both in the United States and abroad and published several books including *Take Another Look at Guidance, The King & You, Fifteen Steps Out, Living Happily Ever After* and *The Purpose of Temptation.* He has also published numerous booklets called *Plumblines,* including *Renegade Male* and a series on *Inheritance.*

Bob has a heart for backsliders, having come to the Lord at age 12 only to stray from God a few months later. During this time, when he was 13, his parents divorced creating the need to quit school and work to help support his mother and five sisters. At 20 years old, he joined the U.S. Navy as a Medic. Bob would go with his Navy buddies to the bar and end up preaching to those in the bar the necessity to repent of their sins and come to Christ. Even then Father God was pursuing him!

While on leave from the Navy, Bob attended a church service one evening. He was overcome by the conviction of the Holy Spirit and literally ran to the altar. After being away from God for 12 years, the Lord cleaned up his heart and gave him new purpose and direction, calling him specifically to "Feed My people."

After completing his High School education in the Navy and then graduating with a Bachelor of Science from Valley Forge Christian College, Bob Mumford attended the University of Delaware and then received his Masters of Divinity degree from Reformed Episcopal Seminary in Philadelphia. Over the years, he has served as a pastor, as Dean and Professor of New Testament and Missions at Elim Bible Institute. In 1972, he founded Lifechangers, Inc. to distribute his teaching materials all over the world where he has traveled extensively to some 50 nations as an international conference speaker. His materials have been translated into more than 20 different languages.

Today he is considered to be a spiritual "Papa" to thousands of Christians. His ministry has been to prophetically proclaim and teach the sufficiency of Christ Jesus and His Kingdom in a manner which promotes reconciliation and unity in the body of Christ. Bob seeks to bring about personal spiritual change and growth in the lives of believers, regardless of denomi-national persuasion. His unique style of humor is designed to keep you smiling so it isn't too painful when the truth of his teaching hits home. Such high intensity in the Holy Spirit, accompanied by his pointed and colorful delivery, enables him to impact his audiences with an unforgettable and life-changing experience.

Bob and Judith reside in Raleigh, North Carolina. If you would like to receive information about Lifechangers, or a catalog of materials available, you can write to us at:

LIFECHANGERS ®

P. O. Box 3709, Cookeville, TN 38502 U.S.A.
800.521.5676 ❖ 931.520.3730
lc@lifechangers.org ❖ www.lifechangers.org